AF574104

The Jazz Image

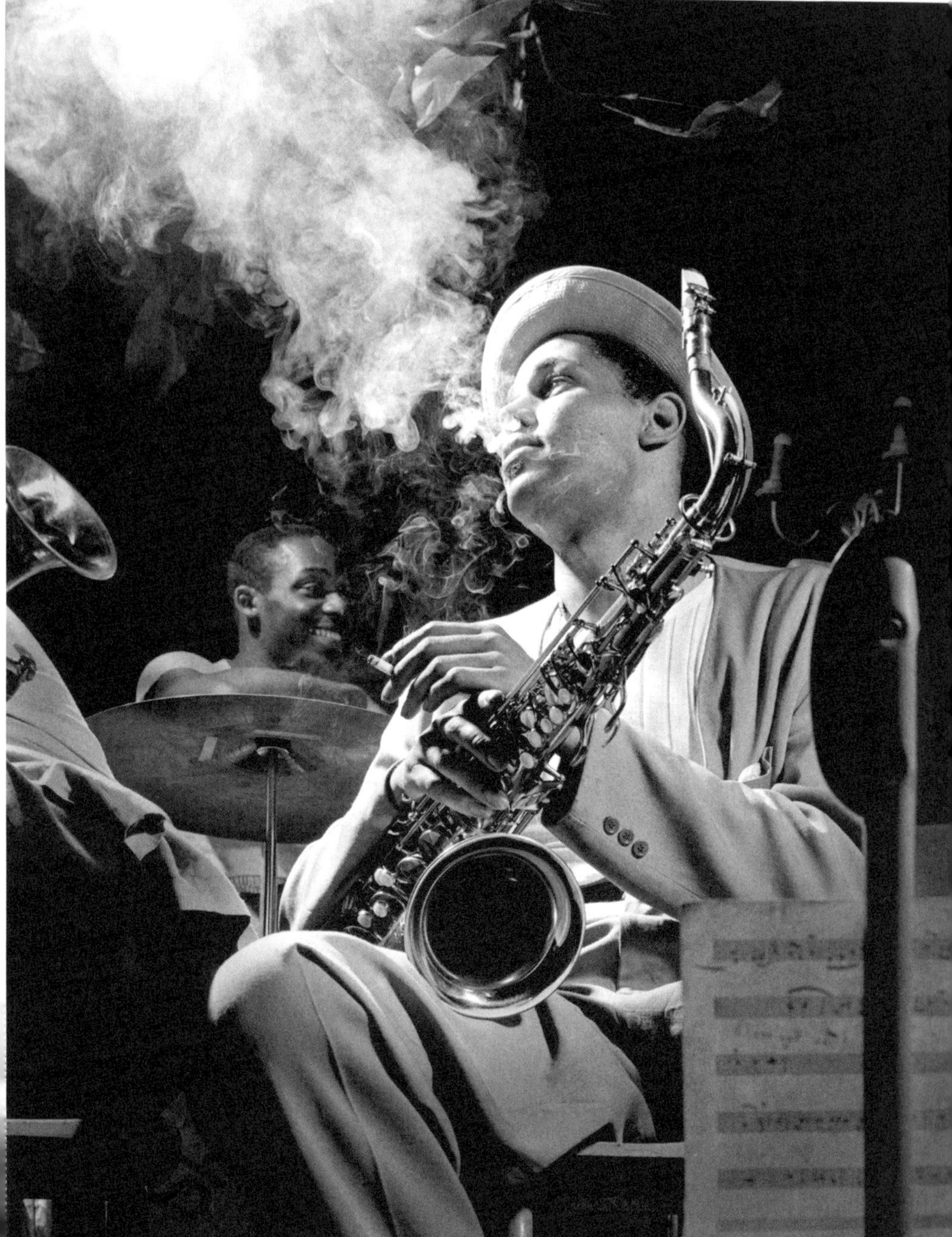

The Jazz IMAGE

Seeing Music through Herman Leonard's Photography

K. HEATHER PINSON

UNIVERSITY PRESS OF MISSISSIPPI • JACKSON

www.upress.state.ms.us

Designed by Peter D. Halverson

The University Press of Mississippi is a member of the Association of American University Presses.

Frontis: *Dexter Gordon at the Royal Roost in New York*, 1948, code #DXG01, by Herman Leonard. © Herman Leonard Photography LLC/CTSIMAGES.COM

Manufactured in the United States of America

First printing 2010
∞
Library of Congress Cataloging-in-Publication Data

Pinson, K. Heather.
The jazz image : seeing music through Herman Leonard's photography / K. Heather Pinson.
p. cm. — (American made music series)
Includes bibliographical references and index.
ISBN 978-1-60473-494-2 (cloth : alk. paper) — ISBN 978-1-60473-495-9 (ebook) 1. Leonard, Herman, 1923– 2. Jazz musicians—Portraits. 3. Jazz—New York (State)—New York—1941–1950—History and criticism. 4. Jazz—New York (State)—New York—1951–1960—History and criticism. 5. Portrait photography—New York (State)—New York. I. Title.
ML3506.P56 2010
778.9'978165—dc22 2009052114

British Library Cataloging-in-Publication Data available

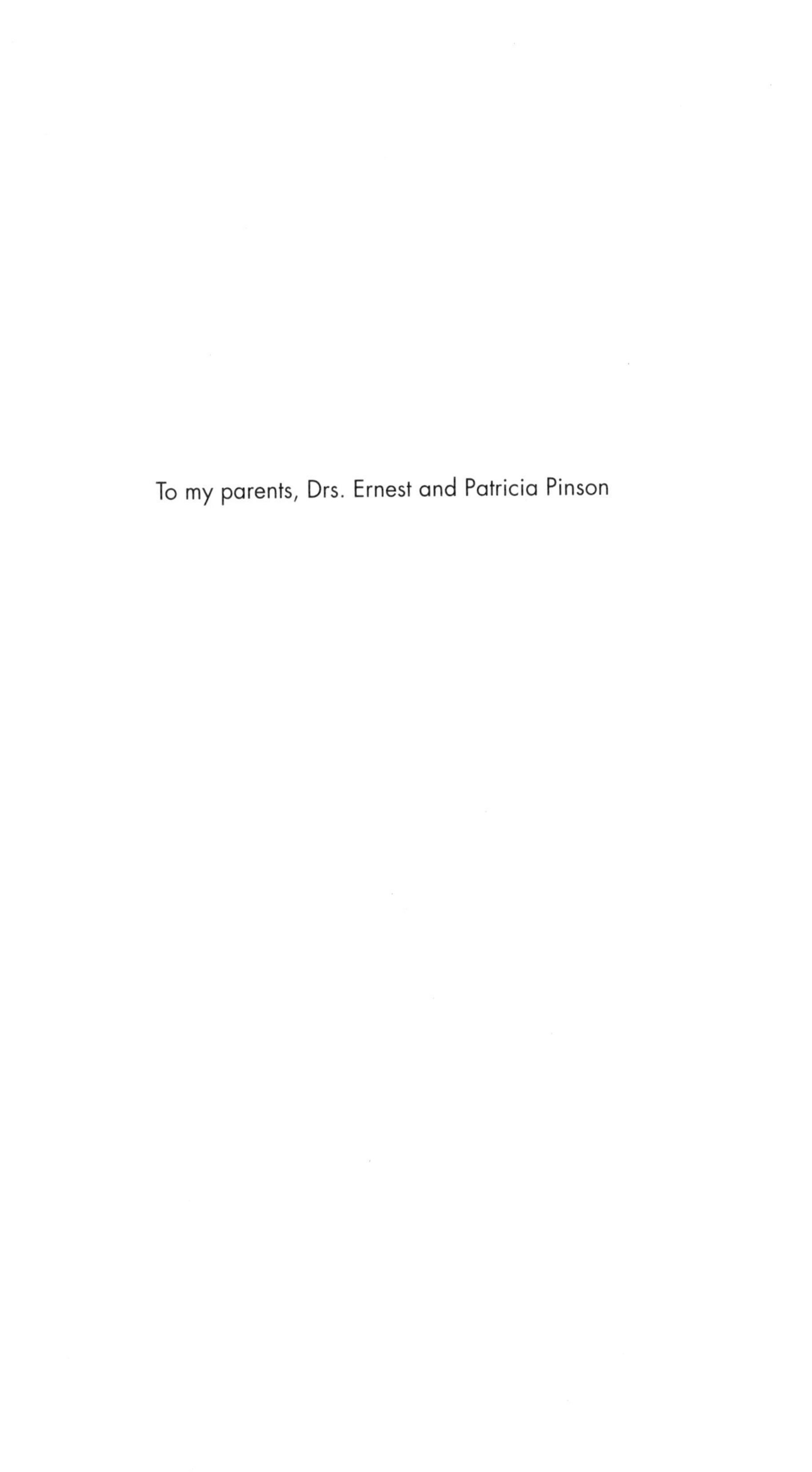

To my parents, Drs. Ernest and Patricia Pinson

Contents

Illustrations

Acknowledgments

This project would not have been successful without the assistance and support of many individuals. Of my close friends who have offered suggestions, comments, and moral support are Rex Crawley, Ann Jabro, John Perrine, Henry McCarthy, and Ryan McCormack. Thank you to the folks at Robert Morris University for supporting me throughout this process. And thanks to Ronnie and Richard Conboy, Brenda Krepol and Eddie Albert, and Pat and Ernie Pinson for making the printing of the images in this book possible. The images found in this publication are dedicated to you for all of your help. In addition, band members and world-class people Nick Long, Matthew Harvey, Grant Cambridge, Zack Quillen, and Ryan Wonnacott had to endure many abbreviated rehearsals and gigs to accommodate my work schedule on this book. Thank you guys for your patience when I had to bow out of practice and gigs.

I also wish to thank Roger Braun, Ernie Bastin, Guy Remonko, Roger Humphries, Herman Leonard, Cynthia Sesso, Gerry Baum, Jenny Bagert, and Lutz Bacher for graciously consenting to be interviewed and quoted for this project. Many writers would pay much for such clear insight as found in the words and music of trumpeter Ernie Bastin. I would also like to thank percussionist and educator Roger Braun for his thoughtfulness and consideration for this project in which his ideas are found throughout. In addition, art historian and professor Charles Buchanan spent tireless hours proofreading pages, for which I am eternally grateful. Now a full-time professor of film and photography, Lutz Bacher has managed many famed jazz musicians from around the globe. His firsthand experience and wide musical palette presented me with a unique opportunity to understand the nature of marketing and performance practice from the true geniuses of jazz. Thank you, Lutz, for sharing your experiences, words, music, and pictures with me.

Like the rest of the world, I have grown to love Herman Leonard through his humor, easy-going personality, welcoming attitude, choice of music, wine, and women, not to mention his photographs. Thanks, Herman, for spending time with me and for your warm spirit. I hope Gerry Baum and Jenny Bagert realize that this book would not have come to fruition if not for them. Thank you for being so hospitable and for accommodating my every whim, email, and phone call. During my research I met friend and colleague Ben Cawthra, whose shared interest, experience, and writing greatly inspired my work. Good luck, Ben, and I look forward to seeing where this idea of visual representation in jazz goes. Finally, Cynthia Sesso is a wealth of knowledge on jazz, American history, image licensing, and photography and remains an inspiration for me professionally as well as personally. She is a hidden treasure that the jazz world is not necessarily aware of. They will be.

The staff at the University Press of Mississippi are walking angels—people like Anne Stascavage, Kristin Kirkpatrick, Valerie Jones, and Craig Gill. Thank you guys so much for inviting me to work with you and for all of the advice, encouragement, and assistance you have given. Thanks especially to Will Rigby, who spent countless hours editing and who has a strong talent for knowing what sounds best.

My greatest partner in this project as well as life has been Matthew Conboy, whose words of encouragement were often the only positive thoughts that echoed in my head late into the nighttime hours. Many times, his plans were averted because I was still working and could not pull myself away from the office chair. He never once complained and instead brought in dinner on a tray with a cup of tea. And finally, this book could not have happened at all if it were not for my mother, Dr. Pat Pinson, and father, Dr. Ernest Pinson Jr. Thank heavens for free cell phone minutes on nights and weekends because we used quite a bit of them. My father read every page of this book several times and offered advice which, if not accepted the first time, was accepted and humbly received the second time after I went back over his comments.

The Jazz Image

Introduction

Herman Leonard's photographs are some of the most recognized images in jazz history. His depictions of predominantly African American jazz musicians in New York City have created not only a visual record of jazz in the 1950s, but have also become the standard by which the musical style of jazz was, and continues to be, visually represented. His photographs have, in effect, established a strong association between the image and music of jazz. The term *image* can be illusive and loaded with multiple meanings, but for the purposes of this book, it means not only concrete visual depiction, but also a mental picture or collective understanding of something. In this case, the visual image as facilitated by Leonard in his photography has come to represent a particular mental understanding of the sound and look of jazz.

Leonard was already successful with his commercial photography taken from the 1950s to the 1980s ranging from *Life* magazine to *Playboy*, but his more recent claim to fame stems from the Special Photographer's Company in 1988. At this London exhibit, Leonard displayed the photographs of jazz musicians he had taken while he was first learning how to use the camera as a tool and creative art form in the 1940s and 1950s. Musicians such as Charlie Parker, Miles Davis, Ella Fitzgerald, Duke Ellington, and Dizzy Gillespie contributed to the vitality of jazz during the mid-twentieth century. Leonard took his photographs at an important turning point in jazz history—the evolution of bebop and modern jazz. He was present as bebop emerged onto the jazz scene and successfully captured on film what the musicians were trying to do themselves: to create a new interpretation from existing standards.

These photographs have had a large impact on both listeners and performers of the jazz community. They have been used in books on jazz ranging from biography to classroom textbook.[1] Leonard was featured in Ken Burns's nationally broadcasted documentary television series entitled *Jazz: A History of America's Music*, and has himself been the subject of a documentary film, *Frame After Frame: The Images of Herman Leonard*, produced and directed by Tika Laudun for Louisiana Public Broadcasting and narrated by

Tony Bennett. The instant success of these images reflects upon the admiration that both the non-jazz and the jazz community have for Leonard's talent for photography. His images capture the very essence of jazz.

Other jazz photographers have also garnered recognition for their work such as William Gottlieb, William Claxton, Ray Avery, Ole Brask, Herb Snitzer, Milt Hinton, Francis (Frank) Wolff, and Lee Tanner. With the work of these photographers combined, one can assemble in retrospect a canon of jazz photography. Although the work of these photographers consists of past jazz musicians, and like Leonard's are as much as sixty years old, the canon of jazz photography is now in a process of being collected and redistributed. Record companies, advertising representatives, agents, collectors, musicians, jazz repertory ensembles, museum curators, and universities have asked these jazz photographers for copies or prints of their work as a part of a revival in classic jazz that began in the 1980s. Spurred by a reissuing of classic jazz CDs and jazz imagery, the visual image of jazz has been on the rise.

Born in Allentown, Pennsylvania, in 1923, Herman Leonard discovered—on the yearbook staff in high school—that the camera could grant him access into many venues. He decided to pursue the photography program at Ohio University in Athens, Ohio, at that time the only university to offer a degree in photography.[2] In 1943 he was drafted into the United States Army, and traveled to Burma with the 13th Mountain Medical Battalion as an anesthetist. For over two years he trekked the Burma Road from Assam to Mandelay, all the while developing film late at night in his combat helmet. After being honorably discharged from the army, he finished school in 1947, the same year he attended one of Norman Granz's traveling Jazz at the Philharmonic concerts in Columbus, Ohio, and took his first few photographs of jazz musicians.[3] He received the remarkable opportunity to serve as an apprentice to the famed portraitist Yousuf Karsh and was influenced by the work of Henri Cartier-Bresson, Irving Penn, and W. Eugene Smith.

After a year under Karsh's tutelage, Leonard opened his first studio in Greenwich Village, and from 1948 to 1956 his photographs appeared regularly on album covers and promotional material for RCA Victor, Decca, Capitol, Mercury, and Verve record labels. Leonard became the personal photographer to Marlon Brando, and in 1956 moved to Paris, where he worked fashion, film, and advertising jobs. In 1960 he began shooting portraits for *Elle* and *Marie Claire*, which eventually led to jobs with *Life*, *Look*, *Esquire*, *Playboy*, and *Cosmopolitan*. At this point in his career Leonard was primarily known as a commercial photographer, traveling worldwide to shoot in cities such as Bangkok and Bombay and countries such as Afghanistan, Bali, Ethiopia, France, India, Iran, Italy, Singapore, Thailand, and Tibet. In 1980 he moved to the island of Ibiza, Spain, to raise his family, and then in 1987, he moved to London. (For a more detailed timeline of Leonard's career and achievements in photography, please refer to Appendix A.)

After twenty-five years of a successful commercial career, he decided to create his first exhibition, "Images of Jazz," at a small London gallery called The Special Photographer's Company. This exhibit ran for over a month and was the cause of a steady rise in his popularity in England. Leonard sold over 250 prints during the exhibit, which was followed by a BBC-TV half-hour special on his work and eight pages in the Sunday supplement of the *London Times*. According to his website, "it was an unheard-of success for a living photographer," and this exhibit spurred Leonard to unearth more images.[4] Since the initial London exhibit in 1988, the past twenty years have been quite successful for Leonard. He appeared on television in the late 1980s, garnering other media coverage and traveling exhibitions, eventually totaling over forty-five exhibitions featuring his jazz collection.[5]

His photos are now collected and sold as fine art prints through several galleries across the United States such as the National Museum of American History in Washington; the Ogden Museum of Southern Art in New Orleans; and the Kennedy Museum of Art in Athens, Ohio. Approximately 700 images in the Herman Leonard library currently are for sale. "Maybe thirty to forty images are our best selling ones," says Geraldine Baum. "They are iconic."[6] Many of those iconic pictures are transferred from print to posters, T-shirts, television advertisements, and not all of the transactions contain permission from Leonard to sell items with his images on them.[7] Other legal forms of licensing Leonard's images are in such scholarly uses as textbooks, magazines, online websites, documentaries, films, and CD covers and interior layouts. According to Baum, the sales from prints make up the majority of the income to run the studios and staff members, and licensing makes up a smaller percentage.[8] Leonard gets some requests for licensing from large corporations like Apple, who used his image of Frank Sinatra for a billboard in Los Angeles. Leonard also displays his works in his own publications, including *(L'Oeil Du Jazz) The Eye of Jazz: The Jazz Photographs of Herman Leonard*; *Jazz Memories*; and *Jazz, Giants, and Journeys: The Photography of Herman Leonard*.[9]

Following his recent notoriety, Leonard relocated to New Orleans, Louisiana, in 1991, but lost his studio, darkroom, and home to Hurricane Katrina in the fall of 2005. With foresight, Leonard called his agent at the time, Jenny Bagert, as soon as he heard about the impending storm and requested her to move all of his negatives from his studio into the vault at the Ogden Museum of Southern Art. He lost about 8,000 of his photographs and exposure records.[10] Remarkably, the negatives in the vault remained undamaged, allowing Leonard to reprint much of what he lost in the flood. He has since moved to Studio City, California, and opened a new studio. He continues to photograph and print.

Leonard recently obtained a grant from the Grammy Foundation to start an archive project, a catalog system with each photograph scanned, copied, digitized, and uploaded into a searchable database. This will be a huge undertaking: there are over 65,000 prints on 2,500 rolls of film that will be catalogued and given a rating system from least to most popular. Leonard's prints mostly include those on 35 millimeter film, 4X5 low to medium resolution, and a two-and-a-quarter-inch square medium format. Leonard himself will be involved in the process, identifying people and describing the circumstances behind each shot.[11]

Leonard's photographs of jazz musicians have come to represent not only great jazz, but also the best of America's original music. He is counted among other great contributors who create an American landscape through photography.[12] These contributions are internationally recognized as a result of his winning numerous awards—most recently the Lucy Award for portraiture, often deemed the Oscar for photography, in October 2008. He is truly an exceptional artist with a keen eye for balance and meaning in a frame. Jenny Bagert notes, "his talents in the darkroom match his talents behind the lens."[13] There is a consistency throughout his collection of photographs, ranging from Ringling Brothers and Barnum and Bailey to photographs for *Playboy*. In the typical Leonard portrait, the subject seems unaware of the camera's presence. No one looks directly at the camera; no one poses. The subject is seen going about his or her business. Every photograph seems to be anachronistic; for example, the Palm Court Cafe New Orleans (Code #PCC01 of his archive), taken in 1996, looks as if it was from the 1950s.

There is an aged look to the images; the photos themselves are razor sharp with detail, but the actions of the people, eagerly engaged in whatever they are doing, have a timeless quality. The works recall the artful qualities of color and balance in J. M. W. Turner's paintings, while positioning the edges of objects to the forefront through sharp, crisp detail with the realism of Jean-François Millet. Among Leonard's models were the sketches of Pablo Picasso, who was able to capture the personality of the individual through the combined lines of the body. Gestures and movement instigate form; Leonard highlights his subject with strobe lights, and then encourages the density of the lines in the darkroom, creating greater photographic effect. The same lighting effect used in the famous Duke Ellington photo taken in Paris, 1958 (Code #DKE02), is repeated in one of Dr. John in San Francisco, 1999 (Code #DRJ1).

His talent has become a signature that graces the presence of viewers through coffee-table books and screen savers. However, it is important to recognize that his influence bears more upon the jazz community than it does for the lover of black and white photography. He has captured Dexter Gordon, Dizzy Gillespie, Lester Young, Charlie Parker, Miles Davis, John Coltrane, Ella Fitzgerald, Frank Sinatra, and Duke Ellington, who are framed in black and white film and frozen in the distinct time and place of the New York from the 1940s to the 1960s. Although many photographers took pictures of the same musicians at the same time with the same technology, Herman Leonard has found permanence within a society known for fleeting fame and short attention spans. The fact that he has been so instrumental in representing what jazz *looks* like deserves further investigation.

Leonard's photographs are so refined in appearance that many have become "classics," representing the standard of jazz photography. His works capture the spirit of mainstream jazz and have contributed to the public's growing awareness of visual imagery along with posters, films, advertisements, calendars, T-shirts, and other commercial memorabilia, as well as textbooks on jazz history, styles, or biographies. The more his images are shown, the more energy he generates or is responsible for generating. This exposure is a direct result of the growing commercial and general interest in the jazz image, that is to say, the visual and mental understanding of what a jazz musician looks like. Leonard's photographs are themselves images of jazz in that they contribute to the circulating knowledge of jazz musicians as well as the style of music.

The image, in many instances, is what a jazz musician looks like in one's mind: a compilation of visual imagery from CD covers, posters, calendars, coffee mugs, tee shirts, marquee billboards, films, television commercials, and photographs. Such principles of jazz as talent, fashion, ingenuity, and personal flair were recognized in the musical geniuses of the swing and especially the bebop and hard bop eras, and have remained the same since that time, regardless of the presentation. There are a variety of ways to interpret the jazz image. But for the purposes of this work, *the jazz image* will refer to the ideals, values, and achievements associated with the mental idea of an accomplished jazz musician, as well as the visual picture of a mid-twentieth-century urban African American.

One of the main reasons Leonard's photographs are popular is that they present idealized jazz musicians at their best. His photographs of not-yet-famous jazz musicians from 1945 to 1959 provide a link to the United States at that time and its cultural and social values. The jazz image acts as a reflection of the tense racial and political atmosphere that faced the African American jazz musician following World War II. Both the struggle by African Americans for civil liberty and the condemnation of middle- and upper-class materialism by the beatnik generation are revealed in the jazz image of the forties and fifties, and gave musicians a parallel reason to fight to be heard. Leonard's photographs recall and promote this idea of freedom. His photographs and portraits of musicians as heroes function as both social constructs and promotional material. Instead of keeping these musicians away from the spotlight, Leonard showcased their faces and framed their personality on stage. Jazz musicians could attest to the social injustices done to them, but now with Leonard as their unelected promoter, they could be seen, heard, and printed. By representing the struggle for equal rights at a time when socially there was no equal treatment for all Americans, Leonard's photographs gain greater meaning by their very existence.

Leonard's photographs also created a utopian image of the jazz musician, including individuals like Duke Ellington, Frank Sinatra, and Dizzy Gillespie, that facilitated social acceptance and respectability. By carefully selecting his subject matter so as to present the clearest vision of the jazz image in bebop era, Leonard gives the contemporary viewer a glimpse into the past, back to the emergence of bebop as art music. He selected subject, setting, lighting, props, and film in order to project an honest image of jazz for this period. By reading these layers of signs, symbols, and representations within an historical context, the viewer can come closer to determining the precise elements and circumstances of the era that Leonard's photographs replicate. At the same time, they were integral in defining the jazz image as including a call for racial equality, an intellectual approach to music, and a return to the more traditional sounds of classic jazz.

Leonard's work is remarkable in its emotional appeal to the audience by capturing essential qualities that are associated with jazz. These photographs capture the allure of the intellectual rebel that existed in the 1950s, while at the same time presenting the jazz musician as a sensual and stylish being. The image of the accomplished jazz musician is constantly recycled in our society, from representations of the beat poet, to visual icons in films such as Frank Sinatra and the Rat Pack, to posters of Miles Davis hung in the practice rooms of aspiring music students. This image of mid-twentieth-century jazz musicians has continued to grow despite jazz's decline as popular music since the swing era.

It is crucial to accompany the visual image with the musical achievements made by a jazz musician. Jazz is typically separated from popular music such as rock and roll because of its increased demand of technical skill, required knowledge of music theory, and experimental spontaneity through improvisation. Jazz also differs from classical music in that it arose from popular music, contains a different repertoire, and focuses on improvisation, or what Charles Mingus calls "spontaneous" composition versus that of the "pencil composers."[14] Jazz musicians such as John Coltrane and Miles Davis pushed the boundaries of tonality, form, and style, none of which can be sensationalized as easily as the latest celebrity breakup. The jazz image is often coupled with racial inequality and depends upon the strength and endurance of the individual. In this manner, jazz is linked with its social and cultural achievements, which in turn spur an association with American originality and perseverance.

While this image of the jazz musician is beneficial, it creates an association of jazz that has been difficult to change. Since the 1950s, the visual image, as well as the mental concept of jazz music that it evokes, has become so canonized that much of jazz today stylistically reflects the tonal sounds of jazz that were created at that time. The music as well as the image from the 1950s is repeated. The era of the bop movement and the following styles that mutated from bop are now understood as "mainstream" jazz. Originally, that term specifically referred to the swing idiom of the thirties and forties; however, *mainstream* has since broadened its meaning from a mere musical style to an adjective encompassing the entire musical approach and sound of jazz as it was established from bebop and beyond. It centers on the combination of acoustic instruments, small combo setting, standard song usage, and manner of playing within the tonal, rhythmic, and harmonic organization of bop.

The definition of mainstream is tenuous at best and varies according to the one using it. There is a consensus among jazz scholars that *mainstream* refers to similarities found within those styles of jazz that cover the end of the swing era to the emergence of bebop, cool, and hard bop; however, they differ sharply with music of the avant-garde or free jazz styles. Because they experiment with new instruments and new timbres, free jazz and the avant-garde are seen as a departure from mainstream jazz. The introduction of free jazz, as seen in the release of Ornette Coleman's album *The Shape of Jazz to Come* in 1959, signified a turning away from mainstream jazz. Therefore, the years 1945 to 1959 indicate the establishment of mainstream jazz now circulated as a canon of music, charts, and chord changes that still serve as the foundation for musical improvisation.

While jazz continued to diversify stylistically into the 1980s, some musicians and listeners looked to the mainstream sound as that which best represents the jazz idiom. There existed in the 1980s a stylistic shift from the avant-garde, fusion, and jazz-rock of the 1960s and 1970s back to traditional standards of mainstream jazz. This growing resurgence of mainstream jazz naturally cultivated a similar resurgence of jazz imagery, promoting the "classic" jazz figure as well as the sound of classic jazz or neoclassicism. It was during this transition that the work of Herman Leonard, gaining in popularity after the 1988 exhibition of his photographs in London, and neoclassicism, gaining in popularity from the reissuing on CD of classic jazz recordings, merged. Leonard's photographs began appearing on the front of books, inside jazz textbooks, magazines, newspapers, websites, and in documentaries, all of which did much to build a core of classical standards for mainstream jazz as well as photographic standards for the jazz image. Through this hesitant relationship, the jazz image and the jazz canon rose into a more stable form.

Just as mainstream jazz has become a collective representation of the entire culture of jazz, so have the black and white photographs by Herman Leonard become the standard repertoire of jazz photography. If these images impart to the viewer the power (however illusory) to know and understand the cultural and musical history of jazz just by viewing one photograph, jazz is thereby reduced to that which can be read, deciphered, and appropriated quickly. The image allows for "swift appropriation without the need to engage with the contradictions and ambiguities of history, the complications of the subject, and in this case, even listen to the music."[15] Of course, the sole extent of a musical genre and established value system do not rely entirely on one or two photographs, so it behooves one to evaluate the circumstances around the visual culture of jazz.

Leonard did not purposely contribute to the neoclassical movement. However, the popularization of his photography in the 1980s was the result of a captive audience already in place and awakened by the stirrings of mainstream jazz. By capturing the feel of bebop in his pictures, Leonard's photographic style complements the recycling of bop standards. They contain far greater meaning than the image presented, and hence are invaluable for this study of the jazz image. And while both the image and the music of mid-twentieth-century jazz has persisted through fifty years of musical development, the importance of the image is measured by how much it is imitated in the jazz community through neoclassicism, and in the visual community by the popularity of Herman Leonard.

Precisely what effect did the image of the jazz musician found in Leonard's photographs have on the jazz canon and vice versa? Although his photographs record the history of jazz as it is actually happening, the image also creates a dilemma by promoting an artifact taken in the mid-twentieth century, the jazz musician of the past. Through the photograph, the jazz musician becomes the object. In actuality, jazz exists as an art form that does not emphasize the object, as one could interpret in the score utilized in classical music. Since most of the creative process involves immediate improvisation and an aural heritage which does not completely rely on a written musical score, the physicality of jazz is seen in the musician and, therefore, the image. The visual image of jazz has become the object. And in this manner, Leonard's photograph becomes as much a part of the definition of jazz as the music itself.

Part of the effect of Leonard's photographs is their connection to mid-century Americana. His black and white film, smoke, lighting, and club settings allow the viewer to step back into time, since most of his famous photos were taken during the 1940s and 50s. Leonard's photographs have standardized this feeling of timelessness and nostalgia. Today, many photographers still use the "classic" black-and-white film to recall a time when jazz was popular music and jazz musicians were at the vanguard of creativity. Of course, Herman Leonard's photography is not the sole cause for America's interest in black-and-white photography of jazz musicians. He merely perpetuates an image of class and style, which is fostered among the jazz community itself.

The portrayal of African American jazz musicians in photography has had a great impact on mainstream jazz, especially with current trends in jazz that recall images of the past. However, due to the fragmentation of jazz into other cultures besides the African American community, one must question the effects of white appropriation. To what extent has white society capitalized on and commodified the images and music of African American musicians—for example, with a white photographer selling pictures of black musicians?

With the technology of the internet and digital music, the music industry in general has been able to produce and exchange ideas faster and with greater accessibility than ever imagined by the musical world; the jazz circle in particular has been able to reach more people and create a larger discourse on jazz, including areas outside of music. During the late eighties and early nineties, a new wave of jazz scholarship bridged aesthetics, musical style, and cultural appropriation, outside of the more common biographical or stylistic analyses of earlier musical writing. This type of scholarship expanded the lens of jazz to include more than the score or the musician; it included the environment of jazz, that is, its history, resources, and culture. Authors such as Ted Gioia, Scott DeVeaux, Eric Lott, Jim Macnie, Ingrid Monson, Peter Townsend, Stuart Nicholson, and Philip Ford began to interpret the role of jazz as a social function in the United States.

By shifting the analysis from the music itself to the social environment of the musician, jazz critics have widened their audience as well. Ted Gioia uses language in his writing that is accessible to both musician and listener.[18] As a philosopher and a jazz musician, Gioia structures his book, *The Imperfect Art*, to incorporate the effect jazz has on audiences of various genres. Through a genuinely interdisciplinary approach, he explains society's understanding of the jazz musician as a means to understand the other arts. In this regard, his book serves as the model for this study.

Other scholars, such as Ingrid Monson and Philip Ford, examine the role of jazz in society by tackling the stereotype of the hipster.[19] They define this term according to how it is used in regard to particular musicians such as Thelonious Monk, whose image personifies the hip jazz artist through his musicianship and his personality. Monson and Ford successfully present a new thread to our understanding of jazz. This book will continue their method of examining jazz through the relationship of image and music.

Scott DeVeaux examines jazz history through a post-structuralist viewpoint.[20] DeVeaux discusses how, in the act of defining jazz, a struggle develops for the "possession" of jazz history, meaning we as scholars often claim jazz in the name of our own agenda. Here, DeVeaux's articles are used as a point of departure for my own thesis by examining the struggle for possession of jazz in both the black and the white communities.

Jazz has developed through the compositions, performances, and audience of the African American community, but it has extended beyond the black diaspora. For instance, the first musicians who were recognized as "jass" musicians through their recordings and radio performances were white: the Original Dixieland Jass Band sparked the general public's interest in jazz in recordings and concerts in 1917. Other performers, such as Arthur Collins, Byron G. Harlan, and the vaudeville minstrel shows by George H. O'Connor, ushered in the sound of jazz, or at least of Dixieland and ragtime, by marginalizing the group of black musicians who created it. The result, however, was a wider span of listeners, many of whom were white.

Throughout its history, jazz retained its ties with the African American community, and the sound of jazz became identified as black music. But jazz also diversified into white communities, young black communities, academic communities, European communities, other musical styles, and, most recently, pop culture. In this manner, jazz has far outgrown its original musical ties with the African American culture. With the ethnic diversification of jazz and the dilution of jazz into such musical styles as rock, jazz has distanced itself from the African American tradition to the extent that now the question arises: how do modern critics define current jazz? Do they still attribute it to the black community?

The association of jazz to race theory is a highly debated topic among jazz critics, primarily because jazz is often marked as a voice for the African American or, more specifically, as a symbol and outlet for the manner, method, and meaning of the oppression African Americans have experienced in an effort to achieve liberation. In the 1960s, scholars of jazz began to incorporate in their writing the fight for civil rights and the Black Arts Movement, thereby codifying jazz music with black national identity. These include Amiri Baraka (LeRoi Jones), Stanley Crouch, Frank Kofsky, Olly Wilson, Albert Murray, and Eric Porter, all of whom marked jazz as a voice for the African American.[21] More recent writers such as Houston A. Baker Jr., Greg Tate, and Kimberly W. Benston examine what it is to be African American while living in a white-dominated society.[22]

The first chapter "The Formation of the Jazz Image in Visual Culture" examines the historical and cultural values underlying the jazz image that Herman Leonard projects into his photography between 1945 and 1959. A brief description and historical account of jazz will be presented at this time, along with an analysis of Leonard's photographs *Dizzy Gillespie at the Royal Roost in New York City,* 1948 and *Duke Ellington in Paris,* 1958, as they epitomize the cultural and social edification of jazz musicians.

Leonard's photographs reflect the musical changes that occur in the 1940s and 1950s. The second chapter, "The Construction of Signs in Jazz Photography," explains this change as it is found in the imagery of jazz musicians. I will then define the style of jazz associated with the image, specifically, photographs by Leonard that exemplify the social significance of the jazz image, after which I will discuss the repetition of image and music in the canon of jazz. This chapter will focus on five photographs: *Max Roach in New York City,* 1954; *Dexter Gordon at the Royal Roost in New York,* 1948; *Ella Fitzgerald, Duke Ellington, Benny Goodman, and Richard Rodgers at the Downbeat in New York City,* 1949; *Frank Sinatra at the Monte Carlo in* 1958; and *Lester Young in New York City,* 1948.

While the first two chapters focus on Leonard's photographs as visual examples of the jazz image, the last two delve into the marketing of such an image in our current society as well as in other styles of jazz. The third chapter, "*Ceci n'est pas jazz*: The Battle for Ownership," compares the jazz image of the 1950s to the current jazz movement, neoclassicism, and explores the similarities held by both in the jazz canon. It also explains the successes and failures of neoclassicism and discusses what effect this has on the jazz image. One large issue that runs throughout this chapter is the prominent featuring of African American musicians in Leonard's photography. Therefore, the central questions which arise include: to what extent is the black community responsible for neoclassicism? Is neoclassicism a natural outgrowth from modern jazz or vice versa? Who actually owns jazz and what are the effects of its white appropriation? This chapter inquires into the authority of the image and exposes the battle for ownership among members in the jazz community.

The fourth chapter, "A 'Style Portrait' of the Avant-garde," offers an alternative to the traditional model of the jazz image in free jazz and the avant-garde. It explores possible reasons why neither avant-garde jazz nor European jazz can be included in the neoclassical movement. The free jazz musician, Ornette Coleman, and the avant-garde artist, Muhal Richard Abrams of the Association for the Advancement of Creative Musicians, have been chosen as representatives of musicians typically thought of as respected icons outside of the canon. Their interest and personal style reflect the initial, distinguishable component of jazz: change. They have, however, successfully reached the ears of a select audience. Again, I believe that Coleman and Abrams have inadvertently established their own separate image away from neoclassicism, one that rebels against conformity; consequently, their image functions differently than the photographs of Herman Leonard. Their pursuit of a new sound, one that may not even be considered jazz, has forced the jazz community to define what they believe to be authentic jazz. In this case, Coleman and Abrams represent the challenge that lies squarely before the jazz community: what is the future of jazz?

Jazz has changed greatly in a brief span of time through its strong relationship with the beat poets of the mid-twentieth century, African American heritage, modernity, cultural expansion, and a stirring political climate. Yet, jazz has somehow managed to retain its identity. The present practice of jazz demands that different styles of music be performed by one or by several different groups of people. One wonders how jazz has been able to retain any sense of its tradition since it is known historically as a music of creativity, modification, adaptation, and improvisation. In truth, it can be identified by its distinct sounds such as those of a saxophone or rhythm section, yet sound alone does not characterize the image of jazz, just as one symphony by Haydn does not represent all of classical music. How then is one able to recognize the peculiar sounds of jazz and to thereby establish the criteria for how a jazz musician appears? That is the focus of this study. The answer can be found in the evolution of the jazz image from 1945 to 1959. Rather than establish a purely historical sketch of jazz, I will use the image of the jazz musician as an analytic instrument for exploring the dynamic and changing influence jazz has experienced in our society.

CHAPTER 1

The Formation of the Jazz Image in Visual Culture

The general consensus of a mental picture of a jazz musician would be a well-dressed African American man playing an instrument, most likely a saxophone or a trumpet, with smoke wafting about the stage on which he is playing at a nightclub. With majors ranging from nursing to corporate communication, my own university students described their ideas of what a jazz musician looks like: "laid back, older man, saxophone in hand with shades on, inside smoky bar," as an "African American male, nicely dressed, with saxophone," and as "a black man, wearing a nice suit probably of unique color, and playing a saxophone or trumpet, and wearing sunglasses."[1] The students' images, along with the perception from others, would likely include a well-dressed individual, usually in profile, inside a club or music hall, either with his band or alone with his horn in a spotlight, perhaps with eyes closed, fully concentrating on the music he is producing. He would exude confidence, individualism, and defiance—the perfect example of the artistic genius. He would be original, yet replicated by other musicians; rebellious, yet marketed by the recording industry; modern, but timeless through his music. He is thought of as a member of an elite community of other jazz musicians who are not part of popular music culture today, but who were leaders in what popular music was considered to be in the twentieth century.

Further images inspired by the jazz musician would appear in our minds, not in linear succession but as one idea occurring as fast as the next, sparking a chain reaction of images that push past the first. Once the images are evaluated, one begins to see meanings that lie far beyond what is first perceived. Other characteristics associated with the jazz musician arise: his demeanor, the noise of the club, the stage, the smoke from a lit cigarette, dry martinis perched on a tray to be served to a patron. Some imagine the youthful energy of swing dancers to fast big band rhythms, or a woman singing sultrily into a microphone. Zoot suits, beat poets, pocket watches, slicked-back hair, cigarettes, button-up white shirts, fedoras, radios, black-and-white televisions, city lights, old movies—all of these emulate the jazz image, and all pertain to a particular time and place: an American city in the mid-twentieth century.

Where does this image come from, and how is it possible to conjure a visual picture of a style of music? How can a picture present what jazz sounds like? The image of a jazz musician in general includes several things: an African American musician standing, playing, or sitting next to his instrument, captured in a black-and-white photograph, usually taken in a club in the mid-twentieth century. This expectation has culminated over years of exposure of jazz through film and photography. The jazz image in photography existed long before Herman Leonard took his pictures during the late 1940s and early 1950s, and clearly existed before and after his photographs found resurgence in 1988. Regardless of the brief twenty-year exposure to the public, Leonard's photographs of jazz musicians have increased in popularity and continue to be a marketable item to the modern public. His images contain qualities that appeal to various groups of people inside and outside of the jazz community.[2] It behooves us to ask exactly where this image came from and how photography propelled it into the most appropriate visual representation of what jazz looks like.

So, we will begin with the introduction of those visual stimulants that cause one to associate them with jazz. Images play a vital role in the collective taste of a society, just as does the spoken and written word; they shape, stimulate, influence, and antagonize those who internalize the sentiments of a particular society at a particular time. This relationship between the image and the society that created it establishes an ideology around the subject presented in the image. Therefore, visual culture includes the act of seeing and looking at something as well as the images composed in various forms of media. However, when examining the visual culture of something, it does not mean that one should evaluate or even notice every image that surrounds a particular subject. Nor should one envision the use of images that occur in their entirety at a particular time period. One should, however, examine those images that have played a part in the development of the subject. Interpretation, information, and inspiration are by-products of visual culture and are part of an exchange between image and viewer and vice versa.

Because it is the "interaction between viewer and viewed," visual culture begins from the point of view of the consumer rather than the producer of an image.[3] However, this book explores the position of both the consumer (analysis of photographs) and the producer (Herman Leonard) of the jazz image, as both play a major role in perpetuating the visualization of jazz. The survival of jazz throughout the twentieth century "depended primarily on the personalities of the subjects and the sensibilities of photographers to create a visual allure that allowed it to compete with other cultural forms."[4] This "visual allure" is typified in the photographs of Herman Leonard due to the ubiquity of exposure to his images. He has become a part of the culture of jazz by being the reciprocator of its visual culture. The more his images are shown, the more attention they generate or are responsible for generating.

Technology and the early strands of jazz began their assent in the late 1800s, and have been perpetuated by the industrial revolution into the format we know today. Technology carried jazz on its back throughout various developments in technology—phonographs, radio waves, records, tapes, CDs, and digital space. Yet, all of these methods of delivery required the auditory receptors of the listener, just as a visual event required interpretation, assumption, and attraction by the viewer. But as the receiving ears have dwindled in number since jazz reigned supreme as popular dance music, the visual representation of jazz has become more important in communicating its meaning.

Technology has accelerated this shift from textual reading and understanding to the billboard, coffee table book, jpeg and tiff files, and other digital icons.[5] And the more an image is repeated in any culture, the more it becomes associated with the information it provides to the viewer. This process of disseminating an image—and then analyzing, interpreting, and learning from that image—becomes instinctual. Instead of reading about experience in order to become knowledgeable, we experience something by *visualizing* it as knowledge. Therefore, visual culture "does not depend on pictures themselves but the modern tendency to picture or visualize something" and, then, the dissemination of that knowledge into society.[6]

The visuality of an object is a mental image of something, our visual understanding of our experiences surrounding that object. This has led philosophers such as Martin Heidegger to describe our surroundings as that which is conceived and grasped through a "world picture" of how we see ourselves,[7] or W. J. T. Mitchell's "picture theory," the idea that Western philosophy and science have come to adopt a pictorial, rather than textual, view of the world.[8] Let us look at the construction of a picture theory around jazz, since so much of the visualization of jazz is tied to the developments of technology.

The history of jazz and the history of photography have much in common, particularly the fact that both were struggling to be recognized as legitimate art forms at about the same time. One of the many idiosyncrasies of jazz is that it began as folk music, eventually garnered the attention of millions as popular dance music, and finally receded into the tomes of scholar inquiry and universities as "art music."[9] Photography was considered, and still is to some, "art" for amateurs. It does not require talent, skill, or experience to take a picture; one can *accidentally* take a good picture or already be standing in front of a beautiful scene. Thankfully, this opinion has changed somewhat over the decades. Both jazz and photography profited greatly from emerging technology; both grappled with amateur and professional status within the discipline.

It was only with nineteenth-century industrialization that photography came into being. The industrial revolution helped propel the popularity of the photograph and encouraged more efficient craftsmanship in its production. The photograph, an expression of progress, became mass produced and achieved the status of mechanically produced art, yet one that was affordable. Photographs became the "general furniture of the environment."[10] Many were able to afford the twelve photographic copies of the *cartes de visite*, a small portrait photograph made profitable in the 1860s.[11] These small photographs, acting in part as business cards for the common person, slowly redefined the photograph as that which presents prestige and entrepreneurship even through limited economic means. The less financially sound public was able to copy the stance, background, or clothing of a wealthier person, thus eradicating differences in status through a picture. Other people were able to hide their own economic means by posing in a lavish setting. Since people with different economic backgrounds wanted their *cartes de visite* to imitate those that were fashionable, little hope was offered for individuality.

The common photographer merely appeased the paying client and took the picture according to the taste of the photographed, which led to uniformity. Still, photography became a sought-after commodity by introducing the phenomenon of taking pictures of any thing or event. "With its low cost and availability, photography democratized the visual image and created a new relationship to past space and time."[12] It provided common people with an easy way to record beautiful objects and offered an affordable way to express themselves. From the 1920s to the 1930s, portable cameras and flash bulbs gave greater possibility to travel with camera in hand,[13] and the Leica, Contax, and Rolleiflex, along with 35 millimeter film, brought greater flexibility and portability to the photographer. Being economically affordable and easy to use, the camera became a way to hold progress literally in one's hand.

Technology also spurred the early formation of American music by not only popularizing the photograph, but also by utilizing electricity and phonographs invented by Thomas Edison, the graphophone invented by Alexander Graham Bell, the flat recording disc to engrave sound vibrations developed by Emile Berliner, and the coin-activated machine or jukebox by Louis Glass.[14] Commercial industries to produce such technology flourished: the Columbia Phonograph Company, North American Phonograph Company, and the Victor Talking Machine Company for sound recording, American Telephone and Telegraph for telephonic communication, General Electric for electricity and radio, and the Radio Corporation of America, the National Broadcasting Company, and the Columbia Broadcasting System for radio. With improvements in sound reproduction, affordable music recording led the way for jazz to be heard nationwide.

Innovations in communication technologies, radio broadcasting, mass print media, and sound recording in the early twentieth century coincided with the rise of American colonialism. Taylor Atkins states: "Jazz, in fact, represented nothing more profoundly than the coevalness of modern time: as they listened and danced to jazz, people imagined that they were experiencing modernity simultaneously with their counterparts in distant lands."[15] By the start of World War I, "the nation had begun to experience intensified economic change, human migration, and technological innovation."[16] So, as ragtime represented the bustling sounds of the city with its rhythmic drive and strange new sound, the "hot" jazz of New Orleans–based music and the "sweet" sounds of Lawrence Welk and Guy Lombardo carried jazz into the movements of the 1920s.

The Jazz Age completely changed the image of jazz as the vast majority perceived it. The soldiers returning from WWI symbolized the end of American innocence, but the increased prosperity of the 1920s projected jazz into instant stardom. As with ragtime before it, "hot" jazz became a symbol to much of the country of modern innovation and city life with its fast pace and progressive sound. Jazz musicians bounced between evolving technical progress and their own harmonic innovation.

Other cultural trends helped launch jazz as an urban sound. An ever greater number of people—drawn by jobs in factory towns and cities, the bustle of movement from cars, planes, and trains, and the lighting of the night through electricity—began to go out in the evening for entertainment.[17] Much like the sexual and radical exploration of the 1960s, the 1920s was a time to embrace a bohemian lifestyle. "The fascination with primitive emotional drives and infancy found expression in jazz nightlife."[18] As Burton Peretti points out, Freud was hugely popular in the 1920s and the public studied infantile and adult behavior and social patterns, exalting jazz as that which represented juvenile expression in dress (large, outsized suits for men), slang (such as "jazz babies" for women), and sound (squealing trumpets and the childlike nonsense syllables often sung in jazz).[19] Jazz became both a pastime for entertainment and a stylistic statement against traditional norms.[20]

More and more Americans were enjoying city nightlife. African Americans were mostly excluded from participating, but the white public became regulars at nightclubs and cabarets, resulting in much of the popular success of jazz. But jazz also received a lot of negative attention from both black and white audiences as a musical style that could corrupt the morality of the young and impressionable. Of course, the original term *jass* or *jaz* had sexual overtones. Interestingly, the supposed origin of jazz is often linked to Storyville, the red light district of New Orleans.[21] Although it is true that the use of the term *jaz* parted with its sexual reference, the music—with its rhythmic drive and romantic lyrics—was never able totally to escape its association with sex. The 1920s dance craze that began to follow the style was thought to incite licentious behavior. This was coupled with the "increasing visibility of blacks in cultural life and the emancipation of women that combined suffrage with the specter of sexual liberation."[22]

Not only did jazz musicians undergo racial discrimination and artistic stereotyping, they also had to navigate a tarnished moral association with sex, drugs, and alcohol (it is well documented that many jazz musicians had a dependency upon one or all three vices). Stories of notorious fights, drug-related scandals, and even death cast shadows over many jazz musicians.[23] Several performers dealt with this negative stereotype of immorality by attempting to raise the standards of jazz, as exemplified by innovative bandleader Paul Whiteman's declaration of the need to "make a lady out of jazz." Jazz of the 1920s and 1930s was also associated with immorality based on the rhythm of the music. Ragtime, Dixieland, and earlier forms of swing pulsated with such dance styles of the age as the Charleston, the cakewalk, and the fox trot. This approach to rhythm was very different from classical music, marches, polkas, and waltzes, which were seen as "safer" music to dance to since they did not carry the frivolous and almost barbaric beats of jazz. The rhythm of jazz long remained an Achilles' heel in its battle for acceptance, as witnessed by this statement in 1924.

> I do not approve of "jazz" because it represents, in its convulsive, twitching, hiccoughing rhythms, the abdication of control by the central nervous system—the brain. This "letting ourselves go" is always a more or less enticing act. Formerly we indulged it in going on an alcoholic spree; but now we indulge it by going (through "jazz") on a neural spree. Just now, the world does not know where to look for some stable principles to cling to, has lost its confidence in the value of ends that it formerly believed in, has been greatly excited, and consequently is not in position to exert the poise and purposeful control that mark the man or the nation that has steadfast ideals, believes in its destiny, and firmly advances towards it. Restlessness, indecision and excitement are characteristic of the interim before we again find compelling aims. "Jazz" is symptomatic of this state.[24]

This quote is taken from Will Earhart's answer to the question, "Where Is Jazz Leading America?" found in a 1924 special edition of a prominent music teacher's magazine, *The Etude*. The magazine's editors printed the responses of a select group of musicians to whom they asked the same question. The edition, titled *Opinions of Prominent Men and Musicians*, is printed in the form of a two-part symposium in August and September 1924.[25] Although written in 1924, such responses typify sentiments toward jazz as it further developed through the decades. Another article states: "We are living in a state of unrest, of social evolution, of transition from a condition of established order to a new objective as yet but dimly visualized. This is reflected in the jazz fad. We can only hope that sanity and the love of the beautiful will help to set the world right again and that music will resume its proper mission of beautifying life instead of burlesquing it."[26]

Of course, the rhythm and general sound of jazz, as Peretti points out, also became a symbol of "global and local black unity," since music was a way to express the concerns of the black community.[27] While black musicians performed for many social events, fund-raisers, and community events, more white musicians were gaining social clout. Peretti singles out Paul Whiteman, who "served as a bridge between the raucous jazz world and that of the small-town brass bands and music teachers." Jazz inspired many young white men to imitate the songs and instrumental solos they heard on phonograph records, which lead to the formation of bands and musical careers. White supporters and admirers helped promote the development of jazz, and "[f]or the first time in almost any American context, whites adopted blacks as artistic mentors, considering them the masters of a worthwhile art and studying at their feet."[28]

Radio also offered a voice to black musicians because skin color could not be determined over the airwaves. Milt Hinton perceives jazz, an "auditory art," as one of the greatest gifts for a black man.[29] But even with radio programming beginning in 1923, and the ability to ship records overseas, jazz did not dominate the airwaves until 1935 with the rise of swing.[30] Technology slowed the live music scene; it was easier and cheaper to listen to a recording or to the radio than it was to pay a band, even a cheaper band of black musicians. But despite a desperate economy, lack of resources after World War I, racism against African Americans, and an unstable job market for musicians, swing became one of the most popular forms of music in American history.

During this time, the visual representation of jazz began to grow along with swing as a national phenomenon. The immediacy of taking a photograph and publication of the photo in a relatively short duration of time increased the circulation of the jazz image with the American public. Photography in general was popularized in the late 1920s by magazines such as *Vogue*, *Harper's Bazaar*, *Ladies' Home Journal*, and *Vanity Fair*. In the 1930s, with the increase of visually based, mass-produced magazines like *Life*, photography became a greater part of Americans' everyday lives. Professional photographers began to emerge through increased circulation in print and elsewhere, including Alfred Eisenstaedt, Ansel Adams, Dorothea Lange, Walker Evans, and Martin Munkácsi.

Edward Steichen, in particular, helped shape America's idea of photography through his ability to photograph icons of his age and create artistic images such as *The Pond—Moonlight*. Steichen, who worked with Alfred Stieglitz in the early 1900s and became known through his work in *Vogue* and *Vanity Fair* during the 1920s and 1930s, also became quite influential as the Director of Photography at the Museum of Modern Art in New York. In fact, when Steichen was approached in 1950 by a young photographer who showed him his photographs of jazz musicians, he could not have known that this photographer would later become an icon in jazz photography. Herman Leonard met with the curator of photography at MOMA at that time to discuss his work on jazz. Steichen said Leonard's photos were technically good, but he rejected them because he "could not hear the music in them," and a disheartened Leonard returned to his studio. In Steichen's defense Leonard says, "he really wasn't all that familiar with jazz."[31]

Jazz photography proliferated through the years as the sound of jazz itself did. The rapid development of the image of jazz coincided with the change that was ongoing in the rest of the country. Interest in photography turned from aiming the camera at oneself to aiming the camera at other communities. Americans became fascinated with photographing the "other"—those who differ from oneself in terms of financial stability, education, heritage, visibility, sexuality, abnormality, and/or skin color. Photography helped people in financially secure classes define their own identities by observing or surveying the lives and working conditions of the poor.[32] Black musicians held much fascination for white audiences, but photographing the black musician was not the first instance of white infatuation. Blackface minstrel shows originated in the 1820s, in which white singers and performers put shoe polish or black grease on their face and skin in order to mock black culture. In some cases black performers performed in blackface themselves, but only as comedians. Although demeaning, this allowed black entertainers such as James Bland, a songwriter, and Bert Williams, a comedian, to become better known and better paid.[33]

With the steady influx of immigrants into New York and the great migration of African Americans moving from the more oppressive southern United States to the North in search of better jobs and a better way of living, musicians began to exchange material to each other. Jazz represented the symbol of the American "melting pot," because musicians of various skin tones and ethnic backgrounds worked alongside one another. Benny Goodman added Lionel Hampton and Teddy Wilson as a part of his show, echoing similar collaborative performance practices that was known over much of the history of swing.[34] The success of swing as an interracial creative act in the 1930s played an important role in the assimilation of African American images onto the public stage, with black athletes such as boxer Joe Louis and performers such as Duke Ellington. Images of African Americans surfaced in the media not for mockery as in blackface during the nineteenth century, but for a more sophisticated category of performer, entertainer, or athlete.

But in America's efforts to consume and understand the real world, photography also became a way to shroud what was considered avarice in an attempt to project better qualities of American life. With the stock market crash of 1929 and the Great Depression in the 1930s, photography was an escape for many individuals into a place that was not their own. It allowed the one taking the photograph to transcend his or her own experiences and replace them with the experiences of those in the shutter. Therefore, the act of documentation became a way to record the lives of others who were going through similar struggles.[35] A trend of photographing on the rise in the 1930s focusing on the target without skirting or hiding unwanted objects in the scene (later called "straight" photography) grew into a form of photojournalism.[36] There was a growing interest in folk cultures and

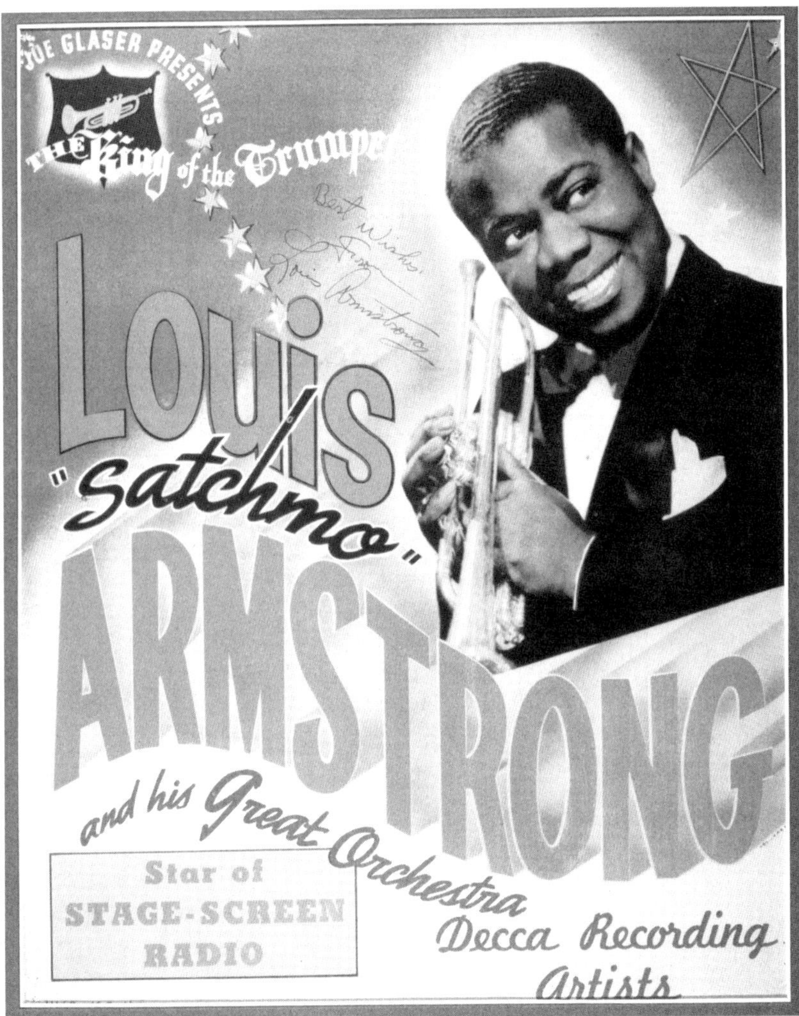

Fig. 1.1. Poster of Louis Armstrong performing in New Orleans. From The Louisiana State Museum Jazz Collection, copyrighted in 2002.

photography was a way to document curiosity with other groups; in the case of jazz, the group was African American. Benjamin Cawthra suggests that "In documenting culture, capturing such folkways as music on film became a recurring theme, whether for mass market magazines or left collectivist social reform efforts such as those of the Photo League."[37]

The musicians themselves offered their own visual complexity as subjects, especially if they were black. Louis Armstrong is the most famous

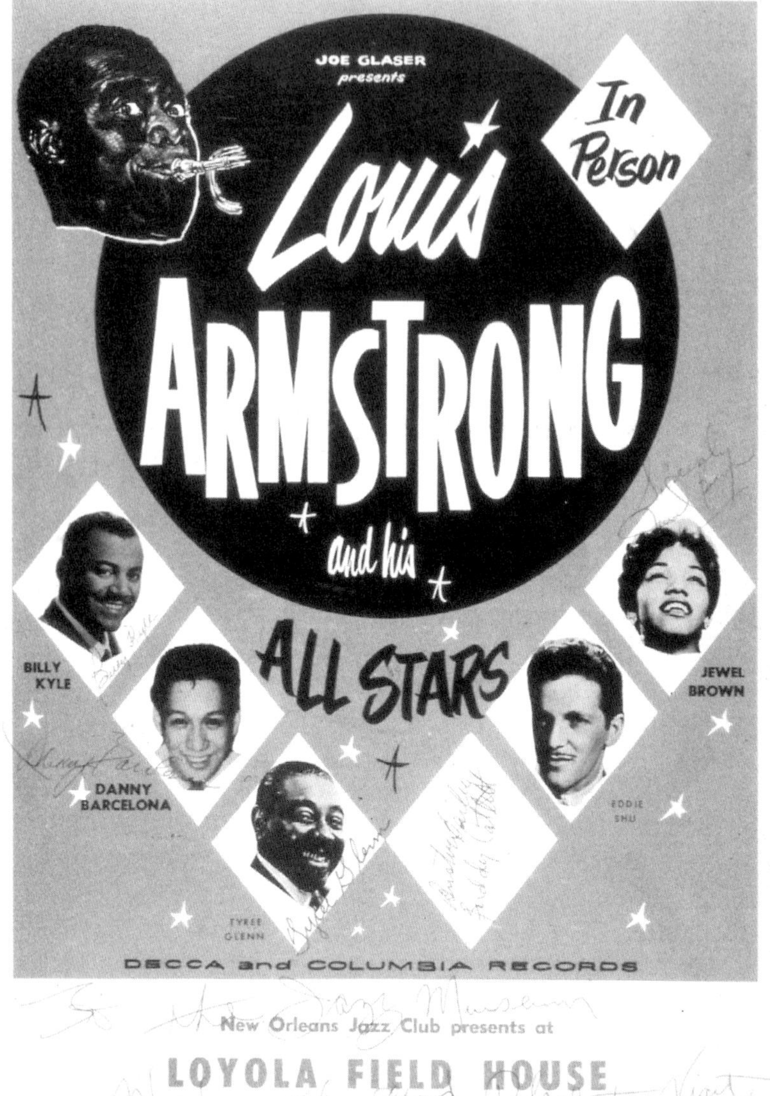

Fig. 1.2. Poster of Louis Armstrong performing with his All Stars at Loyola Field House in New Orleans. From The Louisiana State Museum Jazz Collection, copyrighted in 2002.

example today, as he was in the 1930s. Armstrong presented an easy-going persona, making jazz comfortable to a white audience. As a black musician, he was seen as an entertainer and a jazz ambassador due to his warm smile and various Hollywood film appearances. His picture, thanks to Charles Peterson and others, was cast in magazines, posters, club halls, and flyers as a symbol of black America.[38] His image appeared on posters advertising a particular concert or event, since often these posters would have a picture of the featured jazz musician to draw in an audience. Similar to other advertisements, jazz concert posters helped promote the image of the jazz musician.[39]

The image of the African American musician capable of possessing talents and impulses not experienced by white musicians became an interesting subject for photographers because "black jazz musicians are also policed as a social threat." Further, the African American musician "was also celebrated as the 'modern primitive' because he 'embodied and expressed a masculinity that explicitly rejected the reigning codes of propriety and place.'"[40] *He*, meaning the African American man, was captured in the white imagination much like a caged animal; in both textual and visual media, he was examined, prodded, and poked, and held many fascinations by the white audience (none of which were legitimate skills or intellectual achievements, but instead focused on the craft and intuitive power of the black musician). bell hooks observed, "Any liberatory visual aesthetics of the black male body must engage a body politics that critically addresses the way in which racist/sexist iconography, refigured within the framework of contemporary fascination with the 'other,' continues to be the dominant backdrop framing the way images are created and talked about."[41] But jazz photography offered a way to raise the visibility of black musicians in a positive sense. By making jazz visible and therefore audible, photography, like the radio, followed the stylistic developments of black musicians.

Of particular interest in the 1930s were the emerging photographs as they appeared on posters or in magazines such as in *Life*, the most prominent source of visual information and an early distiller of uniform taste and cultural legitimacy.[42] The work of photojournalists Charles Peterson and Gion Mili, says Benjamin Cawthra, attempted to include the interracial relationship of jazz as it gained heightened attention throughout the swing era.[43] Swing music provided an outlet for critics of all kinds, including the musicians themselves, to openly inquire into this sensational musical form that soon spread across the globe. Even though most of the American public concerned themselves with those musicians who were white, photojournalist like Peterson and Mili saw swing as an opening to document the collaborative relationship between white and black musicians.

Peterson took pictures of Louis Armstrong and became *Life*'s unofficial jazz photographer.[44] Mili took pictures of Duke Ellington in his studio, created a series of photo essays called "Jam session" published from 1943 to 1945, and became known for his fast action photography of swing dancers and musicians, casting him as a leader in jazz photography. His photographs alert the viewer to the fast-paced movement of music in general and jazz in particular. Recalling Eadweard Muybridge's experimentations with motion and photography, Mili used photography to capture a sequence of actions together that aided in our contemporary understanding of movement.[45]

Through their photo essays on swing music in the 1930s, Peterson and Mili attempted to disprove the widespread belief that black musicians learned swing from whites, an impression caused by mostly white musicians being showcased in mass-market media. Cawthra sites such examples of this in *Life*, featuring Pee Wee Russell as the new face of jazz in 1938 and the popularity of swing, which was mostly represented by white musicians such as Benny Goodman and Tommy Dorsey.[46] Articles written on swing tended to focus on the entertaining aspects of black musicians and the seriousness of whites, contradicting the efforts of many supporters. Even the bandleader for the Original Dixieland Jass Band in New Orleans, Nick La Rocca, said "jazz melodies are white man[']s music and not African in origin."[47] Cawthra says, "Peterson's and Mili's photographs make African American art and artist visible in a racially inhospitable editorial and sociopolitical environment, creating images that countered popular racial stereotypes and *Life*'s own editorial practices that portrayed black culture in demeaning ways."[48]

In addition to Peterson and Mili, many references of jazz appear in visual media, including photographs, posters, magazines, and film. At this time, visual representations of jazz, such as in films or on the cover of a recording, depict the musician playing his or her instrument.[49] Album covers featured a posed picture of the musician or a headshot that included colorful drawings in the background. Jazz musicians themselves have appeared in films, including Louis Armstrong, who portrayed himself in many movies of the 1940s and 1950s.[50] Prominent examples of jazz musicians as subjects of films are *The Jazz Singer* (1927), *Young Man with a Horn* (1949), *The Fabulous Dorseys* (1947), *New Orleans* (1947), *Jammin' the Blues* (1944), *A Song Is Born* (1948), *The Benny Goodman Story* (1955), and, more recently, *Round Midnight* (1986) and *Bird* (1988).[51] Through films such as *Blackboard Jungle* (1955), *The Wild Ones* (1954), and *Rebel Without a Cause* (1955) the stage was set for an audience to experience the cultural revolution that introduced bebop.[52]

Several magazines featuring the visual imagery of jazz were published during the mid-twentieth century that included anything from pictures of jazz musicians to suggested harmonic substitutions over a certain chord progression. Magazines such as *Down Beat* (1934–), *Metronome* (1934–), *Jazz Information* (1939–41), *American Jazz Monthly* (1944), which was superseded by *American Jazz Review* (1944–47), *Jazz Quarterly* (1942–), *Universal Jazz* (1946–), *Jazz Journal International* (1948–), *Coda: Canada's Jazz Magazine* (1958–), and *Jazz Letter* (1960–) have fostered the continuing development of jazz, along with images of jazz musicians.[53]

Again the words of Cawthra: "Photographers, musicians, graphic designers, editors, and recording executives created a public image for jazz culture even as the dance halls that brought to jazz as a broader audience in the prewar era receded as primary sites for experiencing the music."[54] In postwar America there was no market for jazz photographs per se; however, there were opportunities for photojournalists to include images of jazz musicians as part of a beat for a magazine or publication. (Herman Leonard's first assignment, around 1950, for *Life* was called "How to make a hit record?") The jazz image began to evolve, from publicity photos and artfully drawn commercial posters similar to the one for Armstrong in Figure 1.1, to represent the musical qualities of jazz through the art of photography. Through the comfortable circulation of the jazz image, fans could gaze upon as well as listen to their favorite musician. "[I]ndustrialisation provided social uses for the operations of the photographer," says Susan Sontag.[55] Likewise, Leonard and other photographers played a role in jazz history by bringing the low cost of high art to the public.

Jazz came into the limelight of the film industry and dancehalls nationwide through the popularization of swing; the bebop era of the 1940s and 1950s boosted the prestige of the jazz musician to nobility, inspiring poets, composers, artists, and filmmakers to integrate the values and freedom exhibited by bop musicians into their own work. The swing era was fading away while bebop was emerging. Simultaneously with the social and political upheaval of the 1940s, jazz was undergoing an upheaval of its own. World War II had devastated the music scene with blackouts, late-night curfews, and a twenty-percent entertainment tax, which caused ballrooms, dancehalls, and nightclubs to close all over the country. Many large dance and swing bands stopped performing because they could not pay their musicians, and with the rationing of rubber and gasoline, musicians did not have enough gas to drive to their venues. Dancing seemed to be generally discouraged, and echoing the morale of the country, no one felt like dancing. There was an increase in women musicians, who often replaced their male counterparts fighting in the war. In addition, service in the armed forces deprived jazz fans of contact for several years. On August 1, 1942, the American Federation of Musicians ordered its union members to stop recording, until record companies like Decca, Capitol, Victor, and Columbia agreed to pay their musicians each time a song was played on the radio.[57]

While musicians' contracts were being renegotiated and fewer performance venues and opportunities were available to record their music, they began to move to the smaller, more intimate space of the nightclub. John Wilson concluded that "The unrest that bubbled beneath the conformist surface of the big bands in the Swing era was fed by after hours sessions that could be found almost every night in Harlem as the thirties drew to a close."[58] Some of the sessions occurred in New York City at the Kentucky Club, Puss Johnson's, and Clark Monroe's Uptown House, but Minton's Playhouse on West 118th Street was the hub of emerging bebop in the forties. Here jazz musicians experimented with the melodies of swing music at a faster tempo, then improvised over the chord changes. The streamlined bop combo offered a more democratic musical setting that allowed for experimentation with form and style, years before the arrival of the avant-garde.[59]

With limited dancers or audience members to perform to, jazz musicians could play how they wanted, and they began by extending the improvisation time over chord changes. At first, musicians cultivated a smaller following of only their collaborators and dedicated fans. When the recording ban lifted in 1944, bebop musicians introduced their style to mainstream music audiences. The new technology of magnetic tape, which was enhanced during the war for radio propaganda and intelligence purposes, allowed the subtle intimacies of bop to come through in recording. These subtleties included a new emphasis on solo artists and solo performances like Charlie "Bird" Parker and Dizzy Gillespie.

Bebop ushered in the transition from entertainment to art music of complexity equal to that of the often-compared genre of classical music. Swing bands featuring Count Basie, Benny Goodman, Artie Shaw, Glen Miller, Cab Calloway, and Duke Ellington provided the kernels for bebop to flower. In 1937 Dizzy Gillespie began to appear on records with Teddy Hill's orchestra, and in 1939 Coleman Hawkins recorded his famous solo in "Body and Soul." Minton's Playhouse and Monroe's Uptown House hosted jam sessions with Thelonious Monk and Kenny Clarke sitting in. One of the main instigators of bop, Charlie Parker, drifted in and out of New York from Kansas City before 1941, but became a regular at the Minton sessions in 1942. In 1944 Coleman Hawkins led the first bebop recording session, followed by the Billy Eckstine Orchestra featuring Charlie Parker, Dizzy Gillespie, Dexter Gordon, and Art Blakey.[60]

The double-time solos and complex harmonic progressions shook the listener with new sounds and rhythms, but many bebop tunes were derived from the chord progressions of other popular songs. The girth of the material that propelled bop onto the music scene came from standards of the twenties and thirties such as "I Got Rhythm," "How High the Moon," "Sweet Georgia Brown," "Star Dust," "Night and Day," and "My Romance," all of which were part of the basic music language known by all jazz musicians. Famous songwriters were also carried over from the swing era, such as Irving Berlin, George Gershwin, and Cole Porter.[61] The strengths of these songwriters came from their lilting melodies and the skilled connection between music and lyrics that was usually perfectly exemplified by the singers who sang them.[62] The songs were recycled because these were the songs that bop players knew and had already studied; however, the collection of songs became the foundation for creating new or what many called "modern jazz." Over the years, these songs became standardized as part of both old and new jazz culture. They were unofficially compiled into an American songbook, now known as the Great American Songbook, and each song is part of the standard repertoire of a jazz musician.[63]

By adding more intervals, more chord progressions, and more improvisation time, bebop musicians became pivotal to the evolution of jazz. Bebop players created a new language that was studied and adapted by more and more musicians. Through the complication of standard tunes, bebop musicians are credited with having saved jazz from oblivion. Recording was a lucrative income for swing musicians by 1940, encouraged by record companies who intended to ride any popularity wave only until there was no further demand. Swing seemed to run its course; during the war, there was little income for musicians except for a cappella vocal groups recorded to lift the spirits of both Americans at home and soldiers fighting overseas. Because singers were not part of the musician's union and were therefore exempt from the recording ban, recording companies stayed in business through their services.

With the emergence of bebop, jazz was again on the market as a commodity, even though its initial intended audience was not the general public. Ironically, because bop players were not dependent on mass popularity to survive, they rejected commercialization and "music for entertainment's sake" even though they were paid to perform in small clubs in New York.

In this respect bop was revolutionary. Musicians happily played for those who would listen and understand their stance toward jazz, which occurred through performances either in loft apartments in New York or on the bandstand in those few clubs who would accept newer music. The movement evolved into what Ralph Ellison called a "revolution in culture,"[64] and this identification as revolutionaries escalated the status of the jazz musician.

Bop soon became associated with an entire generation and, to the surprise of all, became standardized practice. Currently, bop is explained as an accelerant for those who wished to jump start jazz after WWII. But aside from its place in jazz history, bop—along with cool and West Coast jazz—established principles of musical performance, arranging, and composition for others to follow. In addition to its musical components, this ideal of intellectualism, defiance, conviction, and artistry found in bop propelled jazz into the limelight while simultaneously holding future jazz musicians to the musical values and traditions of the 1950s.

Bebop, often seen as a protest against commercialism inspired by the modernist movement, was also seen as a revolt from white society since most people working in the recording companies were white. At the time of bop's rise, jazz was no longer considered music for entertainment, as it had been during the swing era. The struggle for recognition as "serious" music was reached by the bebop players due primarily to three things: the high level of skill necessary to play jazz, the years of study and intensive training required, and the need for a thorough understanding of music theory. The skin color of most bop musicians marginalized them from American society; consequently, issues of race continued to anchor progress among members in the jazz community. Bop musicians, regardless of their rejection or acceptance, played mainly for themselves.

Consumers and jazz aficionados alike could have discredited bop because of its radical nature, and returned to the much more tonal sounds of swing. However, bop entered under the right circumstances and, once established, was embraced by the right people who found each other at the right time. Similarly, its identity with modernity and change translated into a cry for both social and musical freedom. Bebop acquired a voice for those who wished to shout, occasionally drowning out those who held onto the traditional sounds of jazz found in swing or Dixieland. Eventually, it became in the best interests for all those affiliated with jazz to embrace bop as the new, "modern" jazz.

As bebop hurled out from the underground, "its rightful audience was left gasping for breath."[65] As bebop entered the record market in 1944, fans began to flock to see the technical wizardry of their heroes. In New York City, clubs and loft apartments became the breeding ground for small-group explorations. At precisely the same time, a number of great photographers such as William Gottlieb, William Claxton, and Milt Hinton, found their way into the larger jazz scene. Hinton recalls that "[a]t some point, probably in the late '40s, I began to realize that I was experiencing jazz history first-hand. The music was changing rapidly, and there were new faces coming on the scene constantly. . . . For some reason, I felt strongly about using my camera to capture the people and events from the jazz world that I was lucky enough to witness."[66] For these photographers lucky enough to be in the right place at the right time, photography became a way to document the events happening during the development of bebop.

The three photographers recognized for their images during this time period were Gottlieb, Claxton, and Herman Leonard. Gottlieb, like others, stumbled into taking pictures of jazz musicians from 1939 to 1948 and took pictures for *Down Beat* from 1946 to 1948. He had a head start on Claxton and Leonard but was not paid for his photographs, which accompanied articles he wrote on jazz for various magazines. With his Speed Graphic press camera, Gottlieb took pictures of Duke Ellington, Benny Goodman, Mary Lou Williams, Dizzy Gillespie, Miles Davis, Eddie Condon, Charlie Parker, Nat King Cole, Billie Holiday, and Django Reinhardt. But by 1948, Gottlieb could not continue the long, late-night hours of photographing and writing about jazz musicians, and chose instead to focus on raising his family and starting an educational filmstrip company.

William Claxton began photographing as a hobby while attending UCLA, and eventually found himself shooting jazz musicians to create cover labels for Pacific Jazz Records during the 1950s. Claxton, who passed away in October 2008, was known for his photographs of West Coast jazz and his pictures of Chet Baker. Claxton and Gottlieb garnered great acclaim for their work and maintained a significant role in the depiction of jazz during the mid-twentieth century.

Other significant photographers who coupled with the churning developments of Gottlieb, Claxton, and Leonard were Ray Avery, Ole Brask, Herb Snitzer, Milt Hinton, Francis (Frank) Wolff, and Lee Tanner.[67] Tanner has created an extensive list of all the great jazz photographers, including Hugh Bell, Esmond Edwards, Tad Hershorn, Paul Hoeffler, Don Hunstein, Guy le Querrec, Jim Marshall, Robert Parent, Jan Persson, Carole Reiff, Don Schlitten, Chuck Stewart, Dennis Stock, Jerry Stoll, Bob Willoughby, and Val Wilmer.[68] These photographers heard jazz at various periods of its history, and were similarly captured by its sound and by the personalities of the musicians. Some of the photographers were musicians themselves, such as Milt Hinton, an extraordinary bassist who played in many famous groups. In many of these performances, he took his camera and shot pictures. But, says Jerry Jazz Musician, "[f]or many of us, the photography of Herman Leonard is our first link to jazz culture. Ellington in Paris, Dexter with a Chesterfield, a youthful Miles, Satchmo in Birdland. . . . These images, in some cases more so than the music, are responsible for our devotion to preserving and protecting the art the musicians of mid 20th century America created, and Herman Leonard reported on."[69]

Leonard photographed most of the great musicians of the bebop, cool, and hard bop eras, including Charlie Parker, Dizzy Gillespie, Duke Ellington, Lester Young, Miles Davis, and Thelonious Monk, as well as other famous musicians not associated with bebop: Frank Sinatra, Billie Holiday, and Louis Armstrong. Leonard seemed to have known these musicians well enough to have been welcomed into their livelihoods backstage and behind the scenes. His love for the music and people, easily detected in each of his photographs, reveals his kind nature and his commitment to photography. After opening his studio in 1948 in Greenwich Village at 220 Sullivan Street, Leonard used his camera to get into the clubs of Broadway, 52nd Street, and Harlem. In 1950 he moved his studio and residence to 38 East 50th Street. Throughout this time, if he wanted to get into a club to hear jazz, he would bring his camera and tell the owner that he was supposed to take pictures of the musicians; then he would give photographs to the owners in return for access and provide the musicians with prints as well:

> I usually persuaded the club owners to let me install my lights in the afternoon. Then, I'd shoot either the rehearsal that took place that day or the actual performance that night. In the evening, I could put one flash strobe up in the ceiling clamped right next to the main spotlight. I could only afford two lights, so I had another light that I usually placed in an area that would be behind the subject, so they would be hiding it from view. And everything had to be wired. I had to wire my lights through the ceiling to the back of the club, down the wall and then down on the floor to wherever I was and then connect them to my camera. It was all improvised, but it was the only way I could get the results that I wanted since there were no assignments at that point.[70]

He used an old Speed Graphic handheld 4 x 5 camera; in order to create his trademark illuminated smoke image, he wired two strobe lights, one in back and one in front of the musician, that captured the intensity of the exposed light.[71] The slow shutter speed of the camera allowed for longer exposure of images, which is why the film absorbed more light.

After printing the photos he took at a recording session or performance, Leonard would give a print to the owner of the club and to the musicians who were in the photograph. That way, the owners could use the photographs for publicity if needed or simply keep them for their own private use, and Leonard became friends with the musicians, who were glad that people were appreciating their music enough to photograph them. Responding to the question: "When you first started taking pictures of jazz musicians, did you see other images around of jazz musicians such as posters, or photographs of jazz musicians?" Leonard replied,

> There were none. There were none, because there were no other photographers around that were serious about shooting jazz. I mean there were people. But the serious photographers of jazz, there were half a dozen if that many. The only ones I knew about were Bill Gottlieb and Bill Claxton. Well, Gottlieb was before me, and Claxton and I overlapped. There were no posters as such, not photographic, but they were of art work, drawings, sketches and stuff because there were no photos available for them to use. So they did sketches. Even album covers were art works before they used photos—drawing, paintings, or whatever they used before they used photography. So there was no real interest or market for availability of jazz images in photography. I gave the prints out to the club owners; that way I could come back and shoot. I gave prints to the musicians which established a friendship.[72]

In this manner, Leonard unknowingly contributed to the circulation of jazz imagery. His photos were used in an advertisement for the next gig, or they were passed around to other musicians like new baby pictures at a family reunion. His photos, along with those by other photographers, stimulated a change from the more traditional head shots or promotional shots that were used in the 1940s to taking a picture of the musician with their instrument or while they are playing. The more pictures photographers took, the more they were placed on storefronts and in magazines, thus establishing more visual material about jazz.

From 1948 to 1956 his images appeared regularly on album covers and were used as promotional material by record companies including RCA Victor, Decca, Capitol, Mercury, and Verve. He began photographing recording sessions for Verve Records and later was hired as a photographer for Barclay Records. He freelanced for the popular magazines *Look*, *Life*,

Esquire, and *Cosmopolitan* and music magazines including *Down Beat* and *Metronome*. Leonard's jazz photography was given a sixteen-page tribute in a special edition, *Metronome Yearbook* 1950, heralding him as "the favorite photographer of jazzmen."[73]

However while his photos gained greater exposure, at the time they were not the hot commodities they are today. Similar to Gottlieb and Claxton, Leonard worked as a commercial photographer and freelanced for the popular magazines. His images appeared not only on album covers and as promotional material by record companies, but also as a part of other material on jazz that was circulating at that time. In the 1960s, even though he continued to photograph musicians, he began to expand his freelance career to include fashion, advertising and film. Eventually, Leonard stored the negatives from 1948 (when he arrived in New York from studying with Yousuf Karsh) to 1956 (when he began traveling extensively to shoot for fashion, advertising, and film) and focused on his commercial career.

The pictures from record covers, posters, photos, and promotion material slowly began to solidify into a canon of jazz visual imagery that circulated through the mid-century. Photographers such as Leonard, Gottlieb, and Claxton were part of this collection but did not play a huge role until the photographs gained greater importance as the musicians themselves did. Through this process, Leonard transformed the public's image of jazz from the sweet singers of the swing era to the edgy instrumentalists of the bop revolution. As we will see, his signature black-and-white photographs of smoky barroom settings made some jazz musicians look like mysterious alchemists, hovering in an air of artistic splendor, and his training and foresight allowed him to photograph with dignity a number of the most famous jazz musicians at the height of their careers.

Furthermore, the subject being photographed has a lot to do with the presentation according to personal or particular biases.[74] Often, the musicians are not aware of this visual representation of jazz, shaped and molded not only by the photographer but also by editors and authors of magazines, managers of nightclubs, agents of the musicians, radio producers, authors, and the publicity and Artists and Repertoire (A&R) division of a record company. Producers and managers of musicians act as a direct link between the musician and the commercial industry, since they cultivate their reputation alongside the musicians themselves. Their opinions greatly influence not only the direction of the music they are representing, but also the image of the musicians themselves. Managing a jazz musician requires visual evidence, including photography, in order to successfully promote the artist and the music.

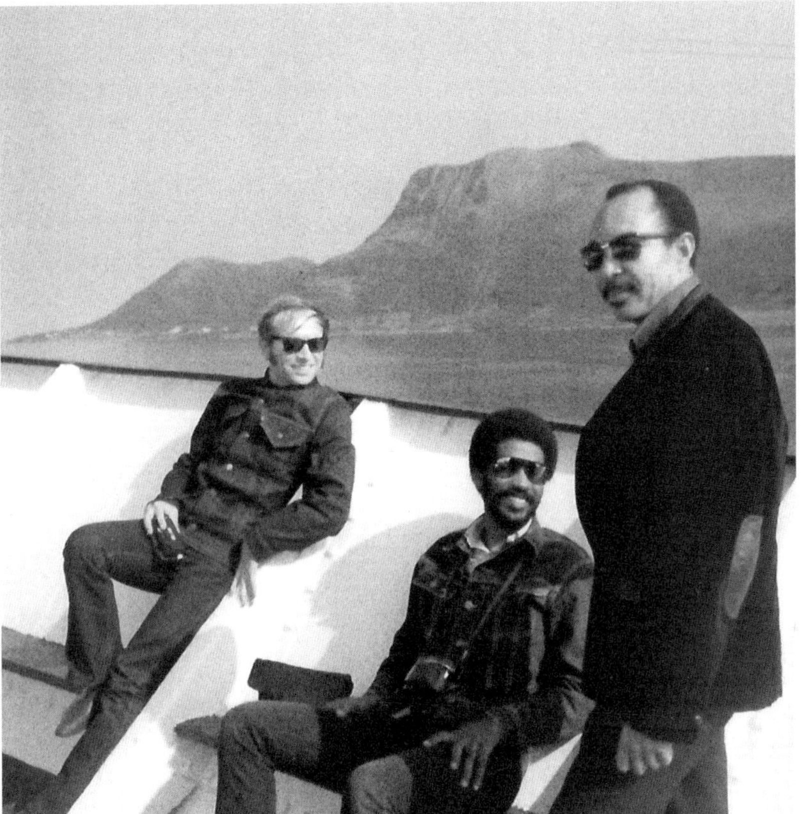

Fig. 1.3. Lutz Bacher in 1969 with Bobby Hutcherson and Harold Land en route to the Molde International Jazz Festival in Norway. Photo provided by Lutz Bacher.

Lutz Bacher, for example, managed many well-known jazz musicians in the early 1970s and is a direct link to the visual imagery on jazz as it developed at that time. Initially, Bacher was a musician and a jazz advocate in college. He contributed to *Coda* magazine and started a jazz society while attending the University of Windsor in Canada. While working on his marketing degree, Bacher began to promote concerts on the campus and surrounding venues.[75] He later started Lutz Bacher Jazz Productions (LBJP) in Detroit, Michigan, and professionally managed American and European clients such as the Johnny Griffith Trio, the Don Friedman Quartet, the Andrew Hill Quartet, the McCoy Tyner Quartet, the Bobby Hutcherson–Harold Land Quintet, the Joe Henderson Sextet, the Freddie Hubbard Quintet, the Pharoah Sanders Quintet, the Kenny Dunell Quartet, the 360 Degree Music Experience, Kenn Cox and the Contemporary Jazz Quintet, and the Karl Berger Total Music Ensemble.[76]

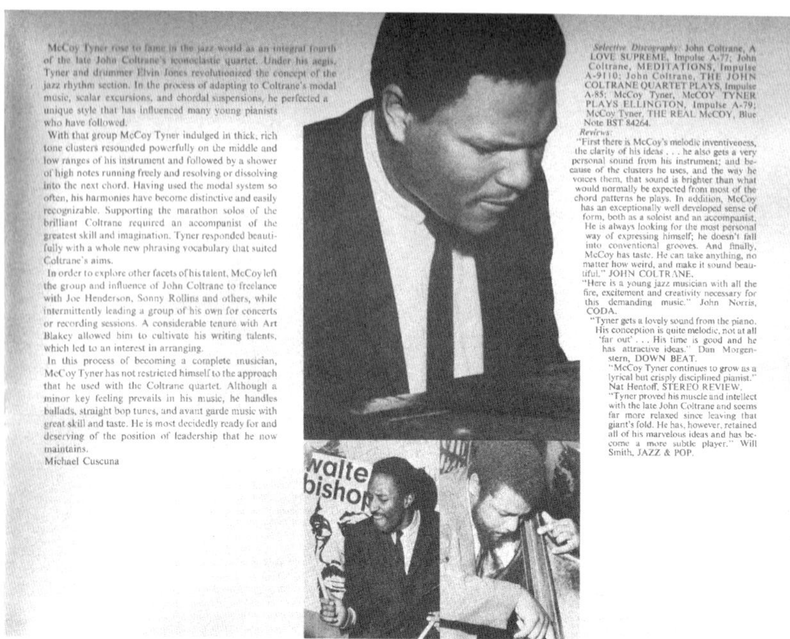

McCoy Tyner rose to fame in the jazz world as an integral fourth of the late John Coltrane's iconoclastic quartet. Under his aegis, Tyner and drummer Elvin Jones revolutionized the concept of the jazz rhythm section. In the process of adapting to Coltrane's modal music, scalar excursions, and chordal suspensions, he perfected a unique style that has influenced many young pianists who have followed.

With that group McCoy Tyner indulged in thick, rich tone clusters resounded powerfully on the middle and low ranges of his instrument and followed by a shower of high notes running freely and resolving or dissolving into the next chord. Having used the modal system so often, his harmonies have become distinctive and easily recognizable. Supporting the marathon solos of the brilliant Coltrane required an accompanist of the greatest skill and imagination. Tyner responded beautifully with a whole new phrasing vocabulary that suited Coltrane's aims.

In order to explore other facets of his talent, McCoy left the group and influence of John Coltrane to freelance with Joe Henderson, Sonny Rollins and others, while intermittently leading a group of his own for concerts or recording sessions. A considerable tenure with Art Blakey allowed him to cultivate his writing talents, which led to an interest in arranging.

In this process of becoming a complete musician, McCoy Tyner has not restricted himself to the approach that he used with the Coltrane quartet. Although a minor key feeling prevails in his music, he handles ballads, straight bop tunes, and avant garde music with great skill and taste. He is most decidedly ready for and deserving of the position of leadership that he now maintains.

Michael Cuscuna

Selective Discography: John Coltrane, A LOVE SUPREME, Impulse A-77; John Coltrane, MEDITATIONS, Impulse A-9110; John Coltrane, THE JOHN COLTRANE QUARTET PLAYS, Impulse A-85; McCoy Tyner, McCOY TYNER PLAYS ELLINGTON, Impulse A-79; McCoy Tyner, THE REAL McCOY, Blue Note BST 84264.

Reviews:

"First there is McCoy's melodic inventiveness, the clarity of his ideas . . . he also gets a very personal sound from his instrument; and because of the clusters he uses, and the way he voices them, that sound is brighter than what would normally be expected from most of the chord patterns he plays. In addition, McCoy has an exceptionally well developed sense of form, both as a soloist and an accompanist. He is always looking for the most personal way of expressing himself; he doesn't fall into conventional grooves. And finally, McCoy has taste. He can take anything, no matter how weird, and make it sound beautiful." JOHN COLTRANE.

"Here is a young jazz musician with all the fire, excitement and creativity necessary for this demanding music." John Norris, CODA.

"Tyner gets a lovely sound from the piano. His conception is quite melodic, not at all 'far out' . . . His time is good and he has attractive ideas." Dan Morgenstern, DOWN BEAT.

"McCoy Tyner continues to grow as a lyrical but crisply disciplined pianist." Nat Hentoff, STEREO REVIEW.

"Tyner proved his muscle and intellect with the late John Coltrane and seems far more relaxed since leaving that giant's fold. He has, however, retained all of his marvelous ideas and has become a more subtle player." Will Smith, JAZZ & POP.

Fig. 1.4. Page on the McCoy Tyner Trio from the Lutz Bacher Jazz Productions brochure on concert artists for the 1969–70 season. Provided by Lutz Bacher.

Like many others, Bacher learned by his own initiative how to manage professional musicians. He attended the National Entertainment Conference to develop his contacts and create bookings for future gigs. He began a mailing list of colleges and universities, who provided the most opportunities for booking. He fostered repeated business with several universities such as Carleton University in Ottawa, the University of Toronto, and the University of Michigan, and booked European tours and club dates.

By 1967, three years after he started booking musicians and two years after he managed professionally under the name LBJP, Bacher created a brochure with the help of an art director friend Baron Hoffar whom he knew from Campbell-Ewald Advertising. This brochure was mailed annually to colleges and universities across America and Canada. Bacher used photography extensively in the annual mailings as well as in the promotional package he created featuring his clients, concert repertoire, bios, reviews, and pictures of the musicians.[77]

One must have a photograph to make a poster or advertisement for gigs, and once agreeing to take on a new client, Bacher asked each musician to

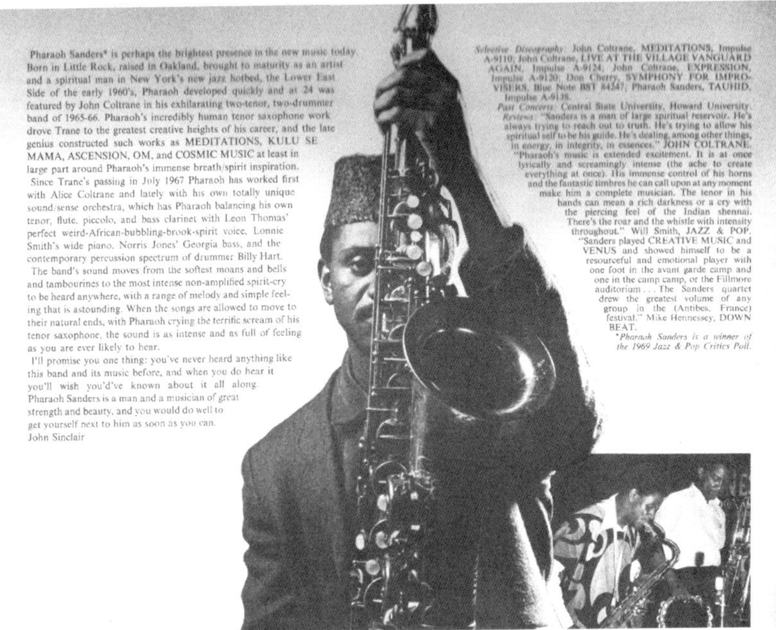

Pharaoh Sanders* is perhaps the brightest presence in the new music today. Born in Little Rock, raised in Oakland, brought to maturity as an artist and a spiritual man in New York's new jazz hotbed, the Lower East Side of the early 1960's, Pharaoh developed quickly and at 24 was featured by John Coltrane in his exhilarating two-tenor, two-drummer band of 1965-66. Pharaoh's incredibly human tenor saxophone work drove Trane to the greatest creative heights of his career, and the late genius constructed such works as MEDITATIONS, KULU SE MAMA, ASCENSION, OM, and COSMIC MUSIC at least in large part around Pharaoh's immense breath/spirit inspiration.

Since Trane's passing in July 1967 Pharaoh has worked first with Alice Coltrane and lately with his own totally unique sound/sense orchestra, which has Pharaoh balancing his own tenor, flute, piccolo, and bass clarinet with Leon Thomas' perfect weird-African-bubbling-brook-spirit voice, Lonnie Smith's wide piano, Norris Jones' Georgia bass, and the contemporary percussion spectrum of drummer Billy Hart.

The band's sound moves from the softest moans and bells and tambourines to the most intense non-amplified spirit-cry to be heard anywhere, with a range of melody and simple feeling that is astounding. When the songs are allowed to move to their natural ends, with Pharaoh crying the terrific scream of his tenor saxophone, the sound is as intense and as full of feeling as you are ever likely to hear.

I'll promise you one thing: you've never heard anything like this band and its music before, and when you do hear it you'll wish you'd've known about it all along. Pharaoh Sanders is a man and a musician of great strength and beauty, and you would do well to get yourself next to him as soon as you can.
John Sinclair

Selective Discography: John Coltrane, MEDITATIONS, Impulse A-9110; John Coltrane, LIVE AT THE VILLAGE VANGUARD AGAIN, Impulse A-9124; John Coltrane, EXPRESSION, Impulse A-9120; Don Cherry, SYMPHONY FOR IMPROVISERS, Blue Note BST 84247; Pharaoh Sanders, TAUHID, Impulse A-9138.

Past Concerts: Central State University, Howard University.

Reviews: "Sanders is a man of large spiritual reservoir. He's always trying to reach out to truth. He's trying to allow his spiritual self to be his guide. He's dealing, among other things, in energy, in integrity, in essences." JOHN COLTRANE. "Pharaoh's music is extended excitement. It is at once lyrically and screamingly intense (the ache to create everything at once). His immense control of his horns and the fantastic timbres he can call upon at any moment make him a complete musician. The tenor in his hands can mean a rich darkness or a cry with the piercing feel of the Indian shennai. There's the roar and the whistle with intensity throughout." Will Smith, JAZZ & POP. "Sanders played CREATIVE MUSIC and VENUS and showed himself to be a resourceful and emotional player with one foot in the avant garde camp and one in the camp camp, or the Fillmore auditorium . . . The Sanders quartet drew the greatest volume of any group in the (Antibes, France) festival." Mike Hennessey, DOWN BEAT.

**Pharaoh Sanders is a winner of the 1969 Jazz & Pop Critics Poll.*

Fig. 1.5. Page on the Pharoah Sanders Quintet from the Lutz Bacher Jazz Productions brochure on concert artists for the 1969–70 season.

send professional photos of him or herself that could be used as a marketing tool to support his business and the musicians. Musicians often supplied their own photographs themselves, since in many instances, the musicians such as Tyner, Hubbard, Hutcherson, and Sanders already had headshots or other promotional material from the recording companies.[78] Bacher then had posters made to advertise them and eventually created a promotional kit that he could send to a venue prior to a performance. On the back of the 1966–67 season brochure (see Fig. 1.6), Bacher provided a section entitled "What makes your concert a success?" Bacher writes, "we supply a COMPLETE PROMOTIONAL KIT including:"

- A Guide to Promotional Activities for Your Concert
- Several Publicity Sets Containing 8x10 Photos, Biographical Material and Feature Stories
- Several Recordings of the Ensemble for Radio Stations and Listening Facilities on Campus
- A Program of Your Concert in Advance
- Attractive Posters at Cost (We Recommend One per Hundred Students)

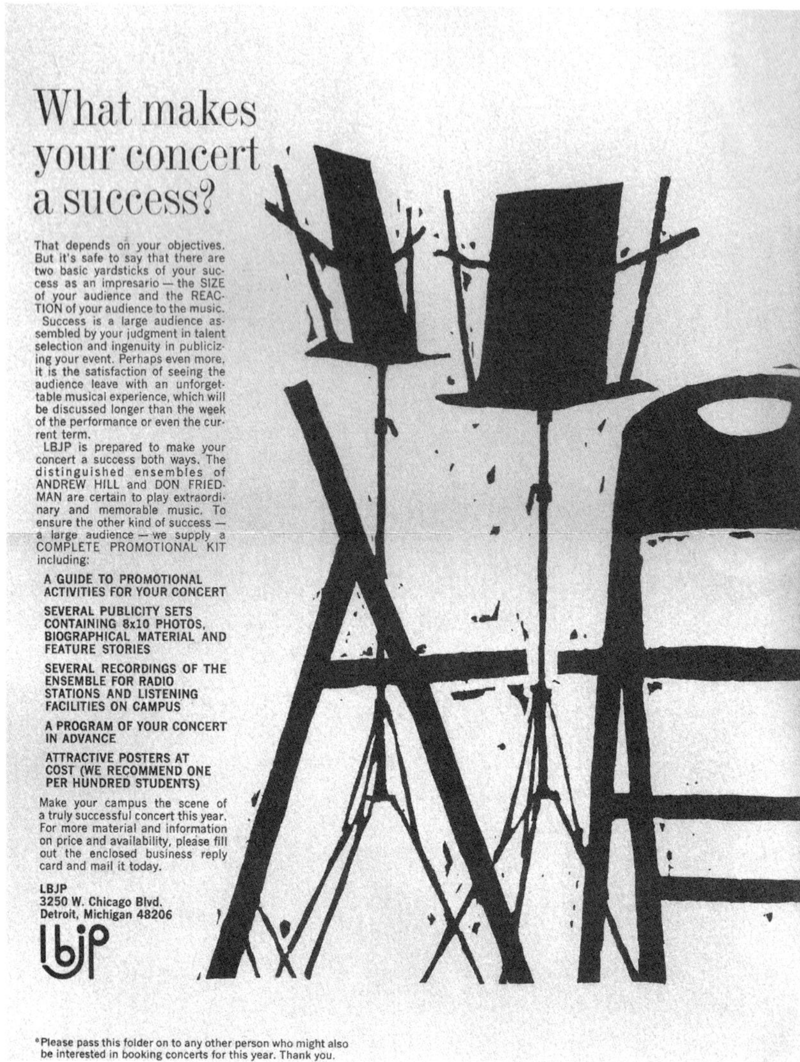

Fig. 1.6. The Lutz Bacher Jazz Productions College Jazz Concerts brochure for 1966–67.

By mailing pictures and promotion kits to countless correspondents, connections were made with other managers and producers, which in turn fostered a circulation of visual images.[79]

Although he did most of the advertising and marketing on his own through LBJP, Bacher also relied on the contacts and skills of others in the same business. He would often receive a letter from a photographer who offered to provide prints of a jazz concert that Bacher had arranged. He

May 2, 1966.

Lutz Bacher Jazz Productions,
3250 West Chicago Blvd,
Detroit Michigan
48206.

Dear Lutz:

Find enclosed rough proofs of the Hart House concert. My rates are $5.00 each for 10" by 8" and $7.00 each for 11" by14" prints. Should you require any, would you be specific about surface finish and number required.

Unfortunately the negatives of Andrew Hill and Bobby Hutcherson were unavoidably destroyed recently, although I do have some 10" by 8" prints of Bobby Hutcherson and Joe Chambers at that same concert. If you are interested, please let me know. Also, you may be interested in other artists that I have in my files; please give me names if you are. I may be able to oblige.

I shall be at Newport this year. Will you want anything from the Festival?

Yours sincerely,

JWMorgan.

JOHN W. MORGAN

Fig. 1.7. Letter from John Morgan to Lutz Bacher, September 1966. Provided by Lutz Bacher.

then had the option to pay the photographer for prints and thus create a new business relationship. This provided an opportunity for freelance photographers to sell their material as merchandise to the audience or, in this case, to the managers of the musicians. For example, in 1966 photographer John Morgan sent Bacher the letter in Figure 1.7, along with proofs (see Fig. 1.8) of the pictures he had taken at a concert managed by Bacher, in the hope that the photos would be purchased and used to market upcoming venues.

Interestingly enough, Bacher did purchase Morgan's prints, and incorporated them into the brochure he was working on for that year. On the page on Andrew Hill, the image in the bottom left corner is the same image

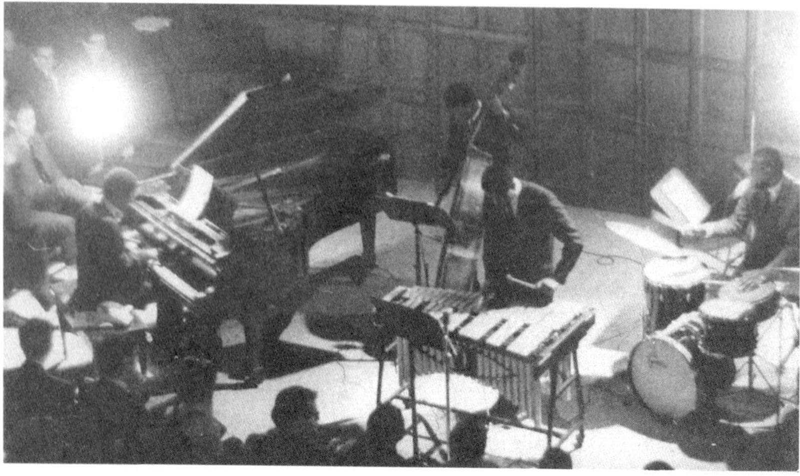

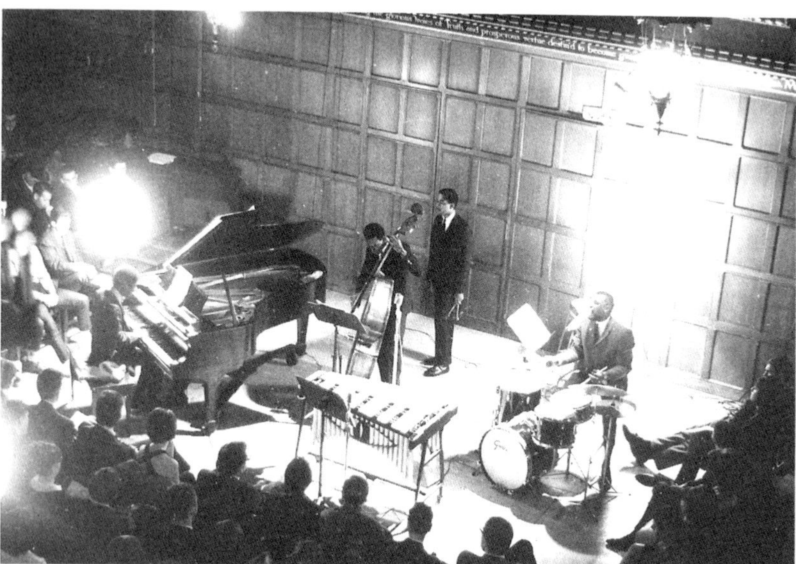

Fig. 1.8. Hart House Concert with Andrew Hill on piano and Bobby Hutcherson on vibraphone. Proofs given by John Morgan to Lutz Bacher, September 1966. Provided by Lutz Bacher.

sent by Morgan with his letter (see Figs. 1.9 and 1.10). By facilitating various images on jazz musicians, both Morgan and Bacher are unconsciously contributing to the visual output on jazz. As Catherine Moore observes, ". . . the visual image is what marketing and publicity staffs use to promote music. Although critics of this practice claim that it has nothing to do with the artistic component of music, it is hard to name a genre that does not use images to entice."[80]

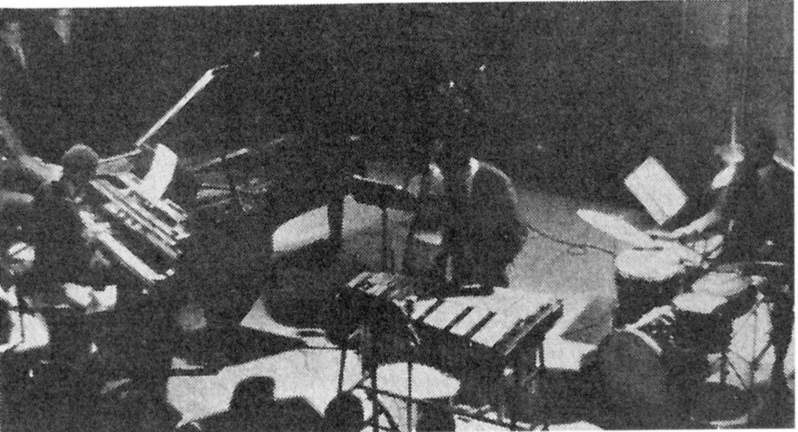

Fig. 1.9. Page on the Andrew Hill Quartet from the Lutz Bacher Jazz Productions College Jazz Concerts brochure for 1966–67.

The Morgan proofs are evidence of a visual exchange not only between musician and photographer, as was often the case with Leonard, but also between photographer and manager as a business transaction. John Morgan does not attempt to create a nostalgic recounting of jazz as we knew it in the past; in this case, he is providing art as a service as do the musicians in the images. However, the photograph acts as a record for the event that happened, and over time, the formation and collection of these "happenings" determine the common taste of a society, establishing an ideology around the subject presented in the image.

In the definition, origin, and development of what we have labeled the jazz image, these "jazz image–makers included not only the photographers but also editors, record company producers, museum curators, and, crucially, the subjects of the photographs themselves."[81] However, the image of the jazz musician did not become an overnight success. The creation of a visual image of jazz occurred historically through the combination of American imagery, ingenious photography, and an almost mythical understanding of the jazz musician. Photographs, in particular, become what Walter Benjamin calls the dialectical image, or the understanding of life as it was in the image. The dialectical image by definition is a snapshot of a particular historical moment in time that acts as a communicative device, a dialectic between the "now" of the viewer looking into the picture and the "then" (i.e., the convergence of all information at the time the picture was taken). It is "us" communicating with "them" and vice versa through the window of the photograph. Through a photograph, one can feel as if (s)he were present to witness Dizzy Gillespie playing in New York. In this

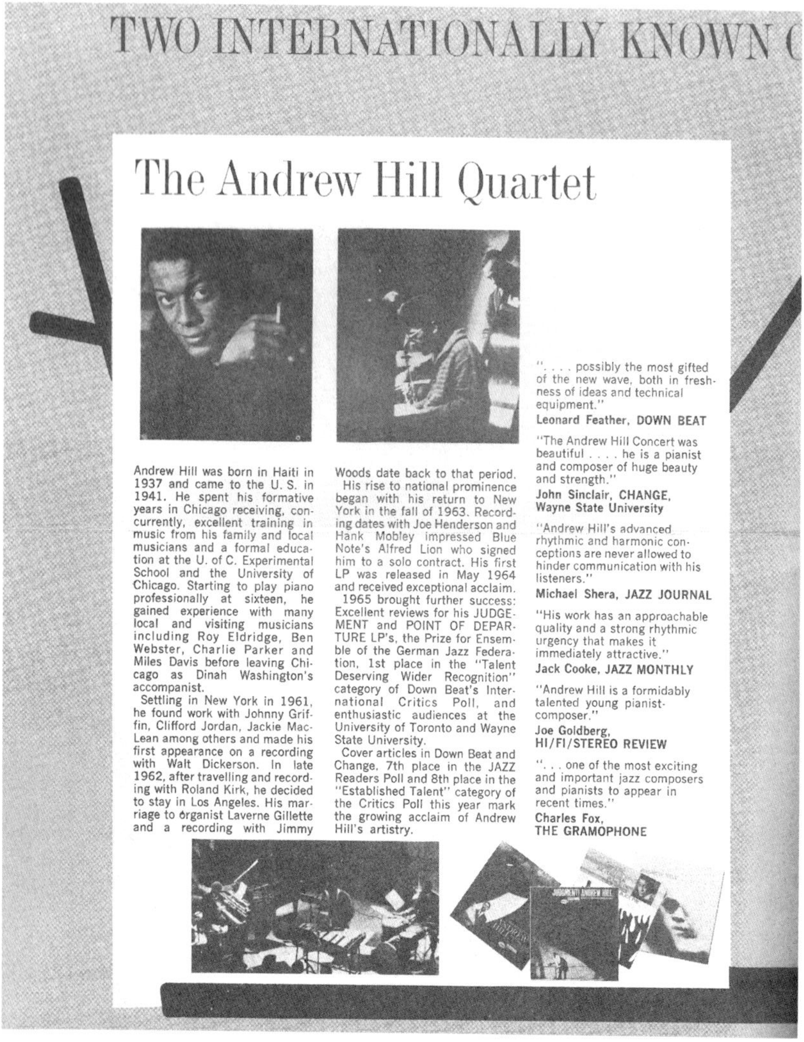

TWO INTERNATIONALLY KNOWN (

The Andrew Hill Quartet

Andrew Hill was born in Haiti in 1937 and came to the U. S. in 1941. He spent his formative years in Chicago receiving, concurrently, excellent training in music from his family and local musicians and a formal education at the U. of C. Experimental School and the University of Chicago. Starting to play piano professionally at sixteen, he gained experience with many local and visiting musicians including Roy Eldridge, Ben Webster, Charlie Parker and Miles Davis before leaving Chicago as Dinah Washington's accompanist.

Settling in New York in 1961, he found work with Johnny Griffin, Clifford Jordan, Jackie MacLean among others and made his first appearance on a recording with Walt Dickerson. In late 1962, after travelling and recording with Roland Kirk, he decided to stay in Los Angeles. His marriage to organist Laverne Gillette and a recording with Jimmy Woods date back to that period.

His rise to national prominence began with his return to New York in the fall of 1963. Recording dates with Joe Henderson and Hank Mobley impressed Blue Note's Alfred Lion who signed him to a solo contract. His first LP was released in May 1964 and received exceptional acclaim.

1965 brought further success: Excellent reviews for his JUDGEMENT and POINT OF DEPARTURE LP's, the Prize for Ensemble of the German Jazz Federation, 1st place in the "Talent Deserving Wider Recognition" category of Down Beat's International Critics Poll, and enthusiastic audiences at the University of Toronto and Wayne State University.

Cover articles in Down Beat and Change, 7th place in the JAZZ Readers Poll and 8th place in the "Established Talent" category of the Critics Poll this year mark the growing acclaim of Andrew Hill's artistry.

". . . . possibly the most gifted of the new wave, both in freshness of ideas and technical equipment."
Leonard Feather, DOWN BEAT

"The Andrew Hill Concert was beautiful . . . . he is a pianist and composer of huge beauty and strength."
John Sinclair, CHANGE, Wayne State University

"Andrew Hill's advanced rhythmic and harmonic conceptions are never allowed to hinder communication with his listeners."
Michael Shera, JAZZ JOURNAL

"His work has an approachable quality and a strong rhythmic urgency that makes it immediately attractive."
Jack Cooke, JAZZ MONTHLY

"Andrew Hill is a formidably talented young pianist-composer."
Joe Goldberg, HI/FI/STEREO REVIEW

". . . one of the most exciting and important jazz composers and pianists to appear in recent times."
Charles Fox, THE GRAMOPHONE

Fig. 1.10. Detail of the bottom of page 2 from the brochure, focusing on the photograph of Bobby Hutcherson and Andrew Hill.

manner of establishing "sight as experience," photographing jazz musicians became a process of understanding the sound and production of jazz itself.

Jazz, ironically and uniquely, cannot be easily reproduced even with musical recordings, because musicians cannot exactly replay the improvised solo they played moments earlier. Similarly, photographers cannot go back to precisely the same place and time of a picture already taken. Both photographer and musician rely on the moment of creation, which inherently provides difficulty when attempting to replicate a moment. Herman Leonard could not return to New York City as it was in 1948 to take more pictures; however, his photographs resurfaced despite the idea that an "image has a finite life."[82] His then manager, Jenny Bagert, was referring to the 1988 rerelease of Leonard's photographs of jazz musicians, which made Leonard's name synonymous with jazz musicians themselves.

Leonard's jazz negatives and prints had been stored under his bed for years and years. He found them during his move to London and decided to reprint them in hopes of exhibiting them. He desperately searched for a willing participant to provide him with the exhibition space. His 1988 show, the Images of Jazz exhibit at the Special Photographer's Company, relaunched his career, not as a commercial photographer but this time as an artist. In the discussion below, Leonard recounts how his photographs found a new audience.

HERMAN: I had my first exhibition in London and through a confluence of events. I had a huge exposure. I sold a lot of prints.

HEATHER: Now how did the London exhibit take off? In '88?

HERMAN: Well, to give you a little background, I had moved from Paris to Ibiza. And then in '88 or '89, I moved to London with my two children. And I had no work. I was 65 already. A 65 year old photographer knocks on the art director's doors, "hello," because I'm competing with 25 year old geniuses, especially this day and age with how easy it is to take a photo with Photoshop, blah, blah, blah. Didn't have that in those days. But I had no work. I had several interviews on the radio calling in, "we love your work" and what not. The only way I could make a living was not through assignments, because it wasn't enough to pay for two kids, school, and you know.

And I went to two of the best reputable galleries in London, Hamilton Gallery was one. And there was another one but, I can't recall. And they said, "oh, nice pictures, but there's no interest in jazz particularly among our clientele." Visual jazz, they like the music, but you know. I don't have a book to announce for a new show. So, I was very depressed, and I really saw no way out. So, I was walking through Portabello Road, and there was a photo gallery called the Special Photographer's Company. And the girl behind the desk, nice-looking, and I showed her my prints in a box. And she said, "Leave these with me, and I will talk to my partner. And I ran into her a week later in the supermarket and she said, "We would like to do your show, but we have expenses that you have to cover: promotion, publicity, the use of the space, all included $5,000."

HEATHER: $5,000! Whew. There you go.

HERMAN: —for a month. Ha! Yeah, "forget about it, lady."

HEATHER: I'll say.

HERMAN: And that evening, I had dinner with an American friend of mine who lived in London, and I told him the story. And a day later, he called me and he said, "Don't worry about it; it's all taken care of." He had a friend in Ford Motor Company who got Ford to sponsor the show in exchange for publicity for Ford Motor. So we came up with the 5 grand and got prepared for the show, started hanging it, and somehow the BBC got wind of it. They came over for the hanging to do some footage for their "Arts and Review" program. Then, they called and said they showed it to somebody upstairs, and he wanted to do a half hour special.

One thing led to another after this, and eventually Leonard's work was exhibited in Europe and the United States, followed by documentaries, publications, interviews, and commissions resulting in more exposure. William Gottlieb, William Claxton, and Herb Snitzer had similar experiences with their own photography, or else they would not be known at all. Their work is also being re-displayed on websites and in publications, but this time the worth of their photographs has increased due to their exposure. Jazz photography has been the beneficiary of a unique approach to marketing in the fine art world.[83]

Consequently, when viewing examples of visual culture from the 1950s such as Leonard's photographs, one does not simply view them for their historical merit. Instead, they are viewed with the knowledge that the photograph represents a transition in jazz history. Visual culture, as Nicholas Mirzoeff states, "does not depend on the pictures themselves but the modern tendency to picture or visualize something."[84] In the twenty-first century our tendency is to look at a photograph with the knowledge of what has happened *after* that photograph was taken: ideas changed, people died, rights challenged, countries invaded, music was recorded, and history was made.

The interesting thing about Leonard's fame as a jazz photographer is exactly the fact that it is recent. Leonard took pictures as he saw jazz at the time the photos were taken. However, he put the prints and negatives away for forty years until he unearthed his negatives of jazz musicians and decided to reprint them. This is the action that propelled Leonard into fame. They did exist between the years of their creation and 1988, but not until Leonard showed them at an exhibit in London did he become known no longer as a freelance commercial photographer but now as the photographer of great jazz musicians. Time is what made Leonard an anomaly. His images are considered representative of the best jazz as it existed in the past—and continue to stand for jazz today.

However full jazz may be of surprises and rich contradictions in its remarkable heritage, it is not the head shots nor artful drawings of jazz musicians that imprint memorable images. Instead, it is those pictures of the jazz musician created during the bebop era and transmitted through the camera lens of Gottlieb, Claxton, or Leonard that captured the hearts of Americans. The success of these images is not solely the efforts of Leonard or the photographer, but is also the result of people buying them. Bebop musicians became icons who rejected the tame and easygoing nature of swing. Indeed, they launched a new method of performing that focused on the individual and the small group setting, and they neither searched for nor desired dancers to intrude on their musical space. They were seen as revolutionaries who were photographed, interviewed, written about, and recorded. As a result, they haphazardly created an image of defiance, and that image of the solitary jazz musician became a marketable item. The music's survival depended largely on the marketing of this image. Bebop would never have left the clubs had it not been marketed as cool, yet edgy for listening.

Ironically, the counterculture spirit from which bebop and cool jazz arose became a marketing tool in itself, as noted by Stephen Struthers in his essay "Technology in the Art of Recording." Once bebop trickled to the ears of jazz admirers across the nation, its status was assured as intellectual music neither artificially manufactured nor slavishly linked to popular culture. Through the strong associations between bebop and the intelligentsia in particular, an ideological framework was created for the jazz musician that came to permeate society. The years 1940 to 1945 saw the rise of not only a new form of jazz but also a new image as a direct result of that form. And Herman Leonard, unknowingly at the time, provided the next key step in marketing the bop musician. Bagert explains, "As the form of music (jazz) was reborn from the 1940s, so was photography's rebirth in 1980s."[85]

The image of the jazz musician was capitalized on during the bebop era with record sales, photography, films, and literary writing. The enticing component of the bebop jazz musician standing proudly playing his instrument is the versatility of the image. The infinite ways to utilize the image became apparent to filmmakers, photographers, visual artists, scholars, and poets alike. Thus, the embodiment of different sensibilities through an image of one solitary jazz figure opened the door for commercialization. But the rise of bebop commercialization did not occur in a vacuum, nor was the marketing of jazz a new idea. Swing provided the foundation for entrepreneurship just as dance music and commercialism, according to Scott DeVeaux, allowed "Swing to be both an authentic jazz expression and a lucrative national fad."[86] Likewise, John Fordham remarks, "If Swing was jazz that went to the public with open arms, bebop was jazz that turned its back on its audience."[87] Fostered by a sense of isolation from the mainstream music world, the energy of improvisational bebop jam sessions came to represent a rejection from the charted, coherent sounds of the swing era.

Jazz, much less bebop, has never regained the popularity it had in the swing era. The development of the jazz image changed radically from the height of its popularity in the 1930s to the rebirth of the jazz image under the guise of modernity in the 1940s and 1950s. Since bebop surfaced, the visual image of the jazz musician has become a commodity, prompting Charles Nanry to observe that "Jazz musicians have always had to articulate their expression within the larger world of entertainment. But in order to do this, jazz must become self-consciousness, to think of itself as a distinct cultural entity."[88]

Albums of the 1950s were marketed to an audience that rejected both the music and norms of popular opinion. A market arose based on the new, socially conscious jazz listener, and record labels gained some profit from the rebellious, adventurous reputation of the jazz artist. Many authors agree with Leonard Feather that bebop was simply the next step in a line of commercialized music: "The story of bop, like that of Swing before it, like the stories of jazz and ragtime before that, has been one of constant struggle against the restrictions imposed on all progressive thought in an art that has been commercialized to the point of prostitution."[89] This may be true, but the difference with bebop is that it has remained at the center of jazz since 1945. Bebop sprang out of the modern era of jazz and created a complex infrastructure of music for generations of musicians to study.

In addition, bop musicians like Dizzy Gillespie are idolized for their spirit and creative energy. It is the bebop image that has permeated the minds of jazz musicians; it is the bebop image that has made the greatest insinuation into the commercialization of jazz; and it is this same bebop image that has been immortalized in the photographs by Herman Leonard.

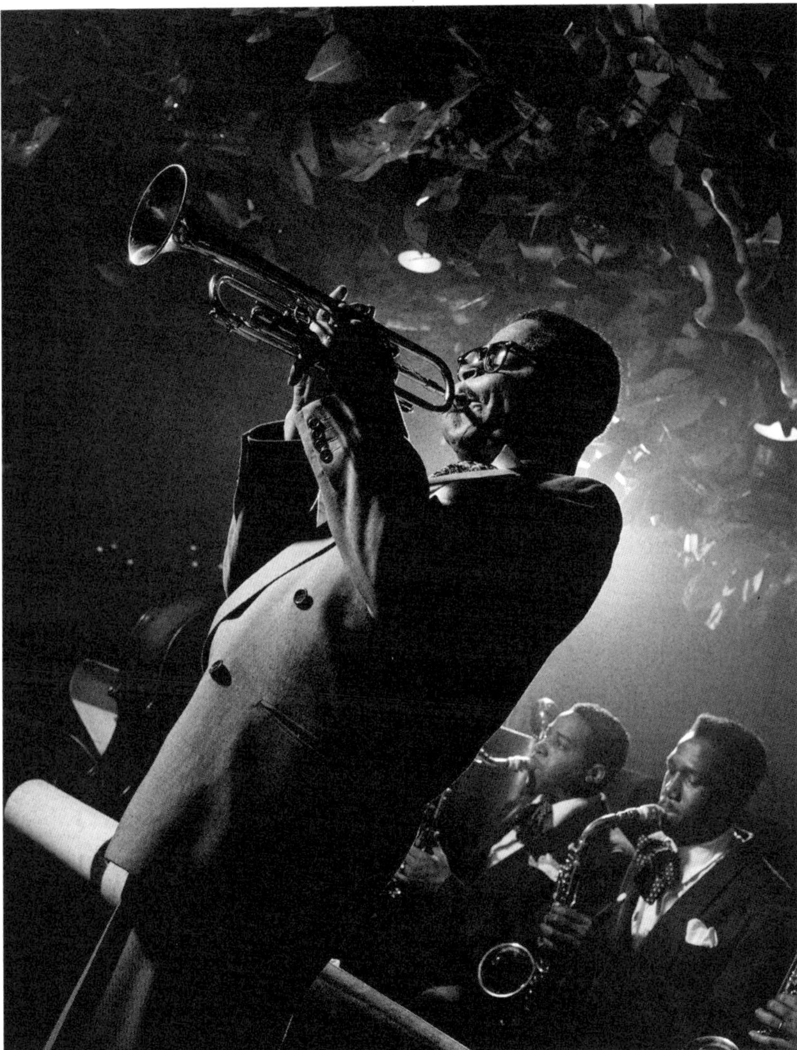

Fig. 1.11. Dizzy Gillespie at the Royal Roost in New York City, 1948, code #DZG04 by Herman Leonard. © Herman Leonard Photography LLC/CTSIMAGES.COM.

In order to understand the importance of the image in jazz history, we must next examine how Leonard's photographs have become so influential in the field of jazz. Leonard's photograph of Dizzy Gillespie taken in New York City provides a ready example. The scene depicts Gillespie standing triumphantly and playing his trumpet in front of other band members. He is playing a solo at a New York jazz club, as indicated by his posture and by his standing while others sit. What makes this photograph unique is the angle of Gillespie and the shimmering plastic foliage at the nightclub, reflected above his head. Leonard has modeled the photograph to create a V-shape from the patterns above Gillespie's head and the men playing below. The implied line of each form extends beyond the photos. Gillespie stands in the middle of the V with light seemingly emitting behind him. The confidence of his stance, mirrored in the other shapes of the photograph, is emblematic of the musicians of this period.

Leonard does more in his photographs than provide a framed vision of well-known jazz musicians; he also enhances certain nuances in shots like the one of Dizzy Gillespie that create powerful, mystic images. Here Gillespie stands tall and firm and his body position is straight as an arrow. The only other musicians in the photograph are seen behind Gillespie, their faces lit by an unknown source of light. In fact, three light sources play major roles in this composition. The strongest light source fittingly pours onto Gillespie himself and his trumpet brilliantly reflects the light in the form of sound escaping from the brass horn. It introduces him as the largest subject and as the center of the picture. The light points to the trumpeter who is not jarred by its strength and brightness but instead absorbs the direct light with his physical stature and heavy suit.

The beam of light pointing to the soloist is interrupted by the strange presence of a second light source emitted from opposite the camera. Gillespie's shoulders and back are illuminated by a shimmering light that projects his frame out toward the viewer. Like the development section of a sonata form, the intrusion of the second light source causes a change in direction of the composition. Gillespie's body blocks the light from reaching the camera and the viewer. The effect of yet another light source begins with the shadow of Gillespie's back and continues to the musicians behind him. If not the same light that first projected Gillespie's frame into the picture, then certainly it comes from the same direction and promptly enshrouds other musicians in his band. Three saxophone players line up but only two are visible. They act as the recapitulation of a musical form by also having the front of their body lit and shown along with their instrument. Although in stark contrast with the brightness and intensity of Gillespie's image, the two sax players catch the beams of light as they play.

As with several of Herman Leonard's photographs taken from 1945 to 1959, this image of the "man with the horn" became central to and a prominent depiction of the new art music. In the minds of many outside of the jazz community, the instrument most associated with jazz is the saxophone.[90] Even though there are a variety of instruments associated with jazz, the most well known are those the sax, trumpet, and trombone.

David Ake reminds us that images of the "man with the horn" flourish on posters, in movies, and in magazine and television advertisements. In these instances, "horns represent sexiness (much to this piano player's dismay), evoking a sultry, smoky, late-night underground."[91]

Again, the association of jazz with dangerous territory, whether it be sexual or radical revolution, can be used to create a profit. In the right hands, a picture of a jazz musician playing his horn is provocative and alluring. Marketing specialists could include a picture of horn players with their instruments in order to incorporate the instrument's attributes of sophistication and allure on album covers. Often unbeknownst to the musician, representatives in the commercial music industry could create a lucrative advertising product based on the success of an instrument. Therefore, the field was ripe at the birth of bebop to re-introduce jazz to a war-torn nation, but instead of emphasizing the face of a singer as with Doris Day or Judy Garland, there appeared the face of the horn player Charlie Parker, Miles Davis, or Dizzy Gillespie. The image of the horn player that was set up in the Jazz Age and the swing era through such musicians as Benny Goodman (clarinet) and Louis Armstrong (trumpet) was re-established in the marketing practices of bebop. The "man with the horn" imposed a certain charm, prestige, and freshness on the general community, in obvious contrast to the a cappella singers heard during World War II.

Once seen as the instrument leading a call to arms or rallying the spirits in a marching band, the trumpet garners a whole new meaning in the hands of a solitary horn player turn jazz musician. The trumpet itself evokes memories of "Taps" played at veterans' funerals or Biblical scenes with pursed lips of an angel announcing God's wrath. However, trumpet players in the Jazz Age like Armstrong portrayed such virtuosity and control as performers that the trumpet was released from any residual association with its earlier loud, clamoring marching band days and moved toward a more sophisticated sound of subtle elegance and clarity in tone.

The jazz image has developed in several ways: first, aggregated from a previous assortment of photos, advertisements, and record covers; second, from the gradual shifting from jazz as popular music to the intellectual, prophetic image it has today; and third, the artistic molding of the black male. The visual representation of the African American man must project a strong sense of masculinity. Even today, the black man frequently becomes successful by means of his physical body; he projects strength, build, dominance, and intimidation by the physical positioning of his body. Speaking to the images of blacks depicted over the years in comics, Fredrik Stromberg has said:

> But we must remember that since the European Age of Exploration, when whites first encountered and entered into sustained relations with Africans, the Negro has been the very special object of the white man's deepest—and perhaps primordial—fears and fantasies; he was seldom conceived as fully human, or culturally and intellectually equal, and was granted by whites superiority in but one area—the physical, i.e., he was placed, ontologically, on the same plane as the animals or brute matter, like the earliest depictions of Mandrake the Magician's hulking assistant "Lothar."[92]

The white ruling majority projects the physical strength of the black man's body by framing him on the screen, on the page, or ultimately in prison. He can remain safe from the white public, and the white public from him, by inhabiting the realm of sports or entertainment. While in the limelight, he is away from racism, or at least, racist treatment.

The old method of presenting the black man in the media as dangerous, unsafe, or capable of violent tendencies remains the same as it did throughout the twentieth century. Theorist bell hooks researched how this stereotype came to be. She quotes white abolitionist Theodore Tilton in a speech made before the American Anti-Slavery Convention in 1863: "In all those intellectual activities which take a strange quickening from the moral faculties—processes which we call instincts, or intuitions—the negro is superior to the white man—equal to the white woman. The negro race is the feminine race of the world. . . ."[93] As sexist as it is racist, this statement by Tilton exemplifies the situation of the black male at the end of the nineteenth century. He was seen as a weaker anomaly, a less than human being, on the same level as a woman or even lower, if possible. He was seen as feminine by white supremacist rhetoric that claimed he was "symbolically castrated, a female eunuch."[94]

His only means of salvation, then, would be to re-masculinize himself. He would have to seek ways to correct his status in order to gain any type of success or accountability. Examples of that success can be seen in black performers in vaudeville or black athletes such as Joe Louis and Jack Johnson. History has shown that it has taken decades for African American men to gain any type of respect from the white population. And instead of helping to establish the black male into a position of success that would benefit all, the white dominant majority subscribed to Jim Crow laws and further persecution as a means to restrict those with different skin color.

In 1946 President Harry S. Truman created a civil rights commission that lasted one year. In 1947 Jackie Robinson broke the color line in major league baseball. The unsteady ground of race relations in the United States was epitomized in 1954 with the Supreme Court ruling in *Brown v. Board of Education*. Jazz musicians, now as African American citizens, advocated for equal rights, a request which was seldom heard until the Civil Rights movement gained ground in the 1960s. As a result, the sound of bop as new music began to be associated with an image of the struggle for equal rights of all individuals. Fused with modernist zeal, the image of the jazz musician as a talented black man, underrepresented by the majority's taste in music, sprouted legs and began accumulating issues, ideas, and beliefs surrounding the beatnik group.[95] Thus, the very sound of bebop became affiliated with the struggle and repression of the jazz musician, the African American, and anyone else who was marginalized or underwent hardship. (Of course, various jazz streams of the 1960s argued for racial equality and furthered black cultural nationalism that permeated the times. This will be discussed in a later chapter.)

Ever since *Life* presented a mythical experience of swing music in 1936, African American musicians have been valorized as the romantic artist. The re-masculinization process that African American men went through in general can visibly be seen in the photography of jazz musicians. Says Cawthra, photographs "visually equated blackness with jazz."[96] As images, black jazz musicians become standardized like the music they play, and photographs of the black jazz musician begin to reconstruct the narrative taken away from them by the white discourses of heterosexual masculinity. This struggle for civil liberties was clearly reflected in jazz and gave musicians a parallel reason to fight to be heard. Leonard's photograph recalls this idea of freedom and stands for the re-masculinization of blackness. His photograph, consequently, justifies its own existence. By representing the struggle for equal rights at a time when socially there was no equal treatment for all Americans, his photographs gain greater meaning by their very existence.

Fittingly, all of the musicians in the photograph of Dizzy Gillespie present a united front by facing the same direction. Jazz musicians could attest to the social injustices done to them; but now, with Gillespie as their leader, they could be seen as well as heard. As if a testament to jazz and African Americans, Gillespie stands tall and proud, resembling portraits of great leaders in the past. Leonard successfully captured the strength of jazz and the racial currents running through the social situation at the time. Undoubtedly, Gillespie would have been required to enter through the back door "for coloreds" to play at various gigs. But in Leonard's photograph, we see no such injustices. The musicians are as free as their music.

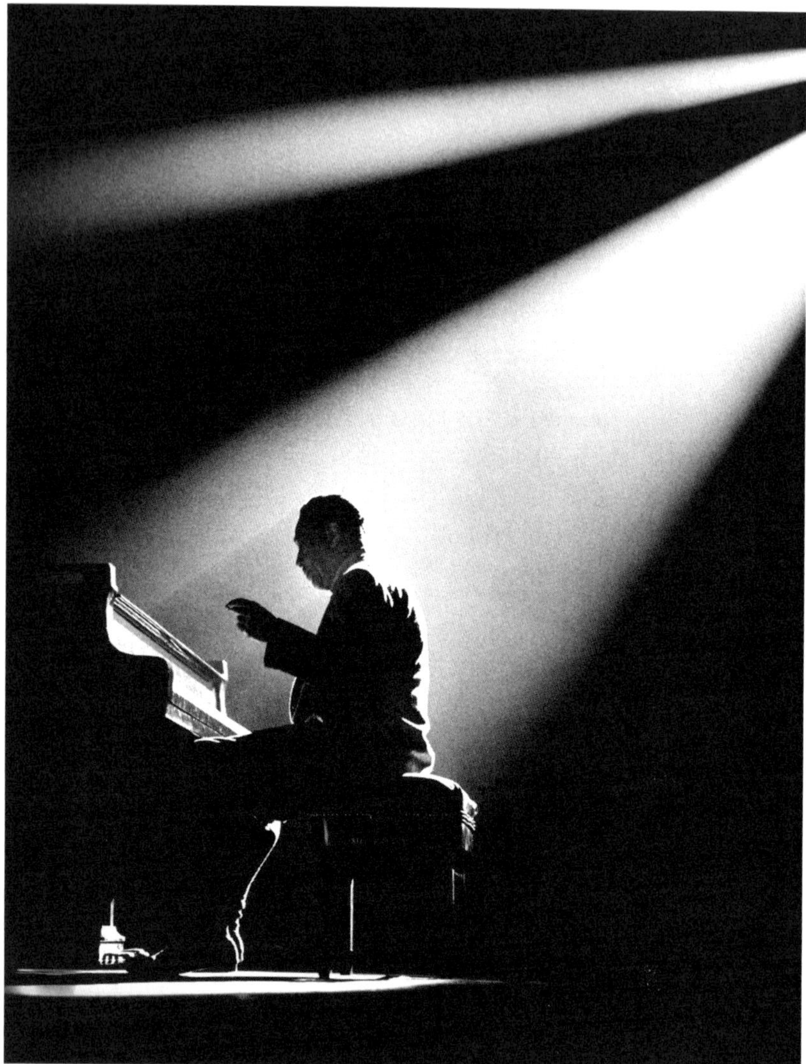

Fig. 1.12. Duke Ellington at the Olympia Theatre, Paris, 1958, code #DKE02, by Herman Leonard.

Even the space around Gillespie is collected, yet non-intruding. The musicians stand as a front line behind their leader, while the mirrored audience and foliage above Gillespie's head implies the fusion of notes and ideas swirling above him and pouring from his trumpet.

Not only does this photograph indicate social tranquility between blacks and whites, it also depicts a utopian image of jazz as it was in 1948. Leonard's image of Gillespie, viewed today, is a link to a past when jazz was promising, artistic music. On the backs of figures like Charlie Parker, Miles Davis, and Gillespie, jazz gradually moved from being entertaining dance music as it was in the swing era, to sophisticated, intellectual music full of technical challenges and rigorous training. Jazz in 1948 was fertile ground for many musicians to explore. It symbolized the possibilities of an American frontier. Thus, the image projected through Gillespie indicates a utopian form of jazz known during the mid-twentieth century. His style of dress indicates the seriousness with which he treated his music. However, Leonard's main emphasis in the photograph is on projecting social acceptance through Gillespie, a poised man bearing leadership and authenticity.

One common component in the discussion of the jazz image is the solitary artist, the hero. This is ironic to jazz, since most of its music depends heavily on the collaborative efforts of a band. Improvisation in jazz requires a band to provide the harmonic movement and rhythm of the piece. In this manner, jazz is unique. It allows several musicians to interpret the music as they see fit while establishing a compilation of songs and standards. This, in turn, establishes a very important social commentary for a democratic society: that even though jazz is based on collective performance, the specific individual achievements within that collective body offers its greatest contribution to the community.

It is, consequently, necessary that we look at another component in the jazz image—the solitary, confident performer. In one of his most famous photographs of 1958, Leonard highlights Duke Ellington through beams of light. In this photograph, Ellington sits at the piano bench on stage dressed in a white shirt and suit. His hands are slightly raised in the air before they land on the black and white keys of the piano, cleverly echoed by the black and white streams of light behind him. In fact, the viewer may see Ellington playing the piano while he sits atop a giant keyboard that is playing him. The viewer cannot see his face, although stage lights outline his body. Ellington, the front end of the piano, and the piano bench are the only objects visible in the photograph. The flatness of the stage symbolically, in fact, repeats the flatness of the spotlight.

Ellington is either in between movements, about to begin, or has just finished playing. His hands are momentarily suspended in the air, seemingly rebounding from the initial force of hitting the keyboard. But here again is a master who, like Gillespie, is confident and self-assured of his abilities as a composer and performer. The perspective of the photograph places Ellington above the Parisian audience, thereby emphasizing his authority as a master musician. Leonard presents Ellington as one who literally rises above all others; even the spotlight acknowledges his contribution to the jazz world by beaming down upon him while he is playing. Another beam searches out into the unknown, or perhaps to find a complementary focus on greatness. The viewer of the photograph acts as another spotlight, gazing with rapt, concentrated attention to the accomplishments of a jazz artist. The focal point is his head, seemingly simmering with creativity and ingenuity while he is or has finished performing. Ellington appears as the solitary figure of jazz, yet one in command of his own destiny, a composer and arranger of heroic stature.

This photograph of Ellington does one other thing—it creates an idealized figure, an iconic, romantic notion of genius. The concept of *genius* was developed in the context of Neoplatonic philosophy, which extended the prerogative of the saint and the prophet to the philosopher, the poet, and the artist—a doctrine that accounted for the superhuman achievements of these secular geniuses by an inspiration from what Plato called "divine madness."[97] This traditional concept of genius has traveled down through the ages to rest on the shoulders of those who carry the greatest intellect. Our society rewards the display of knowledge with grants, money, and prestige such as represented by the MacArthur Foundation Award (often called the "genius grant") and similar awards that address the recipient as one who possesses knowledge and aptitude in a field of study that surpasses the other applicants.

Genius is not limited to the consumption of knowledge, but can be applied to artists who exhibit the utmost talent. The word has often been associated with jazz musicians; in fact, jazz critic Stanley Crouch recently published a book entitled *Considering Genius: Writings on Jazz*. Since Crouch considers several jazz musicians geniuses, the term in this sense refers to the hero-worship characteristic of music making. The sheer skill and mastery necessary to play jazz is thought to require a certain level of intellect not typically found with other styles.

In this image of Ellington, one of the most recognized American composers of the twentieth century, Leonard naturally presents Ellington as a genius. Rendering Ellington's capacity for composing, arranging, managing, band leading, and performing raises him to the level of a Renaissance man. He is often compared to other contemporary American composers, such as Aaron Copland, George Gershwin, Charles Ives, and Leonard Bernstein, all of whom exhibit varying amounts of intellect and musical talent. Unlike the others, however, Ellington has to deal with the additional weight of race at a time in American history when many black musicians, or bands with black musicians in them, received little to no endorsements or financial support. Ellington rose above his oppressive circumstances by becoming one of the best composers and bandleaders of the twentieth century, but only after his compositions were taken seriously by white society. His musical and managerial talents, aided by his classy demeanor, elevated his status from jazz musician to bandleader, and from composer to genius.

After Ellington paved the way for the recognition of jazz musicians, other figures slowly gained awareness for their musical talents. For instance, Thelonious Monk was often scoffed as a musician in his day, but now he is praised for being ahead of his time, a jazz great. Charlie Parker, Ornette Coleman, and John Coltrane have since been called innovators, securing their legacy as leaders of movements in jazz and gaining higher acclaim through the recognition of jazz as an important facet of American culture. Granted, much of the success of jazz musicians rose alongside their appearance in society, whether visually in photographs or posters, or the appearance of their name in print, record releases, and word of mouth. The buzz on the musician through name recognition was unequivocally linked with their image or persona in society.

The rise of the jazz musician as an icon in the 1950s can in part be considered akin to the rising social importance of the movie star at the same time. The end of the decade brought the movie star to an unspeakable height of fame. The fame of James Dean grew immensely after his death. Elizabeth Taylor and Marilyn Monroe, who overwhelmed the movie industry with their celebrity status, sparked a new era for Hollywood fame. By the early 1960s, movie stars were treated like royalty; millions of dollars were funneled into the entertainment business by an American public that could not get enough of their favorite stars. After Monroe's death in 1962, Andy Warhol made his iconic silk screens (the *Marilyn Monroe Suite*) that served to elevate both the Pop Art and the Hollywood industries. The image of the movie star, then, obtained a sacred status that fed on the movie stars themselves, but the image always seemed to remain more unobtainable than the actual person.

Similarly in jazz, the celebrity status of several musicians grew from their image. John Coltrane was widely popularized by his mystical aura, which is also perceived in his music. Charlie Parker's image was personified in his nickname, Bird. Miles Davis not only toppled the jazz world with his forward-thinking concepts of jazz but also kept his position in the limelight through the popularization of his image. Leonard re-enforced the importance of the image in his photographs by presenting jazz musicians in the spotlight, symbolizing the public eye.

Even the names of well-known jazz musicians contributed to this image. Of course, it may be argued that a musician's persona cannot be separated from his or her music.[98] For example, the names Miles Davis and Thelonious Monk awaken the memories of their personal lives, and the name John Coltrane "has come to take on a kind of life of its own, creating a 'shorthand' for a variety of musical, ethical, and spiritual attributes that may or may not correspond to all or even part of 'the real' John Coltrane."[99] David Ake likens the representation of jazz names to Foucault's ideas of author names: "the author's name is not . . . just a proper name . . . [or] simply an element in discourse (capable of being either subject or object, of being replaced by a pronoun, and the like); it performs a certain role with regard to narrative discourse, assuring a classificatory function."[100] Even Parker's nickname established his dominance as a mythical character. Parker was called Bird because that word represented his style of playing. His choice of melodic phrasing on the saxophone simulated the flight of a bird in the air; thus, Parker's identity as a musician is associated with the myth of a free spirit, filling the air with the floating notes sprouting from his saxophone. His style, as free as his nickname, came to suggest a liberated artist who transcends music as it is printed on the score.

The name of Miles Davis brings to mind the simple and brilliant artistry of his playing. Going by his first name, Miles was on the cutting edge of bop in the late 1940s, but he also propelled many styles of jazz such as cool (with *The Birth of the Cool* in 1949) and fusion (with *Bitches Brew* in 1969). He is so well known for his flexibility and open-mindedness that many members of the jazz community disregard his lack of technical prowess. He was not the greatest player on the trumpet, as many mistakes in his recordings testify; yet these mistakes, though ordinarily not allowed for professional musicians, are completely viable for Miles. His ingenuity in jazz has become inspirational, his brilliance is legendary, but his conversation is described as intimidating. His quiet demeanor and stayed tongue posed quite a challenge for those musicians who worked for him. His name holds power unequaled among all jazz musicians. He represents the best, the type of jazz musician who will listen, create, and inspire, rather than overplay.[101] Leonard took many photographs of Davis through the years, and the majority of these photographs present Davis alone—the solitary figure. The most famous of these captures him in New York City as a young musician. Later photographs tended to shock the jazz community by the abrasive nature of his facial expressions, often deemed "the scary Davis," glaring at the camera over his sunglasses.[102]

Many jazz musicians lead a similar lifestyle to that of a touring rock musician, gaining various reputations surrounding their personal life, sexual preference, possessions, habits, and personalities. Such stories and rumors combine to form myths about a host of jazz personalities such as Charlie Parker, John Coltrane, Thelonious Monk, Dizzy Gillespie, Miles Davis, Louis Armstrong, Duke Ellington, Dexter Gordon, Ornette Coleman, Buddy Rich, Bix Beiderbecke, Tony Williams, and Bill Evans. While these musicians are treated like any other celebrity, rumors sprout wherever they go and any events that occur during their late-night carousing are amplified, and thereby become a part of jazz history.[103] Such exaggerated stories serve to dramatize their mystique.

While not all jazz musicians partake in drugs and alcohol, it is this lifestyle that contributes to other romantic notions concerning the jazz image. The social milieu of jazz resonates in the clubs of big cities and within the drug culture of the 1950s. Combined allusions of African American and urban culture, as well as understated celebrity status, created several myths associated with the jazz musician. Playing into the contemporary ideal of a celebrity, the jazz musician is notorious for leading a tumultuous life of alcohol, women, drugs, and late-night carousing. In this manner it can be easily seen how the image of the jazz musician becomes tarnished due to the social attitude associated with each of these.[104]

Dave Liebman, an influential jazz saxophonist, author, and educator, comments on the condition of jazz at the end of the twentieth century as that which is largely dependent on past imagery:

> The jazz subculture has been one of the great tales of the twentieth century, written about and even commercialized in the "hipster" image. . . . The speed of the notes, elusive rhythms and harmonies combined with the appearance of effortlessness on the part of the musicians help to create this image. . . . The jazz image is hopelessly out of date in the late twentieth century. Most young musicians see the past through clear eyes and are interested only in the music and what they can learn from it. But the folklore of jazz is important in keeping a tradition alive. Jazz is music made by living and breathing individuals, not machines. The image of a jazz subculture may seem an anachronism now, but its significance has made it an important part of the twentieth century Western culture and folklore.[105]

The imagery to which Liebman refers is a composite of both clever marketing strategies and actual occurrences in jazz history that were utilized to create an entire set of values and ideas around jazz musicians. Such images are based on African American history and culture, social and political conflicts of the mid-twentieth century, popularization of the Rat Pack, revolutionary concepts of the beatnik, and representations of the jazz musician in Hollywood movies, television commercials, radio, records, and scholarly and creative writing. The identity of jazz is represented through a combination of the visual imagery of a jazz musician and aural recognition of the sound. The visual culture of jazz, including the photographs from Leonard and others, propagated by marketing and business initiatives, have aided in the construction of what Liebman calls the "folklore" of jazz.

The essential issue is whether the jazz image still embodies this time period. We have traced the "hipster image" indicated by Liebman from the height of the bebop era in jazz history.[106] The bop generation of musicians such as Charlie Parker, Dizzy Gillespie, and Bud Powell brought jazz to a new level of high-art status, intrigue, and musical acceptance. They were inspirational not only in their music, but also in their ability to overcome the racial and political tensions of their time. Indeed, their status has extended beyond the jazz community and risen to that of legendary heroes. At the height of their creativity, bebop musicians were photographed by fans, agents, managers, or freelance photographers. Premier among all those, Herman Leonard was able to capture and thus create the ideal image of the jazz musician. These photographs, along with other pictorial items on jazz, have been marketed to both jazz and non-jazz audiences—and it is precisely because of the ubiquity of jazz images that jazz itself has seen some resurgence in American culture in the past twenty years.

In order to understand the profound effect, both aesthetic and commercial, that the jazz image has in our society, it is necessary to perpetuate such images as myth. Jazz needs to be linked with American democracy and the mythic black hero in order to propel its existence. The figure of the black musician creates an exciting story of racial myth. Referring to the black musicians who are the focus in Ken Burns's series on jazz, Ronald Radano states, "They are the mythic heroes who, facing the obstacles of race and the enduring forces of slavery's past, enact an integrationist alchemy."[107] This myth, like those of the Greeks, fits within our system of thoughts and values. It allows us to feel as if we, too, can become a great artist—and that we have insight into the life of other great artists. By reading into the images of jazz's culture, we feel as if we are a part of the myth of jazz, the occurring history.

But at the same time, one becomes more informed about the myth one is investigating. The movement of placing ourselves in the life of the person who embodies one's imagination is a transcendental displacement of the myth. We take what we like of the myth—the romanticism, the lifestyle—and absorb it into our own character. Therefore, close study into the history of jazz demystifies it. It is the myth and folklore of jazz that enables us to feel like we are witnessing the musicians and events. We need to perpetuate this vision of Gillespie on the stage. Even though we were not there, we create a false idol in a world full of American ones.

In *Jazz in American Culture*, Peter Townsend presents the myth of jazz as something that coexists within a social order. Indeed, Townsend establishes jazz as a composite myth, constructed out of a number of sub- or micro-myths (he even gives a list of eight micro-myths). For example, Townsend says, "To study jazz closely in a specific historical context is to begin to demythologize it."[108] The actual history of events does not fit with the stereotype of alcoholics, womanizers, and musical revolutionaries found within the myth of jazz. A myth supplants the historical accounts and the mundane occurrences that musicians face when they do their own booking or play in front of four audience members.

Roland Barthes says, "myth abolishes the complexity of human acts, it gives them the simplicity of essences."[109] Jazz musicians represent freedom (both in terms of race and music), and stand for a utopian ideal; the myth presents the musician as an individual, one capable of genius, and presents the musician as the hero—in Radano's words, "*Jazz* is first and foremost a story of heroes"[110] The photos of Herman Leonard express a desire for utopian ideals and the courage to be unshackled from both social constraints and musical rules. "Rather than celebrating the myths of jazz, historical criticism of this kind gives us a way out of those myths, not to deny the significance of aesthetic experience but to comprehend how our aesthetic responses take shape, so deeply invested as they are in the modern imaginations of race."[111]

Does the myth need to continue to exist for jazz to have greater meaning in society? Krin Gabbard suggests that the myth of jazz has served its purpose in the past and that new understandings of jazz ought to be proposed now.[112] Maybe we need myth as it is presented in visual culture in order to promote high art, since we maintain the same mythical fascination with classical musicians. The attachment of the myth to jazz is continually present throughout its history. We have racial and artistic imagery for which many jazz musicians fought, which is symbolic of what Radano calls the winning of good versus evil. Jazz is an American version of a coming-of-age story. Jazz needs the mythical presentation of our heroes to maintain its prominent role as art music.

It is the author's thesis that Leonard's photographs are not the main reason for this resurgence in jazz, but rather that his photos are the best representation of what is currently understood and marketed as jazz. Leonard photographs of jazz musicians from 1945 to 1959 clearly perpetuate the image of what jazz sounds like, including the folklore of jazz as mentioned before. He has been able to frame many of the characteristics, history, imagery, and people associated with a style of music, and the photographs of these musicians have gained in popularity not only for their presentation of famous musicians, but also for the signification of quality and artistry in the photographs themselves. By posing bop musicians as intellectual artists, Leonard and other contributors to the jazz image have helped glorify and uplift the jazz musician.

Photographers pose their subjects with the intention of framing the individuals as they (the photographers) *heard* them. The musicians are artists; they are capable of taking the listener to another place with their music, just as the photographer is capable of taking the viewer to another realm of reality, one created by the photographer. The viewer accompanies the photographer and becomes fixated for a moment with that reality. It is not that Leonard's photographs are the main visual component of the jazz nexus, but rather that his photos best capture the myth of jazz, the image and the face of jazz musicians as a nostalgic homage. Leonard's photographs have come to represent not only great jazz, but also the best of American music as that which represents originality and perseverance.

CHAPTER 2

The Construction of Signs in Jazz Photography

[L]ike his music, a fine photograph of a musician reflects his soul. I'm very interested in photography and in how the camera can capture personality. . . .

—DIZZY GILLESPIE[1]

How can a picture represent a style of music? What image comes to mind when we think about a musical genre? With classical music, one generally imagines an instrument such as a flute or violin, the thunderous sounds of a symphony orchestra playing the music of Beethoven, or Mozart at the clavichord in the movie *Amadeus*. With pop music, one imagines the facial makeup of Kiss, the Beatles' album covers, or jeans, a cowboy hat, and an acoustic guitar with country. Every category of music contains its own identity, a trait not shared by other genres. Then how is it that, as David Ake says, "we 'see' music as well as hear it?"[2] Wassily Kandinsky used abstract painting to depict musical improvisation, Piet Mondrian recalled the streets of New York and the sounds of jazz with *Broadway Boogie Woogie*, Jackson Pollock's action painting is suppose to emulate the improvisatory nature of ragtime and Dixieland, and even King Ludwig of Bavaria had the plots of Wagner's operas painted onto the interior castle walls of Neuschwanstein.

For centuries, artists have tried to capture visually what they hear in music. With the development of twentieth-century technology, artists were able to trade in their pen and paper for film and digital media, thereby broadening their capabilities and their palette. How could one maintain a career by merely presenting music as it appears? Since there is not a high demand for artists who can do so successfully, it is usually those who are enamored with music to the point that they *must* reproduce their feelings about what they are hearing. Most individuals who found themselves following their favorite musicians around from bar to concert stage did so for the love of the music and not the idea of a self-induced claim to fame. The men who have maintained a niche by bridging the disciplines of music and photography include William Claxton, William Gottlieb, Ole Brask, Lee Tanner, Milt Hinton, Herb Snitzer, and Herman Leonard. They did so by creating a market for jazz photography that was not previously there, beyond merely following and photographing their favorite musicians.

Few photographers receive acclaim during their lifetime; it is remarkable that these few have garnered recognition for their work. Part of their success can be attributed to their ability to transfer their passion for music to the viewer. Leonard, in particular, was able to successfully transmit what he felt for jazz to a broader audience. This chapter will analyze Leonard's photographs through the terminology of Roland Barthes in order to determine those elements in a photograph that create a relationship with the viewer. By analyzing those techniques in a photograph that can effectively communicate to the viewer, one can discover the underlying symbolism of each photograph, and characterize elements that are not always readily visible but contribute to the overall effect.

Roland Barthes, a noted semiotician on photography, image, and text, interprets a photograph based on the messages found within visual elements of the photograph. For instance, a *denoted* message is the literal, obvious meanings of a photograph that are basic to a reader's understanding, whereas *connoted* messages are the interpretations found within the photograph—or as Barthes says, "the manner in which the society to a certain extent communicates what it [society] thinks of it [the photograph]."[3] He contends that the combination of these denoted and connoted messages bring to light the significance of a photograph, and in the process of analysis, one formulates a layered discourse, a language based on the image. This language, which Barthes calls a "meta-language," includes new meanings and words about the image that can contribute to the understanding of the environment outside of the image and the society from which it comes.[4]

One of the qualities that make Leonard's photography noteworthy is the layering of connoted and denoted messages within each photograph. Like a musical composition, each picture contains a collection of several formal structures that holds the composition together. By studying the signs in the picture, one can hypothesize as to the meaning and events surrounding the image and come closer to determining the precise part of reality the photograph replicates. Thus, through Leonard's photographic lens one may decipher how society saw those fourteen years in jazz history, making the photograph a historical artifact. But before one can interpret the specific meanings of signs, one must determine what the photograph as a whole transmits and explore how the photograph by itself has become such an effective communicative device.

Dizzy Gillespie states in the epigraph of this chapter that photography has the ability to capture the personality of whoever is in the photograph. Roland Barthes would agree that the photograph contains realistic threads of the person in the picture. His book *Camera Lucida* is defined by his search for a picture of his recently deceased mother, claiming that only one photograph can truly depict the person his mother really was. Photography can transmit several things from a mechanical record of an event to the nonverbal characteristics of a subject. It can signify a moment that has passed, or it can present timelessness—eternity. Most often, the photograph merely encourages an epistemological discussion or acts as a mnemonic device.

The photograph is "an ensemble of highly disparate images which possess in common the fact that they were created by the action of light on a sensitive surface."[5] Although this description refers strictly to the actions involved in taking a picture, photography is more than the sum of its parts—the mechanical action of the shutter in the camera, the effect of light on a photosensitive material, the chemical reaction that occurs in a darkroom. A photograph contains something indiscernible, unknowable, indefinable, yet we can put together a canon of the world's greatest photographs. If this is true, then how is it that there are so many interpretations of photography while at the same time so little doubt as to what makes a good photograph? And if anyone can take a picture, then is everyone a photographer? Where exactly does one identify the *art* within photography? For that matter, does one attribute the term "artist" with "photographer"? Does "photographer" refer to a skilled craftsperson? Anyone can take a picture, but that does not make him/her a photographer—just as any photographer can take a picture, but that does not make him/her an artist. Similarly, a talented person whose craft lies in the ability to play an instrument or read music is a musician. But some musicians classify themselves as artists rather than musicians. They would rather be associated with the level of the creator, the artist, rather than the level of the musician, the practitioner, because that limits their creativity to a single discipline. (This is discussed further in chapter 4.)

Photography's status as an art form is one of the most debated topics in post-modernity. One reason why photography is such a heavily contested topic emerges from the act of taking a photograph, as Frizot's definition indicated. What is the skill necessary for a photographer if all one needs to do is point and shoot? In this manner, a soldier who is skilled with aiming and firing a weapon could also be a talented artist. (Notice also, that the terms used in correlation with photography "capture," "shoot," "take," and "aim" are engendered with masculinity, referring to soldiers at war.) Is it the combination of pointing and shooting and finding an art-worthy object to enclose in a frame that makes a photograph a work of art? This "snapshot aesthetic" postulates that anyone can click the button to open the shutter on a camera and expose the film. But how does one differentiate from amateur work and that which is considered art? What means do Robert Frank, William Klein, W. Eugene Smith, and Ansel Adams use to make their work stand out from others? In fact, how have Herman Leonard's photographs come to be better known than other skilled jazz photographers?

For one thing, it is not only the photographers themselves but the receptive audience who chooses the qualities of a great photograph. The public asserts value to certain photographs, and other works of art for that matter, that present a greater potential for interpretation, uniqueness, or creativity. By interpreting an artwork, the viewer imposes a subjective view onto material that is not his/her own. This process of interpretation enables viewers to judge, recommend, speculate on, or dissuade others of the importance of the photograph, thus projecting an agency over the artist. Because of its accessibility through technology and visual media, the public seems to be even more scrupulous with photography than, say, with painting.[6] This redistribution of power from the artwork to the patron is a main factor in the discernment of taste. If more people debate the intended smile of the *Mona Lisa*, then more people become informed of Da Vinci's painting, and more contribute to its celebrated status. Ansel Adams has a way of making the viewer feel a part of, yet distanced from, the visions of nature in his photographs, thus provoking thought in the viewer.

The greater the controversy or interpretation of an artwork, the more the public begins to accept that artwork and its universal value into our culture. The most famous of Leonard's photographs are of jazz musicians such as Ella Fitzgerald, Duke Ellington, Miles Davis, Charlie Parker, and entertainers such as Frank Sinatra. None of these musicians are alive today, but all have become emblems of American perseverance, originality, and artistry. By photographing them, Leonard's art transfers this association to the viewer, who then sees the photograph as containing a certain power embedded in the image. Copies of the photograph can be disseminated on posters, postcards, slides, calendars, coffee mugs, T-shirts, books, and album covers. The facilitation of the image into visual culture plants the jazz image further into American culture. In this instance, Julia Thomas smartly perceives culture as that which is textual and visual: the exchange of language on bus tickets, newspapers, Hallmark greeting cards, classified ads, fashion industries, editorials, and grocery lists. "Societies invest these artifacts with meanings, until in many cases the meanings are so 'obvious' that they pass for nature."[7] Photographs are treated as everyday objects; they tell us everything from the events happening in the news to what day it is in a calendar. It is up to the viewer to analyze the images, or as Thomas says, to "denaturalize and defamiliarise" them, because, over time, the meaning of an image becomes assumed.[8]

"Finally," Sontag summarizes, "the most grandiose result of the photographic enterprise is to give us the sense that we can hold the whole world in our heads—as an anthology of image."[9] There are many theories, ideologies, and philosophies aided by a myriad of rhetorical conjectures that grapple with images as they function in society.[10] But a photograph, as Sontag explains, contains various images (visual or mental pictures of something) that assimilate meaning within the viewer. The image is an information-carrying entity that can take the form of a sign, word, sound, or photograph, and construct a relationship to the receiver of that image/sign. The interpretation of an image remains problematic because not everyone will agree on its truest meaning, and thus we are hesitant to declare a universal perception.[11] Human perception of images remains subjective, but when perceptions reach some general agreement, we then claim them as standards of judgment.

Despite the specific knowledge required to interpret images, several generalizations can be made about the introduction of an image into society. One influential thread of discussion centers on how society constructs an image. An image is used constantly in language. A non-smoking sign usually contains the picture of a cigarette with a circle around it and a diagonal line drawn through the circle. The line indicates negation, and we are familiar with the fact that some places allow smoking and some do not. Hence, the non-smoking sign indicates that this function should not be performed at this particular location. By contrast, Leonard's photographs often contain an actual lit cigarette with smoke curling throughout the photograph, and we correctly conclude that the smoke refers to the stage setting of jazz musicians in smoke-filled clubs of the 1940s.

Thus, by determining the relationship of an image as it functions in society, we may gain further insight into our own function in society. The Swiss linguist Ferdinand de Saussure created a theory of semiotics in order to understand the signification between sign, object, and mind.[12] In the process of communication in society, signs are exchanged, ideologies created, and power transferred.[13] All signs rely on the possession of power in the community or through language in order to denote meaning.[14] The complex composite of meanings created by the interpretation of signs creates a discourse, what Foucault calls the production of knowledge through language.[15]

Barthes broadens Saussure's idea of signifier and signified to deepen the understanding of language, literature, and society by focusing on nonverbal signs. Barthes says the word *image* comes from *imitari*, which indicates a reproduction, imitation, copy, or mental picture of something—a conception, idea, or impression. Barthes argues that an image cannot be discussed through just one connection between a photograph of a sunlit beach and the meaning it encompasses. An image can mean several things to different people. But Barthes's goal is to expand the signified or the mental image of an object by examining the composite of several variables found in a photograph. For instance, the mental concept of a tree frog is the signified according to Saussure; Barthes differs in stating that the signified can be more than one mental picture of a tree frog. We can also imagine other tree frogs, the rain forest, wet leaves, the sounds of the frogs, and so on. In this manner, other mental ideas associated with the tree frog also become signifiers: the wet leaves causes one to think of rain, which causes one to think of clouds, wind, sun, and weather. The causation of other images makes the original mental image of a tree frog become a signifier to other images besides the tree frog.[16] Barthes concludes that an image contains several signs that create a chain reaction in our brain, instilling more codes, more signifiers, and more signifieds. Images play a large role in our society because we rely on them to communicate, and the repeated occurrence of images, signs, and objects are further evidence of society's desire to communicate efficiently.

So we find ourselves back to the question: What exactly does an image or photograph transmit? In order to understand this, we must "denaturalize" or decondition ourselves to the photograph itself. We need to treat it as an object that is not familiar in order to understand its meaning. But in order to so, we must naturalize something else. Therefore, I will naturalize the photograph's "mechanicalness," since that is what photography is really known for. No matter what is contained within the photograph, its primary function even well into the twenty-first century remains communication, a mechanical record of something that is communicated to a viewer. Photography can delight the viewer with "accurate" representations of a piece of history, or it can contain, as Barthes indicates, a chain of signifiers that display an artful image. In this light, we need to explore interpretations found within Herman Leonard's most popular photographs. These include (1) the mechanicalness of the photograph, (2) the communicative effects of the photograph, (3) the aestheticization of the object, (4) the presence of time in the photograph, and (5) the presentation of actuality and reality.

In an article defending photography as art, Bernard Shaw confronted accusations by art critics who attempted to prove the superiority of painting over photography by comparing the mechanical elements of photography to the artistic design of paintings:

> The hand of the painter is incurably mechanical: his technique is incurably artificial. Just as the historian has a handwriting which remains the same whether he is chronicling Elizabeth or Mary, so the painter has a handdrawing which remains the same, no matter how widely his subjects vary. And it is because the camera is independent of this handdrawing and this technique that a photograph is so much less hampered by mechanical considerations, so much more responsive to the artist's feeling, than a design. It gives you a direct picture where the pencil gives you primarily a drawing.[17]

Shaw's point is to confront various accusations concerning the mechanical nature of photography. A photograph can exist as a mechanical record because it directly represents a reflection of one moment in time. Yet the photographer's way of seeing is reflected in the subject or the portrayal of that subject through a certain framework, and thus does not exist as a mechanical record. Take, for example, the previously discussed image of Duke Ellington by Leonard. Ellington's presence onstage captures a specific moment in time, either directly before or just after striking the keys on the piano. The camera and photographer were there to catch the event. Therefore, the event is frozen forever in the negative. Obviously, the camera is a machine; however, like a gun, it does not itself shoot. The eye behind the lens remains the sole designer, and the person behind the lens captures the moment of artistic inspiration. The photographer, in this case Leonard, dictates the image produced by the machine. And the simplicity of the machine subtracts many "mechanical" distractions from the process. Leonard has more freedom to incorporate Ellington's style, sensibility, feelings, and mood through the simplified act of pointing and shooting. Photographer W. Eugene Smith stated, "I try to understand before I photograph, then I shoot with passion what I want to photograph."[18] Thus the artist shoots "with passion" and introduces his/her personal emotion into the picture. It is this act that causes Shaw to refer to the camera as "unmechanical," meaning that the nonmechanical nature of photography allows one to focus on the art, in comparison to painting, which is often dependent on the techniques of drawing.

The photograph cannot judge an image; it merely presents the image. Much of the craft is based on one's skill, temperament, and "knowing where to look." And as Julia Thomas puts it, "Deciding where to look is highly political."[19] The camera provides a frame to look through while the photographer dictates what the viewer should see. Leonard says of his own practice:

> You look, you just look. I think that when a musician or a musical composer sits down to compose a piece he will get the general outline of what he is doing and then he'll refine it, listen to it back, and make the changes that he wants. When I'm sitting there in front of a drummer or sax player, I look. I look at the angles. I look at the light. I look at the background. And being disciplined by using a large camera, you have to look. You don't look into the camera, you look at the subject. You feel the composition within the frame within which you're working, and you do it to your own liking. I happen to like a certain style.[20]

The image is captured through the photographer's eyes; however, the image is also shaped by "the composition within the frame." Looking becomes a type of reading or interpreting.[21] In the Ellington photo for example, the angle is taken from below the stage, slightly raising Ellington, indicating that he has an elevated status and is in the spotlight. Along with the pose of the musician, Leonard achieves a greater significance by the embellished setting, black and white film, smoke (or in this case, a cloudy haze over the stage), angle of vision, shadow, and light reflection.

The viewer cannot see the surroundings, and thus the context of the picture is omitted. Instead, the photographer selects not only what he wishes to frame, but he also determines what is omitted. This involves an element of choice. John Berger posits that where one looks or what one looks at is determined by the personality of the individual.[22] In this manner, the direction of the camera is determined by the interests and values of the photographer. Julia Thomas says, "A hierarchical relation of authority and subordination is established between the surveyor and surveyed because those who look can gain knowledge of, and thereby command, what they see."[23] In addition, Michel Foucault has described how, at different historical moments, it is the apparent power of the spectator that allows discipline and control to be regulated and enforced.

According to art critic Joanna Lowry, photography allows one to understand the social dynamic of two entities: the photographer and the subject. Lowry states, "The act of taking a photograph is a communicative act in itself which exposes the social dynamic through which identities (both of the photographer and of the subject) are formed."[24] Similarly, music is situated in a particular social and historical context. This context includes the location at which music production occurs, the prior musical experiences of both performers and audience, as well as their expectations and prejudices. Therefore, music as a communicative art form constructs a dialogue between the musician and the audience. In our examples of jazz photography, the subjects are all jazz musicians; as Lowry describes, these images create a dialogue between the musician and the photographer. In a further step, the photographer instigates a dialogue between the musician and the viewer. Yet, while the viewer is processing information about the subject—which can be interpreted as a "dialogue"—the photographer gains control of how the viewer will perceive the subject. As mentioned earlier, the frame dictates where the viewer should look; therefore, the photographer directs attention, whether positive or negative, toward the subject. However, in the circuitous dialogue between musician, photographer, and viewer in Leonard's photographs, the musician has the last word by the additional association of sound to the image. The sound of jazz recalled by the actual musician in the photograph strikes a chord with the viewer who, even after looking away from the image, remembers how that music sounds. The sound associated by the jazz musician creates an aural memory peg. Music, as a fixed temporal event, seems to reverberate through the fixed, but longer-lived, visual image.

Dialogue continues to be the key in our perception of the image. A dialogue is established between the viewer and the photographer, even though neither can respond to the other as in a more traditional form of dialogue. Mikhail Bakhtin explored the structures of power and authority through the analysis of language, specifically dialogue.[25] Through the act of communicating, or what Bakhtin calls utterances, each individual declares himself or herself as a subject through language, struggling to find a relationship with the rest of the world. From utterances, to dialogue, to texts, to object, we shift our focus from the image to our engagement with or reaction to the photograph. In the context of portrait photography of jazz musicians, Bakhtin's dialogical text is relevant to those photographs that contain a social, verbal, or referential interaction. In addition, a dialogue can be established between the viewer and the social conditioning of the viewer, between photographer and subject, and between the viewer and the subject. Leonard's photographic methods indicate how we, the receiving audience, should perceive the subject, the jazz musician.

Let us take the photograph of jazz drummer Max Roach in New York City. Here, the camera intrudes like a Peeping Tom from backstage to catch Roach performing at Carnegie Hall. According to Leonard, there is an audience present, even though we cannot see them in the photograph. Leonard was backstage to take the photo, "And I just shot it. Well, Max is very small in this. It works compositionally. I didn't create it, I didn't set it up. I just saw it.[26] Compositionally, Roach seems in a world unto himself, surrounded only by his drums and the microphone stands. However, there is a bass player who stands behind a pole and is blocked from our view. The bass player, standing with his instrument, frames Roach on stage and is oblivious to the photographer. Two more outlined bodies stand in the same line as Roach and the bass player and are also obstructed from view by the staircase. The house lights seem to be off and the stage lights on, but there is no streaming spotlight as with the photo of Duke Ellington. Roach is unaware of the photographer's presence and puts his energy toward the audience in front of him. As in the Ellington photograph, we cannot really see his face, indicating that the person is not the subject here but the setting.

Leonard's favorite item in this photo is the drum head, because he sees a circle as the most compositional image one can include.[27] Leonard has created a rhythm by causing our eye to locate the staircase, the drums and other musical equipment, Roach himself, and then the microphones. The viewer's eye follows the curved lines of the staircase and drum heads, then moves to the stretched skin of the drum, and finally lands on Roach. He is simultaneously framed by the items on the stage and dwarfed by the lights and equipment. Does this imply that jazz is overshadowed by commercial success, or does this photograph merely capture a musician performing his craft? The setting of the photograph plays into its aesthetic appeal. The pattern created by the iron staircase onto the drum complements the straight lines of the curtains and equipment stands.

The social dialogue in the photograph, explained by the theories of Lowry and Bakhtin, can be found between Roach and the viewer. At first glance, the viewer is unable to tell who is playing the drums, and must look again to the title of the photograph to see the name of the individual. Max Roach is now a household name (especially for drummers) and his legacy as a stellar jazz musician is secure. Yet one would not be able to

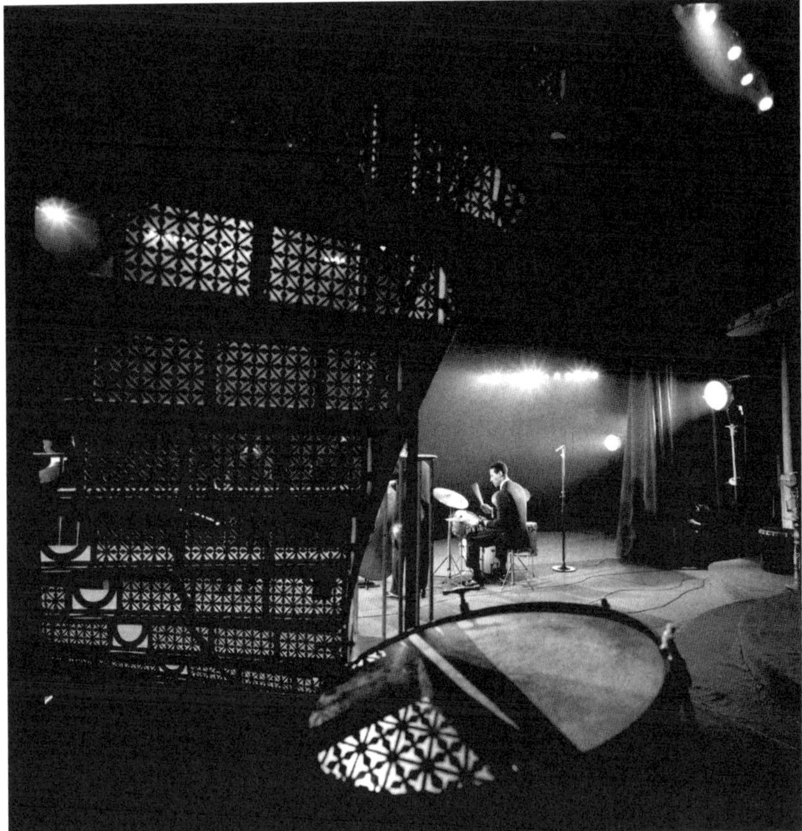

Fig. 2.1. Max Roach in New York City, 1954, code #MXR02, by Herman Leonard. © Herman Leonard Photography LLC/CTSIMAGES.COM.

discern his importance in Leonard's photograph until the entire scene is taken in. The movement of one's eyes around the image from drum rim to staircase, curtains, microphones, lights, and finally to Roach enables one to gather information on his status. By including the equipment used by Roach throughout his life as a recording and performing musician, Leonard directs the viewer how to perceive Roach. Instead of an unknown musician, the viewer is now watching an artist at work. The viewer is almost on the same level as Roach, or slightly elevated, as if the viewer is standing on something to get a better view of him. The fact that Roach is on stage indicates his social status as a musician, but the arrangement and position of the camera implies that the viewer is backstage and in the presence of an artist. Therefore, Leonard becomes a part of the dialogue in his efforts to communicate with the viewer about the subject.

Leonard uses several photographic effects, or photogenia, to employ greater meaning: the performance venu, black and white film, angle of vision, shadow, light reflection, patterning and repetition, and pose of the musician. Each of these is gradually absorbed by the viewer and then interpreted. Barthes labels these devices as those which "connote" meaning, or the connoted message: "Connotation, the imposition of a second meaning on the photographic message proper, is realized at the different levels of the production of the photograph (choice, technical treatment, framing, layout) and represents, finally, a coding of the photographic analogue."[28]

Thus, according to Barthes, the photograph contains two things: (1) a denoted message, which is the subject in the photograph itself, and (2) a connoted message, which can be any combination of the viewer's interpretation of the photograph, a coded message, a visual metaphor, or how that subject is presented. The denotation is what is being photographed. The setting itself is a denoted message, which is to be taken literally and not interpreted, while the process of interpreting the setting is a connoted message. The interpretation of the photograph lies through the analysis of photogenia or the arrangement of objects in the photograph that implies meaning. The analysis of the subject presented is also connotation. "The photographic paradox can then be seen as the coexistence of two messages, the one without a code (the photographic analogue), the other with a code (the 'art,' or the treatment, or the 'writing,' or the rhetoric, of the photograph). . . ."[29]

Leonard arrests the attention of the viewer through the possible interpretations of the denoted messages. His trademark technique of black-and-white film is itself a denoted message, yet it symbolizes artfulness and classic imagery. Photographers for major movie studios, such as George Hurrell, Clarence Sinclair Bull, and Eugene Robert Richee, have used black and white film to construct an aura of the movie star in the photograph. "The key was dramatic lighting and deep shadow, creating a composition of black and white that framed the elegance of the subject, whose dress and hair were the studied creations of skilled studio artisans."[30] Black and white film is often perceived as something that contains art because it is only based on shape, form, tone, and the grey scale. The photographer cannot rely on a striking red sunset or any color that easily catches the eye.[31] Other jazz photographers used black and white for artistic purposes, such as Milt Hinton, who said, "truthfully, I've always been biased toward black-and-white photography. I think it's because when I look at a color photo, I really don't see the same colors I see in nature. Besides, when I got started, color film faded badly after a short time."[32] Even Dizzy Gillespie offers his approval of this technique: "I especially like black-and-white photography. You can see depth in that."[33] Leonard explains his own thoughts on black and white film:

HEATHER: It seems like black and white photographs can make such a statement, but so can color. Do you have a preference for black and white or color?

HERMAN: Yes, black and white. See if I look at this color photo, my brain has to take into account the colors. If I look at a black and white photo like that one, then I don't have to think about color. All I have to think about is shape and design.

HEATHER: Like Picasso.

HERMAN: Yeah, there is a basic simplicity to it that I find easier to read and enjoy. Some people have sent me my jazz photos colorized–

HEATHER: Really?

HERMAN: Yeah! Horrible. I mean, the colors they put were good, but they didn't fit. I mean, think of Dexter Gordon and you put him in whatever. No! It doesn't work. First of all, that age was a black and white age. The movies were black and white; television was in black and white. So your brain thinks that way. At least, mine did.

HEATHER: Hum, that's interesting.

HERMAN: And, I mean, that's the reason I like black and white. I find it a more graphic, simple approach to a given subject. I think its more effective.[34]

Black and white technique creates a feeling of intimacy between the viewer and the subject in the photograph. The lack of color forces the photographer to concentrate on the composition within the frame. And Leonard was typically in a darkened area watching someone on stage in a spotlight, where there was not much color to be seen anyway.

The swirling smoke in many of Leonard's photographs is another connoted message that easily becomes an artful expression, since jazz to Leonard "is a smoky night club."[35] Smoke is extremely difficult to photograph; it takes a bright light shining directly behind the smoke in order to catch it on film. Leonard was aware of the lighting and angles surrounding his subject and frequently put up two additional lights that were wired to his camera, one in front and one in back of the subject. Leonard says of his own photographs: "I like back lighting because it sets the subject off from the background, especially if the background is dark, which most of the clubs were. I like light that goes around the subject and not flat lighting."[36]

The brightness of the additional lights is able to capture the curving air of smoke. The smoke connotes an air of artistic purpose. Leonard seemed to include the smoke for its translucence and absorption of space. If the smoke were not visible, then the background would appear flat and without meaning. But because the smoke takes up the space around the musician, it serves a function other than an indication of the setting. It becomes a decoration, a beautification arranged by Leonard. The smoke takes up most of the picture space, and the viewer must search for the faces peering from behind the smoke. The light contrasts the movement and ephemeral quality of smoke against the solid stability and stronger contrasts of the face. We see Dexter Gordon and the smoke float above him probably on stage and seen in a spotlight. Thus, Leonard is able to conceal the real meaning of including the smoke in the picture: to enhance the viewer's experience of the jazz image. "The photograph," states Barthes, "allows the photographer to *conceal elusively* the preparation to which he subjects the scene to be recorded."[37] The smoke recurs as one of Leonard's greatest artistic devices, so much so that his smoking subjects often connote a memory of the Marlboro man.[38]

Yet, not all photographers consented to the posed-musician-performing-in-a-smoke-filled-bar image. Milt Hinton argues: "Everybody was shooting the band on stage in uniform, and if you went to a professional photographer for your own publicity shot, he'd ask you to smile and put your horn up in the air. I've never wanted to get those kinds of photos because I've never seen musicians that way."[39] Carol Friedman explains it this way:

> I discarded the backdrop of the smoke-filled nightclub and the instrument props early on. For all its visual seduction, the bandstand arena revealed very little about musicians. But away from the sound of the music was a richness of conversation, humor, camaraderie, and warmth that reflected the music more closely than I had imagined. There was an unmistakable connection between personality, character, and musical expression.[40]

For Friedman, the visual stimulation was found with the musicians themselves away from the club or anything that would associate them with their craft. However, her photographs have not received the international attention that Leonard's have. One reason might be because, in Leonard's photographs, the viewer becomes actively involved as a part of the performance. Most of his photographs depict musicians as they are about to play or are playing. They are creating art at the moment the camera flashes. Therefore, the viewer serves as a witness to original art. Many documentaries of Jackson Pollock show him actually painting on a transparent surface. This allows the audience to see the process. It is not enough to see Jackson Pollock's paintings; we are intrigued by their creation and want to witness how he painted them. In like manner, Leonard's photographs of jazz musicians in a club setting allow the viewer to feel a part of the music-making process. Our mind is free to conjure up scenarios of favorite celebrities. We want to relive the moment Sinatra or Ellington stepped out onstage, and imagine what he was thinking.

So our desire to partake in the moment helps to perpetuate the myth of the jazz musician. The setting, again as a connoted message, puts us at the place and time of the photograph. We relive the experience of the jazz musician through the image. Therefore, the photograph instigates mimesis, representing a real act that has already happened. And in this case, the past becomes an ideal, a good memory of what jazz used to be. The time and place of the image become historical markers attributing meaning to jazz through memories of the past. In this manner, reading a photograph is always historical. "[I]t depends on the reader's 'knowledge.'"[41] Dave Liebman says, "serious art needs an educated public and the person who has taken part in the art himself will be the judge of that," meaning, the serious art of jazz requires an educated viewer to understand the importance of the jazz image.[42]

In order to do so one must examine a jazz photograph in comparison to other images of the same caliber. For example, a well-known photographer, Lee Friedlander, took several photographs of musicians with their instruments in their homes between 1957 and 1974.[43] These photographs accompanied interviews being done by the jazz scholars Richard Allen and William Russell for the then new Archive of New Orleans Jazz at Tulane University. Several of Friedlander's photographs illustrate how musicians like Punch Miller and Eddie Morris played the trumpet or trombone (see Fig. 2.2). Both musicians hold their horns up to play them; both are elderly African American men. They appear to be at home; a bright light shines

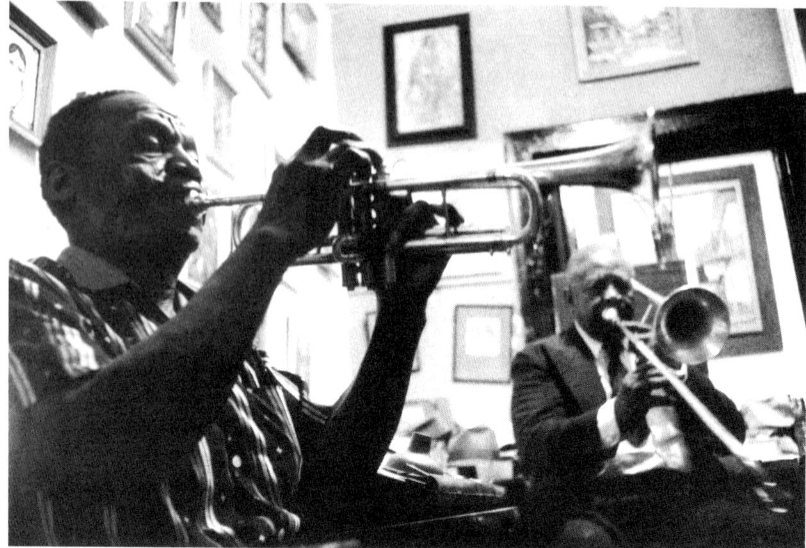

Fig. 2.2. Punch Miller and Eddie Morris, ca. 1959. © Lee Friedlander, courtesy Fraenkel Gallery, San Francisco.

down on their heads. The photograph imitates others taken in the South that captured musicians informally rather than on a brightly lit stage in a New York club. Because the musicians are presented in a down-home setting, the American viewer can postulate their musical style as being country, jazz, or blues.

Stylistically, one may determine that the photograph is black and white, a classic. It frames both men in the picture but concentrates on trumpeter Miller, who is closer and in sharper focus. He takes up the entire left side and middle of the photograph, while Morris occupies the lower right-hand side. The two are angled differently and away from the camera, and neither looks in that direction. While sitting comfortably and ignoring the presence of the viewer/photographer, Miller and Morris hold their instruments with ease and seem to be playing a duet. This connotes friendship with each other—and with Friedlander, since they have obliged him this opportunity to shoot them or at least to enter in someone's home or practice room. Little can be seen except the men and the photographs hanging on the walls behind them, and what appears to be a cluttered desk or table behind them. The photograph is arranged to provide the eye opportunity to gaze from side to side in the room. The viewer imagines Friedlander to be sitting close by, based on the encroaching distance to each musician. The distance between them is adequate; however, the closeness to the trumpet player might create tension or a claustrophobic feeling for the viewer. Regardless, the angle and the setting of this photograph connote informality.

Let us compare a photograph by Herman Leonard with the one by Lee Friedlander. In one of his most famous photographs, Leonard captures the young Dexter Gordon taking a break from a gig at the Royal Roost in 1948. Three musicians appear in the photograph, but only two can be recognized. Gordon, on the right side and facing the left, is sitting with his saxophone resting on his leg, while the drummer Kenny Clarke leans his arms on his hi-hat cymbal and faces the opposite direction to the right. A third musician, who sits to the left of the photo is Fats Navarro, said Leonard.[44] Only his arm and horn are visible. The viewer sees nothing but black space behind all three musicians, and thus the setting cannot be identified. There are many objects to examine in the photograph, such as Gordon's clothing, the instruments, sheet music on a stand, smoke drifting from Gordon's mouth, and his lit cigarette, all of which balance the image.

Note that, although each photograph is in black and white and portrays African American jazz musicians (or what we assume to be jazz musicians, in Friedlander's photo), each is totally different in the presentation of musicians. Friedlander's image depicts friends sitting at home playing music together, while Leonard creates an idealized picture of artists creating more serious work. In Friedlander's picture, Punch Miller and Eddie Morris are proudly rehearsing their music. Friedlander says that during the time of each photograph, "the music was still being played indigenously."[45] The faces of the musicians seem to be weathered by time, but they are jovial during their impromptu jam session. Thus, Friedlander in effect is acting as a photojournalist by documenting the act of these musicians, and the photograph becomes evidence of his field work.

The image, more so than the musician, becomes the subject of Leonard's photograph. In a mythical atmosphere, Gordon appears in the forefront of all three jazz musicians. By using black and white photography, Leonard encapsulates Gordon with his instrument as if he exists in a stilled and ominously autonomous world. He looks young, strong, and capable of real virtuosity just by his presence and poise. With the brim of his hat turned up, his face shines toward the unknown with confidence and patience. The light shining directly onto his face along with the saxophone creates a haloed effect. Gordon stares pensively into space, while the smoke of his cigarette curls around his face and into the air, thereby creating a mystical space of thought and elegance. In fact, the smoke seems to act as a metaphor for the musical sound that will soon escape from Gordon's horn.[46] The

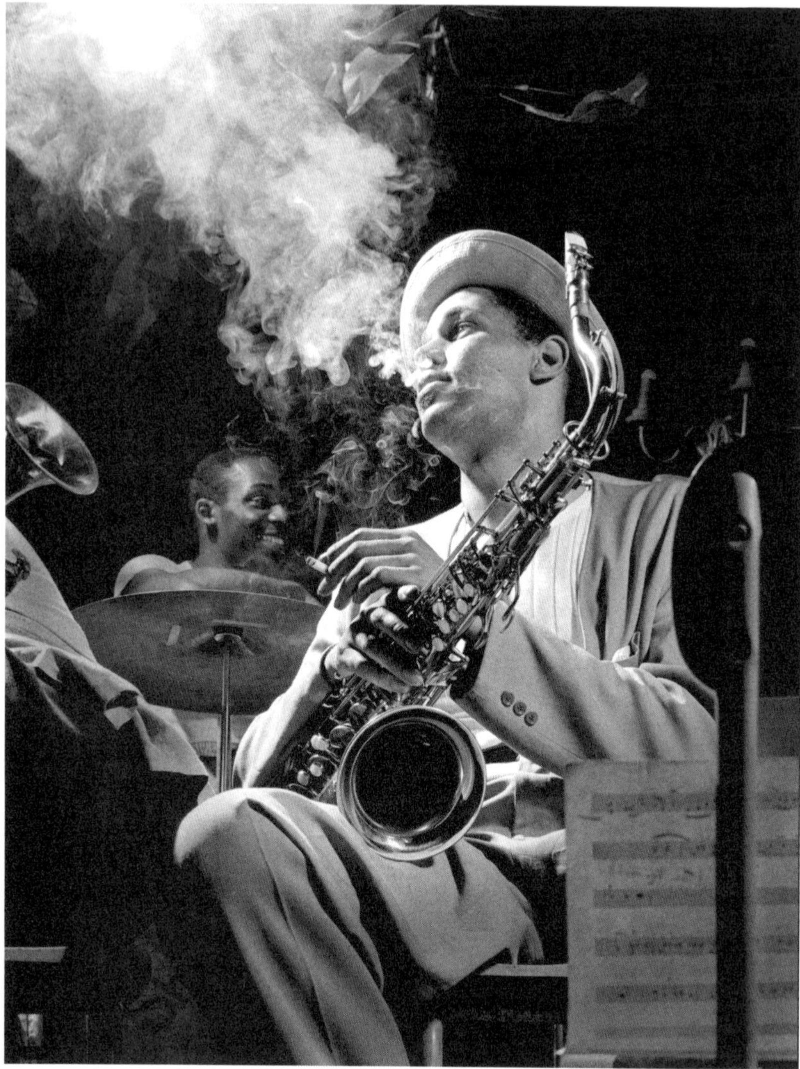

Fig. 2.3. Dexter Gordon at the Royal Roost in New York, 1948, code #DXG01, by Herman Leonard.

saxophone that rests in his lap represents music in a position of rest before the act of creation takes place. The invitation comes from the open bell of the saxophone as it turns toward the viewer, mimicking a black pool of the unknown, and again emphasizing the music that appears out of the depths of art.

Gordon is epitomized as the creator of art in a moment of preparation, not at the moment of creation. One must not pull forth music that is not ready to be performed, and this photograph is intended as an image of music that exists before it is heard. It represents the transience of life, recalling still-life vanitas from the sixteenth-century Dutch paintings. Indeed, Leonard perpetuates the aforementioned myth of jazz as simultaneously sensuous and intellectual.

The grinning face of Kenny Clarke—who hovers in the background between Gordon and the unknown musician—is caught forever in print, and his smile's sense of ease complements the seriousness of Gordon's dreamy stare out toward the lights. The connotation of this image indicates that Leonard perceives jazz as a serious art form and presents it as such to the viewer. While Friedlander's photograph may seem archeological, it is part of a process in excavating New Orleans jazz.

The manner in which the instrument is utilized in each photograph also connotes meaning. Both instrument and musician, can be seen in the same shot; thus, the closeness with which each musician interacts with his instrument creates a sense of security in the viewer. As mentioned in chapter 1, "the man with the horn" has become a staple in the canonization of the jazz image. The instrument, then, becomes as much a part of the character of the musician as does the setting. The instrument is more than a denoted prop; it relays the personality of the musician. For example, consider Dizzy Gillespie playing a folded trumpet with his huge, frog-like cheeks or John Coltrane's closed eyes while handling his tenor or soprano saxophone with grace.

Inclusion of the instrument also narrows the category of music for the viewer. The instrument plays a huge role in jazz imagery since it is one of the major means to identify the genre. Certain instruments are indicative of a style of music: harmonica to the blues, banjo to bluegrass, tin whistle to Celtic music. Not too many styles of music use a saxophone in a nightclub. Thus, the inclusion of certain instruments typically found in jazz, such as the saxophone, piano, bass, and drum in a picture of a jazz musician serves to identify the sound of jazz with the image placed before the viewer.

Musical instruments in Leonard's photographs are also utilized for their shape and design. The circular movement of the drum head is repeated in the winding staircase in the photograph of Max Roach. Duke Ellington looks straight at the piano, and Dexter Gordon's saxophone points instinctively toward the viewer, while Clarke's head weaves in front of his drum kit. The viewer's gaze shifts from the instrument to the body of the musician. Usually in Leonard's photographs, one cannot see the entire musician but can see the layout of the body as well as the instrument. Indeed, the inclusion of the body in a photograph offers numerous interpretations and connotations, many of which are used to evaluate the social condition based on one's physical appearance. Michael Frizot observes:

> From the moment it was invented, photography was dedicated to examining the human body. The knowledge which science would thus acquire about our exterior appearance would, it was hoped, result in a greater understanding of the mysteries of the soul. The body was seen as the visible proof of human differences, criminal tendencies, pathology, and delinquency. Anthropometry and ethnology, allied to photography, were the means by which people hoped to reduce innumerable recorded data to a simple human type.[47]

Leonard, however, uses the body as a frame of reference. To him the body is not a sexual object, but a shape or form that complements his vision of jazz. Fittingly, the body becomes more of the focus in photography when the subject is a vocalist, for the instrumentalist often finds courage by hiding behind the instrument, but a vocalist has no such protection. The vocalist is exposed and vulnerable to all of the gazing eyes in an audience or viewers of a photograph. In Herman Leonard's photograph of Ella Fitzgerald, one may interpret his artwork as an example of the male gaze as defined by Margaret Olin.[48] In this photograph, Ella Fitzgerald is singing onstage for a captive audience that includes Duke Ellington and Benny Goodman in the front row. One could interpret this image as the positioning of female power over male admirers in the audience. The light streams from her mouth as if the sound of her voice enlightens the listeners in the room. The audience members, however, do not appear to be concentrating on her voice, but rather they gaze upon her as a woman in the spotlight.

While Leonard's use of the body in this image may or may not be implicitly sexual, the light surrounding Fitzgerald's head is again used to symbolize Leonard's own position on jazz. He enshrouds the singer with a cerebral light, projecting the power of her voice, as if electrified, onto the listening audience. The setting appears intimate, even with a crowd of people. Fitzgerald's body takes up nearly half of the photograph, yet her blurry figure clearly signals that this is not the photograph's focus. Instead, the viewer's eye rocks from her head back to the entranced, shining face of Ellington. The dialogue in the photograph now has a reaction, the beaming face of Ellington provides a conclusion to the banter between viewer, subject, and photographer.

Through the images discussed in this section, Leonard has illustrated his talents as a photographer who has given prestige to jazz. The more images

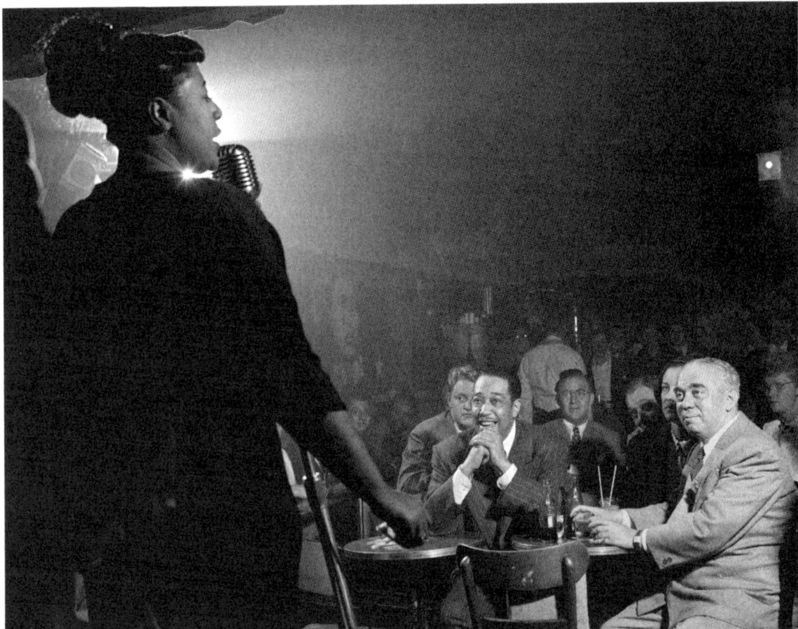

Fig. 2.4. Ella Fitzgerald, Duke Ellington, Benny Goodman, and Richard Rodgers at the Down Beat in New York City, 1949, code #ELF03, by Herman Leonard. © Herman Leonard Photography LLC/ CTSIMAGES.COM.

we see, the more his intent is clear. He wants the viewer to appreciate jazz as he does, to understand what jazz can bring to intended audiences, such as Ellington and Goodman, and to note how jazz can signify quality through the arrangement of musicians in the Gordon photograph.

But one significant point is that Leonard incorporates the values and the customs of the 1950s into his images, which act as a mirror, reflecting social values of the time. The photographs are designed to instigate a dialogue between the viewer and the social culture known to the viewer. As discussed in chapter 1, the social values of the 1950s included the protection of family values, a sense of moral decency that was strengthened by a predominately white middle class, and a surge in patriotism with the return of soldiers from World War II. These values collided with the emerging defiance of the beat culture and its literary giants, such as Jack Kerouac, Allen Ginsberg, and William S. Burroughs, as well as with the eruption of rock and roll with Chuck Berry, Little Richard, Fats Domino, and Elvis Presley.

Leonard's photographs contain elements that signify both the conservative values of the 1950s and the defiance of the younger generation. Depending on which social realm one comes from, each viewer can find something in the photograph to identify with. Leonard's ability to connect to his audience through a strong emotional representation of the jazz musician is one of his strongest qualities. First of all, his black and white pictures recreate a timeless version of the events that they depict. One associates pictures in black and white with the era of the black and white television. Classic TV shows like *My Three Sons*, *Ozzie and Harriet*, and the *Andy Griffith Show* stoically recall that time period; Leonard's photographs similarly transport the viewer to the past, the same way that twentieth-first-century singer Norah Jones's voice contains remnants of Patsy Cline and imitates the timbre found on old recordings. The fact that Leonard's images are valued so many years after they were taken gives even further prestige to their meaning. The term *classic* can be applied to his work simply because it is considered of high taste and of lasting value. This provides another reason to consider the worth of his artwork, especially since the value of his photographs have jumped significantly.

The photograph cannot give the precise judgment of the image; it merely presents an image. Even if a photograph contains a "universal" icon, or something that is understood by everyone, the presentation of the image can be interpreted subjectively. Photographers seem to have their own method of discovery when photographing an object. Much of the craft is based on one's own temperament and "knowing where to look," which ensures simplicity and ease in taking a picture.

> How foolish of me to have believed that it would be that easy. I had confused the appearance of trees and automobiles and people with reality itself and believed that a photograph of these appearances to be [*sic*] a photograph of it. It is a melancholy truth that I will never be able to photograph it and can only fail. I am a reflection photographing other reflections within a reflection. To photograph reality is to photograph nothing.[49]

Or perhaps taking a photo is not as easy as it seems. W. Eugene Smith, who wrote the above statement as a conscientious journalist reporting only the facts, was torn between his role of capturing the presentation of reality in a photograph and literal truth.[50] He knew the limitations of photography, "other reflections within a reflection." But in order to show the conditions of a poverty-stricken country such as Japan in the 1950s to the comfortable American middle class, he had to try to get as close to the literal truth as he could. Thus, in many ways Smith adopted an artificial realism to the world on the other side of the lens. The artificiality of his photography is used to create a stronger interpretation of actual reality as he saw it.

Susan Sontag disagrees with Smith's view; she states, "Photographed images do not seem to be statements about the world so much as pieces of it, miniatures of reality that anyone can make or acquire."[51] Roland Barthes also disagrees with Smith by claiming that photography can achieve a sense of literal truth: "for all the kinds of images only the photograph is able to transmit the 'literal' information without forming it by means of discontinuous signs and rules of transformation."[52] In Smith's defense, one imagines that he would recognize the literal truth available in some photographs; yet he would argue that photography cannot in any way accurately present the real world as seen by the photographer. The debate in this instance is "truth" and what the correct or incorrect way of presenting it is. The interpretation of what reality is and what truth is in a photograph can be found in what Susan Sontag calls the "photographic message" which conveys not one, but two truths: the truth of the time and place of the photograph as set against the truth as seen by the photographer.[53]

Photographers, of course, must interpret truth, and, through this interpretation, they actually alter reality. The subjects one selects, the angle of vision, arrangement, color, focus, proximity, light, relationship—all this can alter or affect the photographer's view of what is real. In some jazz photographs, reality must be altered to create the best picture possible. Let us take, for example, Leonard's photograph of Frank Sinatra at the Monte Carlo. This photograph presents Sinatra completely wreathed in a haze of light and smoke. Dressed in a tuxedo and standing in front of a microphone, we see only his back while he is waving, presumably, to the audience. He seems to exist in a vacuous space composed of only himself. His raised left arm, cigarette in hand, reaches out into the unknown, unable to grasp whatever he sees. The viewer assumes that the smoke and light we have come to expect in a Leonard photograph shields the audience, thus purposely creating the "blind spot" between the light, audience members, and Sinatra. The setting is real enough; the time and place of the event actually happened in real time at a real place. Yet from this photograph, the viewer has no idea of the time and event except for Sinatra's appearance on stage.

The second truth stated by Sontag is Leonard's manipulation of the photograph to fit his particular agenda. First, he has altered the appearance of the photograph through the large aperture, overexposing the light collected by the camera. Second, he has purposely stood behind Sinatra and pointed the camera toward the light, thus blocking the audience (or whatever Sinatra is facing) completely. These alterations create a magical, mystical picture of one of the greatest singers of the twentieth century. Third, he has not included Sinatra's face nor other musicians, which could possibly cause confusion for the viewer. This is one of the few photographs by Leonard that does not display the musician's face prominently. Possibly Leonard saw that the inclusion of Sinatra's face would stifle the greater meaning of the photograph. Sinatra was a cultural icon of the time, a musical deity: complex, vast, unknowable, and, during the height of his popularity, revered by the nation as a man with infinite vocal power. Perhaps Leonard did not include Sinatra's face in the photograph because it would be too limiting. Symbolically, the mystery of his face mimics the mystery of his art and restricts the contents of the photo. Leonard places Sinatra toward the hazy space, implying that Sinatra is alone and bravely faces the unknown. Sinatra, the singer, is made into a hero in this photograph; he now stands for the ideal entertainer who has achieved recognition by metaphorically reaching for the stars.

The mystical atmosphere in the photograph would not be as effective if Leonard had not adjusted his camera or had printed it differently in the darkroom. By altering the shot, Leonard was able to create greater meaning to the image. This does not necessarily mean that Leonard was wrong for enhancing the photo; in fact, he has adequately projected the successful, suave nature of Frank Sinatra's musical career in a photograph. E. H. Gombrich describes our desire for real-life situations in the context of art: "We do not want to see the sitter in the situation in which he actually was having his portrait taken. We want to be able to abstract from this memory and to see him reacting to more typical real-life contexts."[54] Thus our memory of the subject's career, in this instance, is pertinent to our memory of the subject's appearance. The viewer cannot see the face of Sinatra but can project the memory of his face onto the photograph. Therefore, the photograph actually stimulates one's imagination to furnish a picture of Ol' Blue Eyes. Leonard shows that reality in the life of a jazz singer is subjective. The "truth" of his photograph, as Sontag indicated earlier, lies in the adequate representation of Sinatra as an icon known to all in American music.

Photography, as an imitation of reality, transfers the realness of jazz to the picture of the jazz musician. It is both realistic and heightened imagination. Realism, found in W. Eugene Smith's photographs or Susan Sontag's analysis, is often associated with photography as the main method of depicting a situation: "A photograph passes for incontrovertible proof that a given thing happened. The picture may distort; but there is always a presumption that something exists, or did exist, which is like what's in the picture."[55]

However, Leonard used realism to present the world of jazz to the public. In the Sinatra photo, reality lies in the representation of Sinatra's mystical image and household name. His presence is iconic and his voice

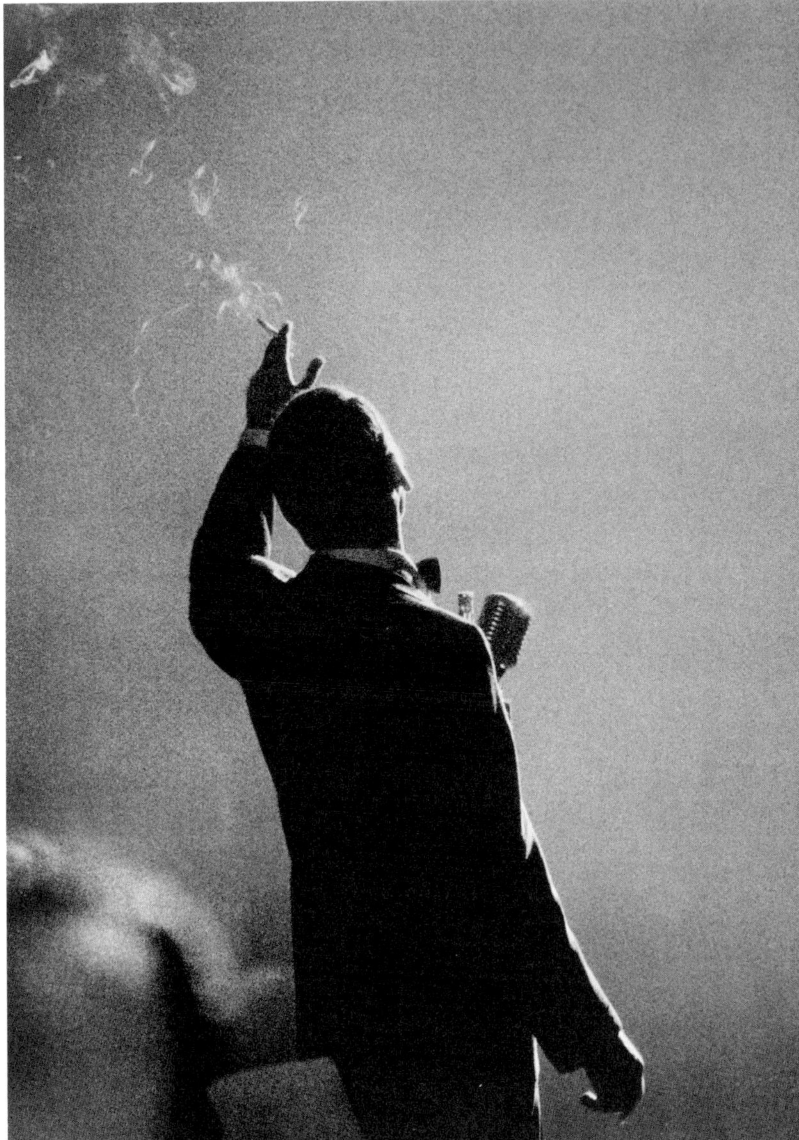

Fig. 2.5. Frank Sinatra at the Monte Carlo in 1958, code #FRS01, by Herman Leonard. © Herman Leonard Photography LLC/CTSIMAGES.COM.

is well-known by society. Leonard effectively captured his aura, as it was known by the public, and posed the great legend within a frame. By establishing a rectangle around the image, the photographer focuses on the material inside of the frame. The object for viewing, in this case Sinatra, is unaware of being photographed and he is not facing the camera or the photographer. Instead, he is acknowledging his adoring public and faces his crowd of admirers. The reality of the moment is found in the light and Sinatra's body facing the audience. Both components are heightened within the photograph and portray the magnitude of the moment, that being the height of Sinatra's career captured on film.

At the same time, a photograph is a limiting experience, as demonstrated by Leonard's decision not to include Sinatra's face. There is no way to capture the entirety of an event in a two-dimensional photograph; consequently, the photographer must rely on our memory of what happened in the past as the best way to relive the experience. As Sontag concludes, "photography [is] the cumulative de-creation of the past," for the photograph "gives people an imaginary possession of a past that is unreal."[56] A picture becomes a search for that which is photogenic, and eventually, a souvenir.[57] Leonard marks the event of Sinatra's entrance (or exit) onto the stage and, like that entrance, introduces his choice of the photo that best demonstrates Sinatra's viability. By depicting the popularity of Sinatra on film, he captured the popular image of Sinatra as a musical icon.

An image, as a sign, should give a glimpse of its significance in our lives; at the same time, the image is, in a certain manner, limiting. In a photograph, one connoted message contains so many meanings that every viewer can find some form of identification to his/her personal culture or life experience. However, by constructing the image of reality being represented, the photographer limits what the viewer can see and interprets reality for the viewer, as explained by Susan Sontag, thus blinding the viewer from the experience of the real world.[58] One assumes that a picture or symbol is universally recognized to be representative of something else. However, as our global view broadens, Western society has come to realize that not everything is universal, especially not signs.

Like many other philosophers, Roland Barthes recognizes the problematic uses of signs as they transfer from one meaning to another. He argues that no one can find a totally agreed-upon meaning of a single image; rather, one can only surmise what the image means to them. "For it is not really the perception of likeness for which we are originally programmed," writes Gombrich, "but the noticing of unlikeness, the departure from the norm which stands out and sticks in the mind."[59] We, as consumers, recognize and perceive those images that bring familiarity. However, in our perception of the image, we project our own set of preconceived values onto the image and then either accept or reject them as part of the image. Because they are not universal, these visual representations determine and perpetuate social values. Louis Althusser argues that "the image can be seen as the inscription of those values and beliefs . . . but [the visual is also] a mechanism that *produces* as well as represents culture to itself, constituting its relations of power and difference."[60]

Through the social framework of the photograph, one can determine which set of presumed values is reflected in the image. For example, as previously mentioned, Leonard uses the medium of photography to illustrate his belief in jazz as a legitimate art form. As Gombrich says, "Perception always stands in need of universals."[61] Thus, Leonard unintentionally universalizes jazz through the artistic production of his photographs. For instance, each photograph utilizes certain arranged elements that enhance the quality of the picture. He constructs the picture around the setting of the musician—usually the stage, as in photographs of Duke Ellington, Ella Fitzgerald, Frank Sinatra, and Max Roach. This setting signifies the place that art was created at a specific moment. The viewer begins to associate place (stage) with the subject in the picture (jazz musician). As more and more photographs are taken of musicians on stage, the public begins to connect jazz with high-class performance. A universal idea is created through the repetition of the image to many viewers of the picture.

Also, Leonard inherently focuses on the universality of beauty. No matter what is contained in the image, we all search for some resemblance to our subjective understanding of beauty. Speaking about the Dexter Gordon photo, Leonard discusses his opinion on what makes his images appealing to so many people.

HERMAN: It's an arresting image with all that smoke. It's an image of an entity that we don't normally see. It's not a great still life of a bowl of fruit, which we have seen, but you rarely see a musician, or any other artist, under these conditions. I mean, he could have been a sculptor with the smoke. It would have been equally as good. It's not the fact that he was a musician. It's a pictorial effect that a lot of people say that I designed it that way. That's fine, but I did not design it that way. It turned out that way.

HEATHER: And I've heard it too that that is the Leonard look.

HERMAN: Well, it is the Leonard look; that's what it has become because of the smoke in that one and in a few others that are pretty strong. . . . And you don't know who it is, and it doesn't matter. There's something about it that stops you and makes you want to look.

HEATHER: So you think it's more about. . .

HERMAN: I don't think it has anything to do with music!

HEATHER: Really?

HERMAN: I really do. I mean, the pictorial value . . .

HEATHER: Like what we said the other day about the composition, the lighting, the . . .

HERMAN: That's it! Think of another subject matter that's not music that entices you with the imagery of it. I can't think of one right now, but there are.

HEATHER: Ansel Adams?

HERMAN: Oh yeah.

HEATHER: He makes it look. . .

HERMAN: He makes it glorious! I mean, it's a *landscape*! And we've gone by that landscape and never paid attention. But the way he presents it . . .[62]

Ansel Adams is regarded as such a great photographer because he is able take an everyday sight and make it extraordinary. As Leonard states above, the "pictorial value" in an image—whether it is in a photograph by Herman Leonard or Ansel Adams—becomes a standard of judgment. We judge the presentation of beauty in a photograph whether or not the beauty of the subject matter is present. The standard perception of beauty is applied towards Leonard's photographs due to their compositional balance, presentation, photogenia, and subject matter, which is why his work appeals to so many people, regardless of their knowledge of jazz. The universality of the jazz image is perpetuated through Leonard's photos.

The reality of human existence depends on humans' engagement with the world. Martin Heidegger equates the German term *Dasein*, literally translated as "existence" or "being there," with actuality or acting in the world. The *Dasein* of jazz occurs in the experience of the music, regardless of setting. Performance settings for jazz musicians are either the concert stage or, in Collier's words, "bars where the cash register rings incessantly,

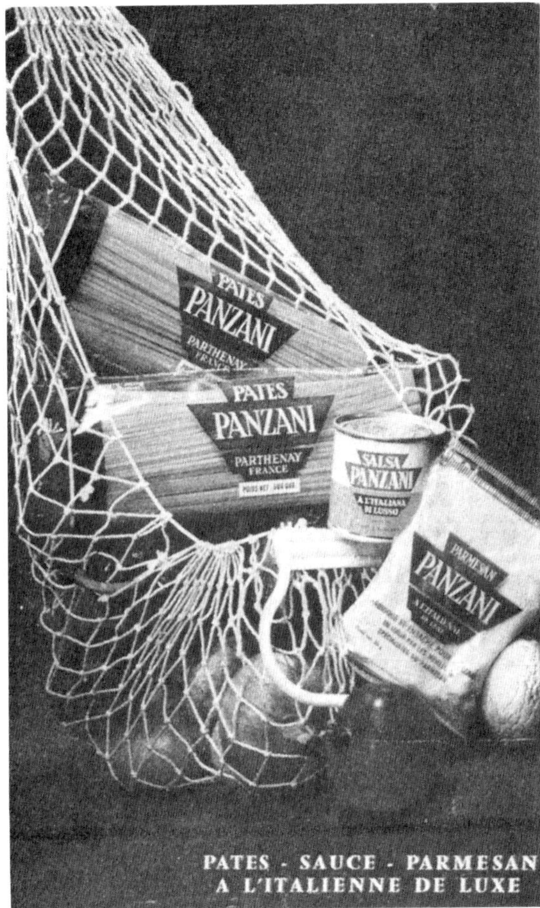

Fig. 2.6. Panzani advertisement discussed by Barthes in *Image, Music, Text.*

where the length of tunes is tailored to the need to sell drinks during the breaks, where the audience is ignorant of the music and drunks badger the band to play tunes totally outside their métier."[63] In a photograph, the viewer experiences the image in lieu of the music, and the photograph therein becomes the reality. The reality of the world appears only as the reality of the artwork appears.

Roland Barthes uses the example of a Panzani advertisement to capture the essence of reality in a photograph.[64] The picture contains some packets of pasta, a tin, some tomatoes, onions, peppers, and a mushroom that are spewing forth from a half-open string bag. Barthes, always the semiotician, points out several messages that are transferred from reality into this image. He says that there are several meanings and signs within the picture. The literal message is found in the caption at the bottom reading: "Pates-Sauces-

Parmesan A L'Italienne de Luxe." In addition, each bag of pasta has the words "Pates Panzani" written on them. Other meanings appear through unspoken language, as seen symbolically with the half-open bag of vegetables "to let the provisions spill out onto the table."[65] The vegetables signify a return from the market which is indicative of Italian culture. Italians are known for shopping for fresh food instead of storing food in a freezer to use later like many Americans do.

Secondary signs are the colors of red with tomatoes and yellow and green with peppers. The colors act as signifiers for Italy, as understood by a signified Italian stereotype and reinstated by the linguistic sign of "Panzani." These combined elements as well as the already noted Italians phrasing, "A L'Italienne de Luxe," firmly communicates a sense of Italy to the viewer. Barthes labels that which represents Italian customs through language "Italianicity." The shapes of circles (onions and can), linear lines (spaghetti), and squares (the net rather than plastic bags) also add to the "old Italian town" image of days gone by. Thus, he establishes Italian culture as a main signifier in the advertisement and several signifiers found within the image.

The perception of signs are based on the previous experiences and knowledge of the viewer, even though many signs are self-explanatory. For instance, in order to understand the Italianicity of the picture, one must possess cultural, almost anthropological knowledge—of the colors of the Italian flag and the Italian language written on the advertisement—to fully comprehend its meaning. However, as Barthes indicated, some universalities assume every viewer would correctly interpret this meaning. The third sign, for instance, is found in the balanced diet for a good meal, transmitting the idea of a "total culinary experience."[66] The produce in the image acts as signifier, and the number and presentation of these objects signify a wholesome meal. Barthes correctly indicates that this is a relatively self-explanatory sign. It does not require much experience to know that produce arranged together represents a healthy meal. In this manner, Barthes hypothesizes that this third sign is a non-coded, iconic message; all that is needed to understand this message is our perception, one that a child could comprehend. The fourth sign is based on the arrangement of the image itself, evoking the memory of still life paintings that are arranged in a similar manner.[67]

The Panzani image contains symbolic, literal, and iconic meanings, none of which are processed linearly. Rather, as we perceive an image, our brain processes several meanings at once, and then, depending on our personal background, we begin to understand certain meanings in order of their importance. An image contains a "floating chain" of signifiers, which the reader can choose to interpret.[68] Through the reduction of images into signifiers, and then the reduction of signifiers into more and more signifieds, the sign becomes diluted into an endless array of other meanings. Jacques Lacan indicates the problems with repeated analysis of images and their signifiers, "[w]here everything is transformed into image, only images exist and are produced and consumed [which] completely de-realizes the human world of conflicts and desires, under cover of illustrating it."[69] This relationship between the viewer and advertisement begins when the viewer attempts to subjectively view the object, and in the process of reading an image, the viewer gains analytic and creative power over the stationary, nonresponsive image that cannot explain itself. And through the exchange of information and ultimately power, the image or advertisement acquires significance and value in society.

In jazz photography, messages can also be combined to create a floating chain of signifiers. In Leonard's photograph entitled *Lester Young*, Young is not even in the picture. Like Beckett's *Breath* (1971), the viewer only sees props littering the stage without the presence of an actor: a Coke bottle with a lit cigarette on top, sheet music, and Young's hat laid haphazardly on the edge of the open saxophone case. This photograph is atypical for Leonard, although another exception lies in his photograph of Stan Kenton's shoes in Atlanta, 1950 (#STK01). Like the Panzani image, the photograph of Young's memorabilia seems to imitate a still life painting. The placement of the objects is crafted for compositional balance in the photograph, but they also imply further meaning.

If one treats this photograph as Barthes did to the Panzani advertisement, one can decipher the historical account of the photograph. The indexical sign of the smoke causes the viewer to locate the source: the lit cigarette. The swirls of smoke detract from the gruff texture of other objects, such as the instrument case and hat. From the title and Leonard's account, we know that the hat is Young's, who has momentarily set it aside during a recording session.[70] Leonard recalls that Young removed his hat, took his saxophone out of its case, put his cigarette down, and walked over to do the session. Each object acts as a sign of Young's presence: the saxophone case signifies the working, performing musician; the Coke bottle is refreshment of the nonalcoholic kind, also signifying an everyday drink; and finally his porkpie hat signifies his return, for Young is always pictured with his hat. Each of these items seems to represent endurance, or more specifically, the performing life of the musician. We are aware of another activity that is obviously going on somewhere else that requires the presence of the

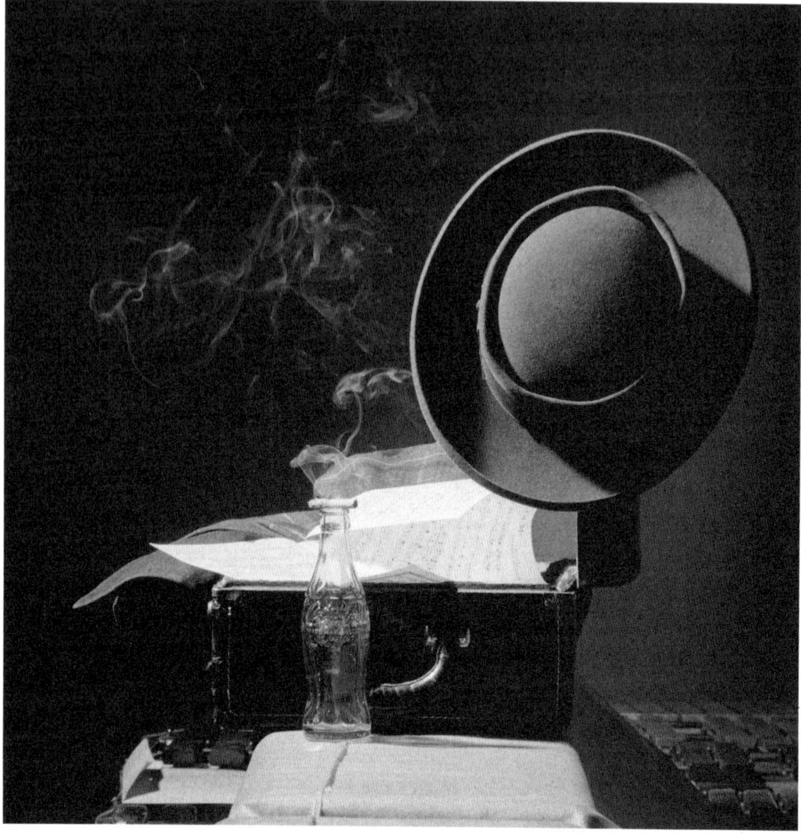

Fig. 2.7. Lester Young in New York City, 1948, code #LSY03, by Herman Leonard. © Herman Leonard Photography LLC/CTSIMAGES.COM.

musician, Lester Young. His belongings are left aside temporarily while he is in another place to record some music. Another important sign associated with the recording studio is the sheet music. Similar to a book, sheet music would not be left open unless it was in use, and here it is waiting for someone to read it. As with finding a hammer but no carpenter, the tool is used to represent the trade of the craftsman. And in this case, we see chord changes written on the music, not tablature, nor a score for the orchestra. This further indicates the musical style that the absent musician plays, since the type of person most familiar with chord changes written in this manner is the jazz musician.

As the Panzani ad indicates "Italianicity," the combination of images here creates what we might call "jazzticity" or an image of Americana. For this reason, Leonard's photographs have come to represent jazz as the best of America's original music. The Coke bottle is clearly an American product, yet the picture does not appear as an advertisement like the Panzani ad. Instead, its emptiness suggests that Young just finished drinking it and walked away, leaving it on the table next to his cigarette. There is a moment of incompleteness in the photograph through the still-lit cigarette, pork-pie hat, open instrument case, and empty bottle, all anticipating Young's return.

As in the Panzani ad, the fact that seemingly random objects are aesthetically arranged implies an intended meaning behind the arrangement. This does not mean that Leonard arranged the objects in this manner. But their arrangement, even haphazardly done, creates an artful experience for the viewer. The first sign is the arrangement of the objects. The positioning of sheet music, a glass bottle, a hat, instrument case, cigarette, and smoke signify composition, order, and balance. The process of bringing the objects together creates a historical account of Young's existence. Thus, meaning is embedded through action that is implied but not seen, for clearly someone had to light the cigarette and drink the Coke. We get the idea that someone was there, but has left so as not to be included in the picture. Barthes would treat this idea as a type of consciousness or what he calls "having-been-there-ness." "What we have is a new space-time category: spatial immediacy and temporal anteriority, the photograph being an illogical conjunction between the *here-now* and the *there-then* . . . its reality that of the *having-been-there*, for in every photograph there is the always stupefying evidence of *this is how it was*, giving us, by a precious miracle, a reality from which we are sheltered."[71]

Barthes continues by saying that the *having-been-there* quality of a photograph probably diminishes the power of the image since ". . . the photograph can in some sense elude history . . . and represent a 'flat' anthropological fact . . . [.]"[72] This photograph does just that by superimposing a reality, Lester Young's personal belongings, and a past, that day at the recording studio. It is an indication of the present, the here and now, but a photo by definition is a record of the past. And Roland Barthes says, "since this constraint exists only for photography, we must consider it, by means of reduction, as the very essence, the *noeme* of Photography."[73] Barthes labels the noeme "that-has-been" or what I would call "that-which-has-been." *That which* is implied in the photograph *has been there* within the frame of the photograph at one point in time. The photograph contains a part of the past in the image, and this representation of a past scene is its noeme.

This photograph is not one of Leonard's best-known, nor is it designed to promote a particular kind of musician like his pictures of bebop musicians

Dizzy Gillespie and Charlie Parker. One possible reason for its lack of popularity is the fact that it does not present the typical image of a jazz musician in person. Even though it replicates the life of a jazz musician through the objects in the picture, and Leonard names the jazz musician he has in mind in the title, the impact of the image is still not received. As mentioned before, there is power and authority in deciphering a photograph; therefore, there is power and authority when looking at a musician in a photograph since that is a standardized image for jazz photography. Because of the musician's absence here, this photograph does not instill the same strength in meaning. The picture does, however, represent jazz differently, through the objects Young uses, rather than through the image of him playing jazz. Young's presence is clear, but this is not enough for the fan of jazz. We want to see the one responsible for the action. We want to relive the adventurous lifestyle he led. We want to emulate the life of Young in our own. But nothing about these things is familiar. Consequently, we are not satisfied, and continue looking for images that allow us to pursue our fantasy.

Susan Sontag comments upon how both the ambiguity of the photograph and the greater meaning of the image are compounded, depending on who owns the photograph.

> A photograph is both a pseudo-presence and a token of absence. Like a wood fire in a room, photographs—especially those of people, of distant landscapes and faraway cities, of the vanished past—are incitements of reverie. The sense of the unattainable that can be evoked by photographs feeds directly into the erotic feelings of those for whom desirability is enhanced by distance. The lover's photograph hidden in a married woman's wallet, the poster photograph of a rock star tacked up over an adolescent's bed, the campaign-button image of a politician's face pinned on a voter's coat, the snapshots of a cabdriver's children clipped to the visor—all such talismanic uses of photographs expresses a feeling both sentimental and implicitly magical: they are attempts to contact or to claim to another reality.[74]

As we have seen, Herman Leonard does capture a particular kind of reality through his photographs taken from 1945 to 1959. According to the present organization of jazz history, Leonard's photographs recall the "good" time of jazz history, back when musicians fought for justice, equality, and concepts worthy of being called "art." Thus, if the noeme of photography is the past, then Leonard's particular noeme is "the past that was good." The reality presented by Leonard stems from the circumstances in the United

States that shaped the new sounds of jazz, and as a result, musicians moved from playing in nightclubs to playing for the hearts of thousands.

By reading into these layers of signs, symbols, and presumed meanings found in each photograph, one may come closer to determining the precise part of reality the photograph replicates. We have determined, in this chapter, that there must be in all observations a dynamic dialectic occurring between viewer and subject and photographer and subject. In a real sense, no art work comes alive without this back-and-forth dialectic. Just as each viewer "creates" his or her own "reading" or interpretation of the work, so does each artist participate in the dialogue through the selection of subject, angle of vision, and other tools used in the trade. The resulting oscillating dialectic insures a responsive and creative dynamic between artist and viewer.

When answering the question in an interview, "Do you think that you made the best photos from the musicians which played music you liked most of all?" Leonard replied: "The 'best' photos I've made were never by design or preference for that musician. It's that they were great visual subjects . . . like Dexter Gordon who gave me my most popular image."[75] He recognized Gordon's handsome appearance as a potential good shot, and chose to photograph him based on this possible artful image. Leonard guessed correctly, because this image is his best-selling published print.[76]

It is interesting to note that Leonard chose Gordon not only because of his sound. Leonard stated, "He was extremely interesting to photograph but not necessarily my favorite tenor-man"; he was a "good visual subject."[77] Apparently, Leonard made a decision based on what would be the most provocative or exciting subject to represent in a photograph. His goal was to find a visual stimulant that matched the aural significance of the music. This is the talent of his craft. He has come the closest to providing a visual representation of an entire musical force, and he achieved that by correctly choosing the subject, setting, lighting, props, and film that best reveal the mental image of jazz in the mind of the public. And by merging the mental with actual image, Leonard has been able to find an audience outside of the jazz community as well as within. His presentation of Gordon as the epitome of jazz symbolizes his own feelings towards the music; by putting Gordon in the same light symbolically as he does jazz, Gordon thus becomes the physical representation of the music.

Leonard's photographs contain meaning that is greater than the image presented. He gives a visual representation to the sophisticated sound of jazz music, thus achieving the impossible: casting a musical genre in a visual image. As Susan Sontag states, "To photograph is to confer importance," and Leonard has indeed conferred importance on jazz photography.[78] By matching the same prestige found in the sound of "high art music" to a visual picture, Leonard clearly has acted as an artist himself, sculpting and manipulating the image of jazz. He has struggled to find the best way to showcase jazz musicians, and in so doing has created a canon by which other jazz photographers can do the same. Arguably, he has as much influence among the jazz community as some musicians.

CHAPTER 3

Ceci n'est pas jazz

The Battle for Ownership

After the free jazz and fusion eras of the 1960s and 1970s, the pendulum of musical taste shifted from the avant-garde scene to more traditional norms of mainstream jazz. The fusion era seemingly ran its course, and a new generation of musicians pursued the musical standards of bop in the early 1980s and dedicated their albums to past heroes such as Thelonious Monk, Charlie Parker, and Lester Young. This resurgence in the 1980s of the classic jazz of the 1940s and 1950s is seen as the neoclassical era.[1]

Leonard's association with jazz was also being reborn at the same time as the rise of neoclassicism. The main body of his jazz collection stems from 1945 to 1959; from 1960 on, his career focused on commercial work for *Life*, *Look*, *Esquire*, *Playboy*, and *Cosmopolitan*. Most of Herman Leonard's jazz photos were not well known before his 1988 exhibit in London, at the same time that jazz was going through its own transformation. Leonard's photographs have become as much a part of the definition of jazz as the music itself. His photographs recall the "good" time in jazz history when musicians stood for racial equality, intellectual approaches to music, and a diversification of styles from swing to bop, cool, and hard bop. In addition, Leonard's images are remarkable in themselves regardless of the subject matter. His photographic depictions of African American jazz musicians not only have created a visual image of a black musician of the 1950s, but also have become the standard by which the musical style of jazz from 1945 to 1959 is represented. His photographs established a strong association between image and music: the *visual* image, Leonard's photos, came to represent a particular *musical* period and style of jazz, the age of bebop.

However, this visual depiction creates a dilemma by promoting as an artifact the jazz musician of the past. The jazz greats of the 1940s and 1950s have had such influence in jazz history that most of the music, instrumental arrangement, and performance practice has continued from the mid-century to today. In essence, the history of these musicians has not only survived but also become the staple for what is known and understood to be jazz. Herman Leonard's pictures of great jazz musicians like Miles Davis, Dexter Gordon, and Dizzy Gillespie retain the heroic appeal identified with the music they were making during this time. Consequently, this image of great jazz musicians of the past has become firmly planted into both society and the jazz community, and has aided in the solidification of a distinct musical tradition of jazz. As an artifact this image has rejuvenated the ideals and values stored in the past while providing a visual depiction of the jazz canon.

But some questions remain. What is neoclassicism in jazz, and how has Leonard's image of the jazz musician affected contemporary musicians? This chapter will trace the influence of the jazz image by explaining its relationship to the current cultural influence of jazz. The role of Wynton Marsalis as the unofficial "spokesman" for this style will be evaluated, as will the successes and failures of neoclassicism.[2] By examining neoclassicism as a safeguard of the quality of jazz music and the jazz image, one may understand the impact the jazz image has had on the social and cultural history of jazz. It is also the purpose of this chapter to explain how the image of the jazz musician has come to mean so much to the jazz community as well as to the rest of society—or more specifically, how the jazz image functions as part of the jazz canon.

The development of jazz to its current elevated status as intellectual music is largely due to the musical qualities found in bebop. Three things occurred that greatly affected jazz history from 1945 to 1959: (1) the switch in social status from entertainment to intellectual music; (2) the introduction of several new styles as the result of bebop, such as cool, West Coast, and hard bop; and (3) the rise of the jazz icon as exemplified by Charlie Parker, Dizzy Gillespie, Thelonious Monk, Miles Davis, and John Coltrane. It is historically self-evident that the bebop movement encouraged musicians and listeners to recognize jazz as high art, the result of which sparked the absorption of jazz into academia, promulgated by predominately white jazz enthusiasts. But let us now turn to the events that occurred after bop, which helped in solidifying its presence in the jazz canon.

Jazz lost much of its popularity with the general public once the dance bands stalled during World War II. The 1950s brought a new type of popular musician through the rock and roll revolution, but, as Paul Lopez says, they did not adopt the same professional ethos utilized by previous popular musicians.[3] Jazz musicians were not as eager to bounce and thrust on stage as their rock counterparts.[4] Elvis's shiny pants, coiffed hair, and intoxicating smirk were no match for Parker's mellow attire and small club setting. Moreover, the intellectual complexity of jazz that developed during this time could not compete with the repetitious dirge of rock and roll that became the new dance music. Thus, rock ushered in the new era of the pop star and increased the distance between professional and popular musician. Bop was, as Ed Enright says, "the musician's music," with zigzagging melodies, complex chord structures, and instrumental virtuosity unprecedented for any kind of popular music.[5] Jazz found itself isolated, losing its hold on the popular music market, and, arguably, it has never returned to the status it had during the Jazz Age. For all its glory and complexity, bebop is seen as having dampened the prominence of jazz as popular music, at least in the eyes of the general pubic.

Ironically, the hipster attitude adopted by bop musicians gained a marginal appeal that was disseminated throughout New York City. The jazz community feverishly began its assimilation of new sounds, people, and styles from recordings released during the late 1940s. Young, white, professional musicians soon joined the bebop style and helped to influence later developments in the 1950s, but it is more common to discuss the black professional musicians of bop, the stylistic innovators who incorporated extended and chromatic harmonies as well as new rhythms. While forfeiting jazz's association with popular music, bebop simultaneously was creating a new, smaller market for the socially and politically conscious listener. This group of listeners, educators, musicians, record producers, and club owners has grown into the jazz community we know today, and the same group has perpetuated a canon of musical values that reflects the contribution and stylistic innovations of the bebop movement.

The qualities of the bop movement—and the ensuing styles that drew from bop such as West Coast, cool, and hard bop—are now considered mainstream, modern, or staight-ahead jazz, commonly understood as the approach and sound of jazz as it was established from bebop and beyond: a combination of acoustic instruments, small combo setting, standard song usage, improvisation, knowledge of theory and technique, and manner of playing within the tonal, rhythmic, and harmonic organization of bop. Of course, the definition of mainstream jazz is tenuous at best and varies according to the one who is defining it; however, similarities are found within the contrasting styles of bop, hard bop, West Coast, cool, and modal jazz that differ sharply from avant-garde or free jazz. Jazz musicians themselves use the term "mainstream" when referring to a sound or style of jazz from this period; for instance, Stan Getz would be considered mainstream, while Ornette Coleman would not.

According to some critics, the recording of "good" jazz came to a halt in the 1960s due to the invasion of popular music and the shift to free jazz, fusion, and jazz-rock. With the release of Ornette Coleman's album *The Shape of Jazz to Come* in 1959, the introduction of free jazz signified a turning point away from mainstream jazz. The years from the emergence of bebop in 1945 to the release of Coleman's album in 1959 solidified mainstream or modern jazz through the circulation of music, charts, and chord changes into a canon that serves as much of the foundation for musical study and improvisation of jazz today. This canon includes a collection of blues and standard tunes from the American songbook that borrow the Tin Pan Alley song model and employs a series of ii-V-I harmonic progressions usually structured in a type of 32–bar form.[6] The canon contains songs of varying styles such as Lee Morgan's tune "The Sidewinder" and Horace Silver's "Song for My Father" and "Filthy McNasty," which are categorized under hard bop. The modal jazz numbers of Miles Davis, such as "Freddie Freeloader," "All Blues," "So What," "Milestones," and John Coltrane's "Impressions" are listed in any jazz Real or Fake book, as with Coltrane's more adventurous "Giant Steps," Charles Mingus's "Goodbye Pork Pie Hat," or Herbie Hancock's "Dolphin Dance," "Maiden Voyage," "Cantaloupe Island," and "Watermelon Man." Each of these standards was written after the bop era, yet all are included among the canonical list of jazz favorites.[7] Like any other standardized list that is generally agreed upon, it takes time for materials to be written, played, recorded, dispersed, bought, heard, and then reproduced, imitated, or studied in order for a song to be remembered in the minds of many.

It is important to realize that bop's assimilation into artistic status was proven, in theory, by the events that followed after bop's arrival onto the New York jazz scene. Such events include the rise of another popular music, rock and roll, and the introduction of free jazz and fusion, all of which are said to have contributed to the "death" of traditional or mainstream jazz. Mainstream has, thereby, come to represent not only the time period of standardized jazz, but also the nostalgic feeling associated with end of the swing era.

Mainstream is now more of a method of performing standardized music in, or as part of, the jazz canon, while neoclassicism in jazz is a movement or group of musicians, educators, and critics who share a common taste and ideology. Mainstream or traditional jazz is more idealistic than just the confirmation of accepted pieces into a canon. One of the main reasons a canon is constructed is that "it suggests the complete construct of activities, values, and authority that surrounded the music."[8] Mainstream music ensures that a musical style contains a likeable sound that is not offensive to the general populace. The term is used vaguely, but it is always associated with that which is ideal, or that which has become commonplace. It can be used broadly in distinguishing the figureheads within jazz, such as "Dizzy Gillespie sounds more mainstream than Thelonious Monk"; or to suggest that a young musician sound more "mainstream" in order to find a place in the music industry; or to compare undiscovered artists to those known within the mainstream.

Another important characteristic of mainstream is that it includes jazz standards. As mentioned in chapter 1, the recycling of older songs played in the 1920s and 1930s into standardized tunes helped solidify the new presence of bop. David Ake suggests that mainstream reflects the ways and places that standards were recorded, published, or written about in the past: "beyond describing simply the popular song-based repertoire of many musicians, 'standards' in jazz also began to imply a statement—revealing an awareness of and reverence for a legacy handed down by the music's forebears."[9] Again we are provided with a sense of awareness of the past. Standards, as part of mainstream jazz or traditional jazz, are the foundation for common practice which, in turn, establishes a general taste for judging music.

By having a set of rules or standards already in place, jazz musicians can compare which types of jazz or which jazz compositions meet these standards. By having a previously established set of chord changes (as with "All or Nothing at All") one can compare how far a musician chooses to deviate from these chord changes or how closely these changes adhere to the traditional layout of the tune. If one musician slightly alters the chord changes to "All or Nothing at All" in a recording, the jazz community can deduce the creative alterations for the better or worse of the song. If a musician decides to change the instrumentation of a traditional jazz standard from the acoustic instrumental arrangement to an electronic arrangement by adding an electric guitar or synthesizer, the jazz community can compare the original version of the tune to the modern alterations as creative choices of a particular musician. Thus, standards not only give the jazz community a collection of songs from which to draw inspiration but also establish a method of performing and judging jazz.

There is much more to mainstream jazz than just the collection of tunes. The term *mainstream*, reportedly coined in the mid-1950s by English critic Stanley Dance, arose from "the belief in some quarters that bop, and modern jazz in general, was something of an artistic wrong turn."[10] At that time the term referred to the older swing music of the 1930s, and bebop was deemed a maverick through the label "modern music." The birth of bop in the 1940s offered an alternative to dance band music. Bop was flashy, stylistic, and modern, and by 1945 had emerged in the stylistic nuances of the Dizzy Gillespie Quintet with Gillespie playing fast licks over "Shaw 'Nuff" and Charlie Parker over the changes of "Ko Ko" with the Reboppers. As soon as bop became as commonplace as swing had been, the term "mainstream" shifted to include the newer styles of the 1940s and 1950s.

Larry Kart believes that the original labeling of swing music as mainstream was as much an expression of aesthetic preference as it was an inclination to make those preferences, in fact, permanent values. The association of mainstream as swing music of the past—which, according to the categorizers, was not getting the recognition it should—contains a certain nuance of nostalgia or, as Kart says, "ideological wishfulness."[11] Even as the term "mainstream" began to include the canon of bop licks and standard chord progressions, the nostalgia associated with the term was still in place. Part of this nostalgia has absorbed itself into the current realism of neoclassical jazz, which holds to "the belief that within shifting stylistic boundaries a majority of musicians still agree on how the music can and should be played."[12]

Labeling a style "mainstream," much in the same way as labeling a musical style "classic" or "traditional," implies that this musical style contains a set of values or tastes, as well as a "wishfulness." The difference is that jazz musicians are more likely to use the word "mainstream" to describe a sound than to use "neoclassicism" or "neoclassical music." "Mainstream jazz," says Larry Kart, "is a term to use when referring to jazz primarily influenced by bop, cool, and hard bop and sometimes used in place of those original names."[13] Conversely, the term "neoclassicism" is used more by jazz critics and enthusiasts who reference the ideology and "wishfulness" concept found in the sound of mainstream jazz.

Jazz musicians have acquired the aesthetic sensibility that stresses originality, creativity, and emotional expression, the same attributes that were carried over from the Romantic period. According to Eric Porter in *What Is This Thing Called Jazz*, "[T]he ideological framework set in place during the early nineteenth century permeated institutional and informal musical discourse and education and affected the way some jazz musicians understood the arts of improvisation and composition."[14] Porter discusses the system of musical ethics that was passed down from the Romantic era and has continued through the establishment of the jazz canon. The same values toward music in the Romantic era, such as virtuosity, harmonic composition, chordal arrangement, originality, and a sort of *Gesamtkunstwerk* or complete art experience, lingered into the twentieth century. The dexterity, skill, and personal flair of Franz Liszt and Niccolò Paganini is also seen with Charlie Parker and Dizzy Gillespie; the pursuit for originality and creativity of Giuseppe Verdi and Igor Stravinsky with Miles Davis and Thelonious Monk; the lyricism and extended harmony of Pyotr Ilyich Tchaikovsky and Johannes Brahms with the arrangements of Bill Evans and John Coltrane; the revolutionary work of Beethoven, the tragic artist, with Charles Mingus; and the shadow of Richard Wagner, whose work encompassed many art forms at once, with the large compositions by Duke Ellington that conjured up paintings and color just by their titles: "Black and Tan Fantasy" (1927), "Mood Indigo" (Dreamy Blues) (1930), "Old Man Blues" (1930), "Symphony in Black," film score (1935), "Diminuendo in Blue/Crescendo in Blue" (1937), "Azure" (1937), "Black, Brown and Beige" (1943), "The Blue Bells of Harlem" (1943), "Blutopia" (1944), "Golden Feather" (1946), "On a Turquoise Cloud" (1947), "Red Carpet" (1958), "Paris Blues," film score (1960), "The Golden Broom and the Green Apple" (1965), and "Beige" (1965).[15] Of course, the comparison between jazz and classical is also a double-edged sword. Does the comparison imply that jazz needs to be "raised" to the level of the white musician by comparing it to classical music? In *Jazz in Black and White: Race, Culture, and Identity in the Jazz Community*, Charles Gerard asks this same question.[16]

One can make several connections between the taste of the audience in the 1800s and the twentieth-century jazz community. The favored type of music is mainstream, that which is chromatic but tonal, expressive but smooth, rhythmic but not abstract. But there are many influences that shape what is understood to be the canon of jazz. Simply performing familiar songs does not automatically make them part of the canon, says William Weber: "the musical culture has to assert that such an authority exists, and define it at least to some degree in systematic fashion."[17] For instance, both performers and composers generally share musical values and an understood level of excellence through musical training obtained in universities, private tutoring, or from other musicians. The jazz canon, then, contains the reflections of many who agree, more or less, on the qualities that jazz should contain. Jazz criticism also contributes to the canon as a means of discourse and cultural review. Criticism asserts an ethical value and ideology to views about music, and, as stated earlier, the values found behind the instigation of mainstream reflect the Romantic notion of high art within music and the skill of the musician. The canon is completely embedded in one's assumptions about music, and controls much of what the jazz community deems "good."

The sound of mainstream jazz continued in the 1960s with the West Coast style of Gerry Mulligan, the Brazilian bossa nova played by Stan Getz, and the hard bop swing of Horace Silver. Obviously there is much overlap within styles and influences during this decade. But it was the introduction of free jazz, particularly the release of Ornette Coleman's album *The Shape of Jazz to Come* in 1959, that gave cause for alarm for many traditional jazz musicians. Because Coleman's music does not rely on tonality (as well as other aspects of musical production) in the traditional sense, much of his music is difficult to listen to for those who are conditioned to Western harmony; the squeaks and howls heard from Coleman's saxophone and musicians such as Cecil Taylor and Don Cherry caused controversy within the jazz community. Attention was given to Coleman as an example of how *not* to sound as a jazz musician, disregarding the fact (discussed in the next chapter) that Coleman was not attempting to sound like a jazz musician at all, but instead was creating a new form that redefined the very idea of what music is. As a consequence, the years 1945 to 1959 historically mark the solidification of mainstream as it was established with arrival of bop, ended by the departure from traditional models with free jazz. Now, says Christopher Porter, "The status quo in jazz is music that sounds like it was made between the 1940s and the 1960s."[18]

The year 1963 marked the global success of the Beatles and introduced the British Invasion into American culture the following year. Rock continued to reign supreme on the charts, and jazz musicians such as Chet Baker, Don Cherry, Jimmy Heath, Bud Powell, Ben Webster, Art Taylor, Phil Woods, and Dexter Gordon sought refuge in the recording studio or in Europe. Others began to explore new methods of playing jazz. The experimentation with harmony and structure on John Coltrane's *A Love Supreme* in 1964 revolutionized the jazz world with long and freer improvisations spiritually channeled through themes of "Acknowledgement," "Resolution," "Pursuance," and "Psalm." Band members on the album, McCoy Tyner and Elvin Jones, were launched into an era of progressive jazz, joining other musicians like Charles Mingus, who included non-jazz instruments[19] and poetry in the song "Scenes in the City" and demonstrated his opinions about racism and capitalism in America through such compositions as "Free Cell Block F, 'Tis Nazi U.S.A.," "Work Song," "Haitian Fight Song," and "Oh Lord, Don't Let Them Drop that Atomic Bomb on Me." Innovation continued with the introduction of electronic instruments, as Miles Davis did on *Bitches Brew* in 1969.

The decades that followed are still highly contested within the jazz community. In addition to the experimentation of Cecil Taylor and Ornette Coleman with tonality in free jazz, Chicago avant-garde musicians such as Anthony Braxton, Joseph Jarman, Kalaparush(a) Maurice McIntyre, and Muhal Richard Abrams grappled not only with tonality, but with provocative performance practice and ensemble-based composition. Abrams joined with other musicians in 1965 to form the Association for the Advancement of Creative Musicians (AACM) and later the Art Ensemble of Chicago.[20] The notions of change and innovation in jazz have always been epitomized in the music regardless of the form. But in the 1960s and 1970s this new strain of experimentation offered jazz a more radical departure from convention, combining and sometimes deconstructing elements of rhythm, tonality, and structure. In fact, avant-garde music became synonymous with open-ended forms that were often much more difficult to characterize than even free jazz. The incorporation of popular music into jazz became another means to explore the depths of jazz, and with the introduction of Miles Davis's *Bitches Brew* and the "fusing" of electronic sounds with Chick Corea and Pat Metheny in the 1970s, it resulted in the new labeling of their music as "fusion."

Precisely these three areas—free jazz, fusion, and avant-garde—that sprouted from the jazz tradition but exceeded the traditional classification of jazz, have become the unofficial boundary lines for many jazz purists. These new styles are often viewed as detrimental to the progression of jazz history for several reasons: electronic instruments and technological manipulations were not seen as preserving the traditional sound of mainstream jazz or the sound of acoustic instruments; the integration of pop music into jazz devalued the intellectual nature of classic jazz; and those musicians, both black and white, who worked so hard to establish free and avant-garde jazz as legitimate music were seen as refusing to acknowledge the African American roots of jazz and as violating the traditional tonality, harmonic progressions, or standards in the American Songbook. With regard to fusion and other combinations of electronic jazz that emerged out of the 1960s, the Jazz at Lincoln Center website posts this statement: "Most serious jazz fans agreed that jazz-rock fusion had, from the beginning, been nothing more than a devil's bargain: these musicians, critics contended, had achieved success by selling their soul. Accordingly, there was a growing consensus among fans, critics, and many performers that, while jazz certainly did need to move forward, it shouldn't have to abandon the more mainstream traditions of its past."[21] The problem with this citation, of course, is that the phrases "most serious jazz fans agree" and "a growing consensus among fans, critics and many performers" are subjective assumptions. It is true that three genres, which flourished mainly in the 1960s and 1970s, did anticipate the revival of traditional jazz in the 1980s.

Dexter Gordon's return to America after fifteen years in Europe in 1976 is considered a major catalyst of a revival of interest in mainstream jazz, which, according to Geoffrey Ward and Ken Burns, "never had died completely."[22] "He still played straight-ahead jazz, without the synthesizers and electric bass and drum machines of fusion, and within the boundaries of swing, lyricism, and blues feeling that had been at the heart of the music he'd played since boyhood but that many avant-garde players discarded."[23] Gordon's live recording at the Vanguard for Columbia Records, *Homecoming*, was pivotal in the reaffirmation of jazz to a new audience. A new generation of mainstream jazz musicians began to surface; an affectionate name, the young lions, was taken from a recording by that title made by Lee Morgan, Wayne Shorter, Frank Strozier, Bobby Timmons, Bob Cranshaw, Louis Hayes, and Albert Heath from 1960. At the Kool Jazz Festival in New York City in June 1982, Wynton Marsalis, James Newton, Chico Freeman, John Blake, Anthony Davis, John Purcell, and Paquito D'Rivera ushered in a new generation of exceptional musicians.[24] These musicians were college-trained, in their early twenties, and had musical foundations set in classic bebop and hard bop styles. Other lions were later added to the list, including John Scofield, Bill Stewart, Michael and Randy Brecker, Joshua Redman, and Brad Mehldau.

The young lions are cited on the NEA website as a "cadre of bold, talented young musicians, all of them rigorously trained in the entire jazz canon, from what will come to be called the neo-mainstream movement."[25] Wynton Marsalis, often deemed the spokesperson for the neoclassical movement as well as for the young lions, represented a return of the purity in technique, melodic and harmonic standardization, choice of instruments, and performance practice that was treasured in the bop period. This talented musician of both classical music and jazz epitomized the intelligence associated with mainstream jazz.

This new infusion of older ideas with young, developing musicians created a bouquet of talented traditionalists, fueled by the growing appetite of the general public. The blossoming of albums onto the market established a new wave of musical acceptance with what has been labeled neoclassicism, referring to the resurfacing of the music and image of jazz icons of the past (such as Miles Davis, Charlie Parker, Thelonious Monk, and John Coltrane), combined with the standardization of set forms, chord changes, and melodies and the canonical methodization of performing, arranging, and maintaining the jazz image. Of course, the prefix *neo-*, or new, indicates a revival and adaptation of an older style or way of thinking, and implies that the new form is not an exact imitation of an older one but is based on the same or very similar basic principles as the old one. Neoclassical art, for example, is art based on the principles of balance, order, and harmony manifested in ancient Greek and Roman sculpture and architecture; but these Greco-Roman principles were transformed and adapted at different times in different ways in later eras, like the Italian Renaissance and late-eighteenth-century France. The difference is that jazz musicians are not likely to use the term neoclassical to describe their music.

This period of resurgence in the jazz community followed several themes: a reexamination of the American songbook; a heavier study into the musical contributions of bebop, Dixieland, and ragtime; and the solidification of a jazz canon of music. However, much of the characterization of conservative practices lies in what is not accepted. Many of the neoclassicists consider neither free jazz, nor the infusion of funk, rock, ethno-pop, or hip-hop, to be worthy of the term jazz; in other words, these styles were not art-worthy. It is often thought that the "tributaries" of jazz styles after 1960 are more fanciful deviations from the main model of jazz as it was established in bebop. Mainstream is a "pure" form of musical activity, placing emphasis on the art of the improvised soloist and acoustic rather than electronic instruments, and presenting jazz in a historical context based on the contribution of great past artists. In recent years, progressive jazz musicians have dipped into the broadening world market, fusing jazz styles with more "exotic" sounds. It will be explained in the next section that neoclassicists *do* appreciate other forms of jazz beyond traditional jazz, such as free jazz, for its contributions to the musical community, but do not necessarily endorse recognized players such as Coleman to be legitimate jazz musicians. Ward and Burns, in their seminal book *Jazz: A History of America's Music*, reiterate, "No Great Man can be said to have towered over everyone else, as Louis Armstrong and Charlie Parker could be said to have done in their time. . . ."[26]

The establishment of mainstream jazz relies not only on the spoken or written words of the jazz purist, but also in the selection of music performed at jazz venues. More often than not, the song choice for jazz musicians comes from the Real Book or Fake Book. These tunes are familiar with all of the musicians on the bandstand, and they offer fresh reinterpretation each time they are played. The circulation of these songs is not detrimental to jazz; for that matter, neither is the establishment of the jazz canon. But the repetition of this selection defines the general taste of American musicians and the American public. The performance repertoire of jazz musicians do the same: choose from the bop era, immediately before with swing, or immediately after with hard bop, soul, or bossa novas under the tutelage of Stan Getz, cool, and West Coast musicians. Much of the dissatisfaction with jazz purists stems from the struggle to keep the status of jazz as intellectual art music rather than entertainment. Jazz enthusiasts have always struggled for jazz to be recognized, along with European classical music, for its "refined" beauty. Many jazz musicians look to classical composers for inspiration, reveling in the improvisatory nature of Beethoven and Bach.[27] Even jazz educators have connected the development of jazz to that of classical music. Such comparisons restrict jazz to traditional molds.

"There is nothing new about the neoclassic impulse, which first surfaced in jazz in the early 1940s, when Lu Watters and Turk Murphy tried to recreate the music of such 1920s masters as King Oliver and Kid Ory," says Larry Kart. "What is new, though, is the nature and extent of the neoclassicism that runs through so much of jazz today."[28] The neoclassical movement began to reinstate jazz in the general population by further expanding the jazz idiom through marketing tactics and media exposure. Throughout the 1980s there was a steady growth in the sales of jazz recordings and a general increase in the production of documentaries, remastered videotaped performances, films, commercials, advertisements, interviews, and publications, all featuring jazz artists. Most of this acclaim is in response to the basic principle of neoclassicism—going back to the social, historical, and musical source for great jazz. The success of the movement can be measured by the sudden financial gain achieved by marketing jazz effectively.

Unmistakably, jazz is on the rise, and this recent popularity has arguably been the result of neoclassicism, which has strengthened jazz primarily in four ways: (1) by producing a large number of new, talented musicians on the market;[29] (2) by incorporating integrative marketing tactics featuring both jazz heroes of the past and young musicians who emulate these classic figures; (3) by having several neoclassical jazz musicians and critics in powerful positions that can promote and financially support the neoclassical movement; and (4) by establishing a set of criteria for jazz that respects the contributions of African American men to its development. The result of these collaborative approaches toward jazz has helped establish the image of the African American musician in popular society.

The success of neoclassicism was created "in large part by talented young musicians who had undergone a rigorous program of instruction encompassing the entire history of mainstream jazz."[30] These young lions, who burst onto the music scene in the 1980s, were welcomed by record companies looking to hire younger and cheaper musicians instead of older and more costly jazz legends. The unspoken leader of the young lions was, and continues to be, trumpeter Wynton Marsalis, son of the great pianist Ellis Marsalis and brother to the great saxophonist Branford, drummer Jason, and recording producer Delfeayo Marsalis. The entire Marsalis family has been blessed with self-determination, talent, and persistence, which has projected them onto the jazz scene.

Wynton Marsalis, in particular, launched himself from his noteworthy gig with Art Blakey and the Jazz Messengers to a successful career in both classical music and jazz. His most prominent achievement was the award in 1981 of not one but two Grammys for a classical recording, *Trumpet Concertos*, and a jazz recording by his quintet, *Think of One*. Columbia Records foresaw the marketing appeal in Marsalis as a new phenomenon in jazz. He has received many awards for his works, which has led to various commissions and performance invitations. Marsalis's most influential achievement was his appointment as artistic director for New York City's Jazz at Lincoln Center.

In that position Marsalis has grown into an immensely important figurehead. His charisma and positive charm are ideal for fund-raising, and he soon reached out to corporate sponsors to support the efforts of Jazz at Lincoln Center.[31] The center worked in collaboration with the National Endowment for the Arts to develop a web-based curriculum, that can be accessed in any school, to educate children and young people about jazz as America's music; Marsalis also organizes and performs in jazz programs held at the Center and develops education-based jazz programs like WeBop! for children.[32] Marsalis directs a weekly radio broadcast of performances from Lincoln Center, hosted by Jazz at Lincoln Center board member and CBS News correspondent, Ed Bradley (recently deceased). He has been interviewed countless times for news articles, journals and publications, television broadcasts, and even fund-raising efforts for Hurricane Katrina victims.

Marsalis has reached the rank of a musical icon similar to Leonard Bernstein or Louis Armstrong. His looks, and more appropriately his debonair stature, have made him ideal for marketing classy goods. His face is everywhere in New York City on billboards and public transportation ads, and he travels constantly for master classes, sponsored speeches or workshops, and performances around the globe. With unprecedented credentials, Wynton Marsalis has become "the symbol of the rebirth of mainstream jazz" and has led jazz back into the popular eye.[33] Many wonder whether jazz would have found such a boost had it not been for Marsalis's likeable personality, obvious musical talent, and graciousness. Intentionally or not, he has become the next leader of jazz. His position of authority at Lincoln Center, one of the most prestigious performances centers in the world, has earned Marsalis the right to speak on jazz; it is his opportunity to broadcast to a captive, wealthy audience.

The establishment of neoclassicism does not rest entirely on Wynton Marsalis's shoulders. In January 2001, Ken Burns took an active role in the blossoming resurgence of jazz listeners. Burns's film for public television, about the history of jazz as an American art form, not only interviews actual jazz musicians but also depicts the styles of jazz through narrative accounts, recordings, photographs, and film. His costly project, *Jazz: A History of America's Music*, included ten episodes divided into ninety-six chapters, lasted more than nineteen hours, contained an array of chronological information on jazz greats, and was a huge success for PBS.[34]

Wynton Marsalis was interviewed extensively for the series. The repetition of Marsalis' image enhanced his reputation, not only as a *Wunderkind* of jazz, but also as a spokesperson on behalf of jazz musicians across the country.[35] Of course, increased record sales for jazz albums cannot be attributed entirely to Wynton Marsalis, but rather reflect the influence of neoclassicism.[36] Of course, categorization plays a large role—Kenny G and other easy-listening performers are included with jazz recordings. Regardless, there has been a significant increase in the jazz audience, in jazz education, and in sales for jazz recordings since neoclassicism began in the 1980s.

The increase in jazz sales has played an important role in the rise of neoclassicism, and, likewise, the rise of neoclassicism has played an important role in the projection of the jazz image. The instant success of the Ken Burns series propelled Marsalis's face onto the TV screens of millions of Americans; and with his leadership at Jazz at Lincoln Center, Marsalis has become a big influence on the marketing and distribution of jazz to the public at large. Even events like the flood of New Orleans in 2005 have extended Marsalis's influence. He garnered much attention and support for the victims of Hurricane Katrina, often sacrificing his own tour dates, concerts, and personal schedule to raise money for New Orleans.[37] Marsalis now seems to be responsible in part not only for the salvation of jazz, but also for the survival of its birthplace, New Orleans. In equating the survival of jazz with the survival of New Orleans, Marsalis is connecting the history of jazz with the *expression* of certain people; jazz is that which expresses "the feelings, values and ideas" of an entire group of people—mainly African Americans.[38]

"Jazz is black music, but it is not just the music of black musicians."[39] Often jazz is identified not only as a voice for African Americans but also as an outlet for the oppression experienced in their efforts to reach liberation.[40] Jazz developed largely during the system of mandatory segregation in the United States. Suffering from several forms of racism throughout the twentieth century, African American musicians expressed feelings of oppression through their music. Jazz has functioned as a part of Afrocentricity, or, as Sherrie Tucker says, a "sign of blackness"—in fact, to such a degree of blackness that it has become the source of debate for many musicians.[41] Jazz continued to be associated with the African American community well into the 1970s, but since then, it has diversified rapidly into white communities, young black communities, academic communities, European communities, other musical styles, and most recently, into pop culture. One wonders whether this diversification has diluted the African American contribution, and whether jazz may no longer be associated with the African American tradition. The components of jazz that are African American, such as call and response, shout choruses, communal creativity, spiritual and gospel influences, West African rhythms, and improvisation are firmly embedded in the jazz tradition. But do we still use these characteristics as a way to define jazz today? If the sound of jazz was taken from the Blue Note stage and put into a Nissan car commercial, does it retain its association with the African American community?

To Wynton Marsalis, the answer is "yes." He has firmly indicated throughout his career that jazz, as black music, should always be black music. In one particular article appearing in the *New York Times* in 1988 entitled "What Jazz Is—and Isn't," Marsalis separated jazz from classical and popular music and then described the exploitation and commercialization of the aesthetic principles found in jazz.[42] He structured his argument around the "pursuit of quality" found in the study of past heroes such as Ellington, Monk, Gillespie, and Armstrong. He praised the accomplishments of past African American musicians, and rightly so. However, Marsalis has repeatedly indicated that jazz should remain black music.[43] Even as he first gathered ground in his appointment at Lincoln Center, Marsalis was criticized for hiring only African American musicians to perform on the center stage. He has since rectified this arrangement by adding several white musicians.[44]

In all the hysteria of skin color on or off of the Marsalis bandstand, Charles Gerard asks, what exactly are Marsalis's obligations to the jazz community? Does he need to hire black musicians due to the strong ties jazz has in black culture or does he need to hire white musicians to prove that he accepts the contributions of white jazz musicians? Because of his leadership position in New York, Marsalis probably will be criticized no matter who is invited to play; so should he present a "race-neutral program," and how would one go about doing that?[45] Jazz seems to be constantly divided by race.

> Jazz is somehow able to be both an African American ethnic music and a universal music at the same time, both an expression of universal artistry and ethnicity. Black musicians lash out at whites, and yet invite them into their bands. Wynton Marsalis refuses to accept white accomplishments in jazz, but proclaims the genius of Beethoven. Amiri Baraka heaps scorn on the art of the white world, and in the next breath praises Roswell Rudd.[46]

Marsalis's actions and words do not mean that only blacks should play jazz, which is how his statements have often been interpreted, but that the historical cultivation of jazz remains solely the contribution of great African Americans. While his claim that jazz history comes from the black community is accurate, the degree to which Caucasian, Cuban, Brazilian, and European performers have contributed is often overlooked.[47] Marsalis believes that both white and black musicians can understand jazz if the musician has a deep understanding of the African American contribution. In other words, anyone can enjoy and perform jazz as long as one is familiar with those parts of jazz and blues that remain the intellectual property of African Americans. He claims, for instance, that jazz should remain close to its African American ties, and music that stems beyond the pure form of classic jazz or the mainstream sound is not adhering to these roots.[48] And, as this book has been arguing, through the presentation of the history of jazz and the photographs of Herman Leonard, the jazz image is key to solidifying the place of jazz in American history. By grounding jazz in the past through images and music of the black bebop musician of the 1950s, the jazz community clings to roots that distinguish jazz from other forms of popular genres.

Marsalis sees the diversification of jazz into free jazz and fusion as trivializing the contributions of the black community.[49] Herbie Hancock, for instance, is known for playing straight-ahead jazz with Miles Davis, Ron Carter, and Tony Williams while at the same time being on the fusion/funk forefront with his band the Headhunters. In a conversation with Ben Sidran, Hancock discusses the catchy nature of fusion in the 1970s because it fuses jazz with rock and roll, allowing a wider audience to appreciate and encompass both genres. Sidran responds to Hancock's statement with "some years later, we saw a tremendous serge of popularity for, and interest in, the so-called return to straight-ahead jazz, which was theoretically signaled by the success of players like Wynton Marsalis. . . ."[50]

In a similar interview between Marsalis and Hancock, Marsalis divulges his biased opinion concerning the placement of jazz today and the divisions between pop music, fusion, and jazz. This conversation concerns two accomplished jazz musicians with two completely different positions on jazz and pop music.

HANCOCK: Wynton is not an exponent of the idea that blending of musical cultures is a good thing.

MARSALIS: Because it's an *imitation* of the root. It loses roots because it's *not* a blending. It's like having sex with your daughter. . . . What disturbs me is it's the best people. When somebody is good, they don't have to do that. I was so happy when Stevie's album came out. I said, damn, finally we got a groove and not somebody just trying to cross over into some rock 'n' roll.

HANCOCK: I understand what you mean about a certain type of groove, like this is the real R&B, and so forth. But I can't agree that there's only one way we're supposed to be playing. I have faith that . . . whatever's happening now is not a waste of time. It's a part of growth. It may be a transition, but transition is a part of growth, too. . . . I'm finding a door that hasn't been opened. That's exciting to me, and I'm given the opportunity to use some elements from the "farthest out" jazz stuff in this music, and have it be unique.

MARSALIS: How do you get human feelings in automated, computerized music like that?[51]

While he is friends with Hancock and has played with him, Ron Carter, and Tony Williams collaboratively, Marsalis finds himself quite disturbed with Hancock's explorations combining rock and jazz. And though several of the free and fusion jazz artists were black, Marsalis contends that they did not contribute to the "pure" form of jazz. Purity equals blackness to Marsalis, and anything that deviates from this distinction is not qualified to be called jazz. He is not alone in this opinion. The jazz critics Stanley Crouch and Albert Murray have formed an alliance with Marsalis based on their shared views toward African American authenticity and the jazz canon.[52]

By instilling jazz with strong ties to black culture, Marsalis, Crouch, and Murray are essentially strengthening the African American community. They have created a close communal unit between the African American community and the jazz community. Through the Marsalis-Crouch-Murray line, many African American jazz musicians are finally getting the recognition they never received in their lifetime. Throughout the history of jazz (and any other type of musical genre, for that matter), African American musicians have always gotten less pay, less recognition, and less respect among the dominant white majority. During the swing era, countless examples can be cited of white musicians receiving greater acknowledgment.[53] Ingrid Monson provides several examples of racial acts against jazz musicians.[54]

- In 1945, Benny Carter successfully defeated an attempt by his white neighbors to evict him from a house he owned in an exclusive area of Los Angeles.[55]
- In 1946, Charlie Barnet protested the Hollywood film industry's decision to keep two of his band members, Al Killian and Paul Webster, off camera on account of their skin color.[56]
- In 1946, Cab Calloway was arrested in Kansas City after attempting to visit Lionel Hampton at an engagement at the whites-only Pla-Mor ballroom. Hampton, who had invited Calloway to the club, refused to play after intermission, forfeited his guarantee and percentage for the night, and forced the management to refund admissions charges to the patrons.[57]
- In 1947, Billy Eckstine lost a job at a Boston nightclub after he exchanged harsh words with a white female patron who had hurled racial insults at him. A brawl broke out after the woman's escort kicked Eckstine. The club reported that they had been having "trouble" with the band all week. Eckstine's group refused to stop playing "jive" and continuing to use the front entrance to the club after they had been told that all employees were to come through the rear.[58]

Because the performance on stage or in a public event is so essential to jazz, any African American musician who was on stage during a performance became a target or an invitation for racial prejudice. They were often thought of by the white community as disturbing the peace or characterized as "asking for it."

In the early formation of jazz, black musicians had to balance European- and African-influenced musical practices.[59] Black musicians then saw white musicians who had appropriated black music gain greater rewards both financially and culturally. Often record companies were seen as part of the white collective who owned and profited from the music while the blacks played it.[60] This created a greater drive for legitimacy in African American professional musicians. For the connection with jazz to benefit the African American community requires all musicians to acknowledge the ties to black music and associate the intelligence and artistry of jazz with African Americans. It makes sense, then, for Marsalis to reject the diversification of jazz into other musical styles that do not have strong ties to the African American community. In this way, he has helped to preserve a culture. As Paul Lopez explains, "[i]n this quest, black professional musicians played a central role in creating a tradition that was an alternative to classical music. . . ."[61] Marsalis, Crouch, and Murray witnessed white musicians obtain greater financial rewards and cultural recognition just by being white. This has created a greater drive for legitimacy among black professional musicians.

It seems almost as if Marsalis acts as what Theodore Gracyk calls a "cultural gatekeeper" by treating jazz as the intellectual property of the African American community or assuming that all black experiences can be summarized in jazz. It can be borrowed by white musicians but not necessarily shared.[62] Similarly, Joel Rudinow argues that white people cannot adequately express the blues because they have not experienced the struggle for freedom in an oppressive society that black people have.[63] As these reviews of the influence of black jazz musicians have demonstrated, jazz and blues contain certain privileges that only a select few have earned the right to play. Jazz itself has traditionally been a device of social ordering; but as we have seen so far, the icon of the jazz musician unintentionally participates in this ordering by idealizing the black artist.[64] Even though white jazz musicians were as prominent as black musicians, black musicians are seen in American visual culture more consistently.

The success of neoclassicism is also due, in large part, to the marketing of the jazz image. The recirculation of Leonard's images beginning with his first jazz photography exhibition in 1988 accompanied the resurgence of mainstream or neoclassical jazz that began in the 1980s. Like the neoclassical resurgence of mainstream or "classic" jazz from the 1940s and 1950s, Leonard's photography popularized the appearance and attitude of musicians from the same period. Besides their recordings, they are the clearest and most familiar tie we have to jazz musicians of the past, and provide visual evidence of the importance of the jazz image. Because of the combined success of the neoclassical music style accompanied by jazz photography, one may assume that Leonard's images contain the same authority we give the jazz musician through neoclassicism. Leonard, of course, did not purposely contribute to the neoclassical movement; however, the popularization of his photography in the 1980s was the result of a captive audience already in place and awakening to the stirrings of neoclassical jazz. By capturing the sounds of bebop in his pictures, Leonard's photographic style complements the recycling of bop standards. They contain far greater meaning than the image presented, and hence are invaluable for this study of the jazz image. Leonard gives a visual representation of the sophisticated sound of classic jazz, thus achieving the seemingly impossible: casting a musical genre in a visual image.

Image licensing specialist Cynthia Sesso witnessed the reissuing of jazz memorabilia of the 1980s. She was cataloguing for Ray Avery, noted jazz collector, historian, and photographer who had twenty-seven filing cabinets full of visual material on jazz going all the way back to the 1920s. In his store, Ray Avery's Rare Records in Glendale, California, he had at one time one of the largest collections of jazz recordings in the world, from which he held an auction four times a year with a worldwide mailing list.[65] Avery's collection included his own photographs as well as large amounts of physical inventory that he had been collecting, and Sesso's relationship with jazz grew into a specialized career of cataloging, archiving, preserving, and maintaining jazz recordings, images, and other material.[66] Sesso recalls the reissuing of jazz recordings in the late 1980s: "All of a sudden with the resurgence of the CD reissues popped up, all of the record companies were scrambling to find new photographs to put on the new CDs. And that's how Herman and Ray and all of the great photographers really got a second wind in their career, because they were being asked for new images."[67] The fact that Leonard's photographs began to appear in magazines and on book covers makes an even more important statement about the developing jazz image.

Leonard's prints were not accessible to the public between the years 1945 to 1959 since he was known only as a commercial photographer. It was nearly forty years later that he, and Ray Avery alike, rummaged through his negatives and decided to reprint his best pictures. Ironically, Leonard's photographs probably would not have found an audience if the jazz community had not gone through the neoclassical period. They would have appeared poetic, but would not have met with the extraneous meaning given to them by contemporary jazz sympathizers. Leonard was fortunate to have his photographs appear at the right time and place. Waiting to view his pictures was a jazz-savvy market that agreed with his approach to photography, and a general public who, although not informed on jazz history, experienced the wave of bop repopularization along with the jazz community. Leonard found listening ears for what he had to say, and steadily his name began to carry the vision he had for jazz.

There is a core group of photographs that are the staple of his collection: (1) Dexter Gordon at the Royal Roost in New York in 1948, (2) Billie Holiday in New York City in 1949, (3) Duke Ellington in Paris in 1958, (4) Ella Fitzgerald, Duke Ellington, Benny Goodman, and Jack Robbins in New York City in 1949, and (5) Frank Sinatra at the Monte Carlo in 1958. Other popular images are of Miles Davis and Charlie Parker.[68] Some of these are not bebop musicians at all. Previously discussed icons such as Frank Sinatra, Ella Fitzgerald, and Duke Ellington were taken at the same time that Leonard photographed the rising bop players. Sinatra, along with Billie Holiday and Ella Fitzgerald, were more easily seen in the spotlight since they were vocalists. The general public has always been more favorable to vocalists in any musical format because they maintain a celebrity appeal and because they engage the audience.[69]

As we have seen so far, other famous images from the bebop era are primarily instrumentalists because the hard driving melodic lines found in bop were not easy for vocalists to follow. Instrumentalists helped shift the emphasis from the single melody line usually sung by the vocalist to the improvisation and virtuosic technique displayed by the instrumentalist. This was an important shift in the progression of the music but also certainly had an effect on the arrangement of Leonard's prints. As Leonard's image licensing representative, Cynthia Sesso provided her professional experience and opinion on the importance of jazz imagery in a telephone conversation in March 2009.

HEATHER: Now what do you think people are looking for when they want to purchase a print or, you know, a photo from someone? And I'm not talking about the photographer's side, I mean more from the collector's side. Do they request something more often than others? What is it that they're looking for?

CYNTHIA: I think in that aspect, it's the uniqueness of an image, plus artists themselves. There are certainly artists that will always sell, in particular Miles Davis, Billie Holiday, Ella Fitzgerald, people who recognize an artist even outside of their own realm, people who know nothing about jazz. The more recognized the artist is, the more likely people will want a photograph, a print, of that person. That seems to be predominantly what's requested.

However, then you get some real aficionados who want the most unusual picture of an artist of people that you don't often think about. They'll want that picture, or things that people read on something, like I was telling you earlier about Gold Star studios. You'll have collectors who will want something that is specific to a place or of a club. "You got any pictures of Billie Holiday singing, at . . ."

HEATHER: Yeah, at the Royal Roost or something like that.

CYNTHIA: Yeah, that kind of a thing. And then there are people who want something specific to an event. So people have different definitions of what they are looking for, but I think in answer to your question, it's usually about the recognizable artist plus the unique place.

HEATHER: I was talking with Jenny Bagert and she said that with Herman, there seems to be a repeated set of images that people liked for some reason or other, and kept getting such as the Frank Sinatra one, the Dexter Gordon, etc. . . . Pretty much the ones I am using in my book because I keep seeing them all over the place. Perhaps it is because of the uniqueness of the place like you said earlier or because they really feel that they identify with it.

CYNTHIA: And I can add that Herman's images are unique. They are so iconic and dramatic and even on a technical level, they're perfect, but it's his mastery at printing to make them as unique as they are. There is nobody who can do what he can do with printing: his vision of what he saw, what he heard, or his friendships with some of these musicians and people. I mean, that's what it is all based on when you look at these photographs from him. They're full of high drama, iconic, and high art.

There are photographers that go everywhere and shoot everything, and maybe on a historical level, they got some picture at Slug's in 1960.

HEATHER: (laughs)

CYNTHIA: But, it's just a photograph, you know. And it's important because it documents a certain place at a certain time, but Herman's images are just so dramatic. Because that's how he saw these people that he was photographing; that's just how he looked at them while he was doing it. And that's why they are everywhere, and people say, "that's what I feel when I think of a Billie Holiday recording," or, "that's what I thought she would look like when she was singing," and so forth. There are very good photographers out there, but there are none better when it comes to evoking that whole expression when you are looking at one of those pictures. . . .

HEATHER: And do you think the market of jazz, being where Leonard and cohorts of the era couldn't sell his photographs, even when he took them to Edward Steichen the director of photography at MOMA who rejected them, has changed? But now, it is a commodity, a high-priced item.

CYNTHIA: Absolutely, that was an interesting evolution. Music photography has only risen in the last ten to fifteen years to be taken seriously. Before that, it was dismissed. I think that when enough time goes by, that's when things become more valuable. It's a process, just like any other art form. It's a process of realization that people get. And in music photography, it has been *less* time that people have taken it seriously.

It's been an interesting evolution. And then, of course, when private collectors get into the mix who actually do appreciate music photography, then it became interesting because the more that's out there for people to see, the more they realize that it's available. The more things happen. But I have to be honest, I think, in the total picture, it's still a long ways to go.

HEATHER: I never thought of it like that.

CYNTHIA: Oh yeah, even Herman. Everyone knows they're of quality. So everyone is looking for those images when they are looking for something to use of quality. So my intention, as proctor of those things in his world as well as the other photographers, is making sure that the value remains very high.

HEATHER: Right, right.

CYNTHIA: And that's hard to maintain that when people are dragging it down [referring to our earlier discussion on the theft of images from the internet].

HEATHER: And you need to keep the quality high because the relevance of it is high. I mean it pertains to two forms of art: visual art and in a musical form. So that in essence doubles the worth of the image.

Leonard's quality can be measured by the current cost of his photographs. Because photographs are easily and cheaply reproduced, one could merely print another copy. However, the escalating cost of Leonard's photography indicates smart marketing.[70] Of course, the economics involved in print making and purchasing are not one-sided. Leonard himself must be able to make a living. His studio used to be located at 200 West Robert E. Lee Boulevard in New Orleans, but after Hurricane Katrina, like so many others, he was washed out of his home and studio. He lost about ten thousand prints that he had accumulated over the years, but managed to put his negatives in the vault at the nearby Ogden Museum of Art in New Orleans.[71] Other negatives of his work were out of harm's way and away from New Orleans. Leonard, now 85, has moved to Los Angeles, California, to live close to his family and recover from the storm, and will make California his new home. Arrangements have been made for two studios to produce and sell his work: one in California and the other in London, England.

Leonard's sole income comes from his photographs; as he stated in an interview, "I stay alive by selling my old jazz photos."[72] His previous agent (and herself a talented photographer) Jenny Bagert commented on the link with jazz photography and neoclassicism: "As a form of music was being reborn from 1940s, so was photography being reborn in 1980s."[73] But Bagert explains that, even as famous as Herman Leonard is, he struggles to sell his photographs; most of the sales come from museums purchasing prints and royalty fees, mainly because, like jazz itself, Leonard's general audience and exposure is broad but the audience for his source of income is limited. Many people who see his work are familiar with his photographs without knowing who took them—they have somehow become second nature to the general public. But Leonard's target audiences are those who are intimately aware of jazz history, especially during the bebop, cool, and hard bop years.

His pictures come the closest to presenting jazz as a marketable item to the public. Because they are the clearest and closest tie, besides musical recordings, we have to jazz musicians in the 1940 and 1950s, they are invaluable for any study of jazz history. These photos of past experiences in jazz are a direct link to the neoclassical resurrection of these images in the late 1980s and early 1990s. In many ways, his photographs recall the atmosphere of the era because first, Leonard is faithful to the music of the times, and second, his vision of jazz has found a home in the hearts of the general public. He is not avant-garde or "difficult" in his approach to the photograph. His training with Yousuf Karsh taught Leonard the range of skill necessary to become a noteworthy photographer, and his work with big-name magazines such as *Life*, *Look*, *Esquire*, *Playboy*, and *Cosmopolitan* demonstrated that Leonard knew how to appeal to the public.

Aided by his personal affiliation for jazz, he applied his talents in photography to broadcast a new type of musician to the world. Leonard's technique, with the camera and in the darkroom, combined with personal motivation elevated him from photographer to the status of artist. His photographs provided an image for the neoclassical movement to grow from, yet not much has been written concerning his contribution to jazz. Since Leonard took his pictures in the mid-twentieth century, his photographs have been received with growing enthusiasm. (See appendix B for Leonard's exhibition list.)

Any leading group, in politics or in art, is destined to reach its dominance at the expense of others. The "other," in this instance, is any musician not affiliated with neoclassicism, presumably fusion, free jazz, jazz-rock, and the avant-garde. Concerning the selection of any artists (in the case of jazz, Louis Armstrong, Duke Ellington, and Charlie Parker, among others) who have contributed to a canon of art, it is not just the contributions of the artists that are collected but also the most basic principles of how jazz functions as a genre. Recordings, compositions, improvisations, and stylistic characteristics are collected and gradually adapted as values in the jazz community. As a sub-group of the large umbrella of jazz, neoclassicism focuses on those qualities of a musician that contribute to the canon of mainstream jazz. In addition, neoclassicism, as with Leonard's photographs, focuses on the *image* of the jazz musician, not the actual musician who exhibits the characteristics of the canon. For instance, not all black jazz musicians adhere to the Marsalis-Crouch-Murray approach to jazz, nor do they believe that black music can be summed up in one style.

The neoclassical image represents the great black jazz musicians of the past, and the more this image is repeated in society, the more jazz becomes linked with this image. The image presented in Leonard's photographs, that of a talented, black musician of the 1950s representing qualities of intellectualism, freedom from oppression, modernism, and American values, are also found in neoclassicism. Musicians who affiliate themselves with neoclassicism are linking themselves to the qualities of the jazz image of the past. By promoting mainstream jazz in Jazz at Lincoln Center, Wynton Marsalis is also promoting neoclassical values that, in turn, highlight the image of the jazz musician. In the same light, Marsalis himself is enacting the persona of the black genius. However, as Amiri Baraka said, the critic of jazz has always been white, "but most important jazz musicians have not been."[74] The majority of educators and, arguably, performers now are white, as are the majority of jazz photographers and television directors. So are we all chasing the black musician of the past? Does the image of the jazz musician promote what Andrew Ross calls a "romantic version of racism"?[75] Are they romanticizing stereotypes of primitivism and sexuality as well as problems of gender, as Ingrid Monson notes?[76]

Baraka points out that jazz musicians are often characterized by the myths surrounding them.[77] Casting jazz musicians as "untutored, natural geniuses" easily invokes primitivist ideas of the African American artist unspoiled by culture or civilization. Winthrop Sargeant wrote, in 1938, that "the Negro, like all folk musicians, expresses himself intuitively."[78] But Baraka's argument is that the modern black jazz musician is still stereotyped unjustly. Ted Gioia understands the more familiar and racially unjust characteristics of the primitivist myth surrounding the early jazz musician of the 1920s and 1930s, but argues that this same attitude, although in a milder form, continues to be part of discussions about modern players.[79] Will the modern black jazz musician ever escape the idea that he is talented, not just "born with it"? And will jazz critics, as well as the rest of society, ever leave behind the language that surrounds primitivism and racism when referencing African Americans? Or, asks Charles Gerard, is the goal to gain the status of "genius" just another way of seeking white approval?[80]

In addition, African American musicians still represent the "struggle" and "tragedy" of their historically repressed social position. Parenthetically, it seems that a black musician makes a better picture, especially in a photograph or film, than a white musician. This is a possible reason why the photographs of Leonard have gained in popularity at the same time neoclassicism has. The shared qualities, values, and historical references in his photographs have promoted the African American and have promptly set the stage for Wynton Marsalis to become the next leader in the jazz movement.

E. Taylor Atkins argues that the primary mission of jazz history is to identify significant figures and works, thus facilitating the construction of a canon and establishing standards of taste for judging future works. Texts by the jazz community detail a natural stylistic evolution, guided by a select handful of geniuses, who captivate the world with the sounds they have produced.[81] As early as 1982, Gary Giddins anticipated that Wynton Marsalis would not become the innovator desperately needed in jazz. This negative prophecy from Giddins was aimed at the rest of the young lions as well. Instead, Giddins warned that the dominance of neoclassicism in jazz was something that could be expected, since the pendulum had been swinging away from the mainstream for quite some time.

After the turbulence of the past 20 years, however, with the avant-garde rooting out clichés only to be followed by fusion mercenaries and their middlebrow posturing, the neoclassicists have a task no less valuable than innovation: sustenance. Not unlike the popularizers of swing in the 1930s and soul in the 1950s, musicians such as Marsalis are needed to restore order, replenish melody, revitalize the beat, loot the tradition for whatever works, and expand the audience. That way we'll be all the hungrier for the next incursion of genuine avant-gardist, whose business is to rile the mainstream and keep it honest.[82]

Giddins chastises Marsalis's claim to fame as a resurgent neoclassicist, and correctly describes the relationship between Marsalis, jazz culture, and the rest of society by suggesting that the average music listener needs someone like Marsalis to relight the jazz lantern. Louis Armstrong served not only as a spokesman for jazz, but also as an ambassador for jazz to other nations. He carried a message supporting jazz by performances in other countries throughout his lifetime. Armstrong did not endorse, however, the "new" music (bebop) that was coming from the younger generation of musicians, such as Bird, Miles, and Dizzy. Armstrong remained steadfastly loyal to his style of swing mixed with New Orleans Dixieland.

Stuart Nicholson pinpoints the noticeable absence of leadership in jazz after Miles Davis's death in 1991, which plunged jazz into a "crisis of confidence."[83] He argues that the construction of the jazz canon is based on the teleological "great man" theory, and that the absence of a great man after Davis died caused a momentary stillness among jazz musicians, who lacked leadership. Jazz, according to Nicholson, seemed to be "waiting for Godot," thus articulating a general need for a leader to take jazz in a new direction. Marsalis filled all of the necessary requirements: he was talented, articulate, knowledgeable, and had paid his dues among the jazz community. However, Marsalis' neoconservative approach to jazz included the aforementioned return to the harmonic and melodic values of the bop and post-bop improvisers of the 1940s and 1950s, and went back even further to Duke Ellington and Louis Armstrong as well.[84]

Nicholson explains that Marsalis codified jazz as a music form which must include 4/4 swing and the blues as necessary ingredients. Jazz, according to Wynton Marsalis, must stem from the mainstream tradition, be played on acoustic instruments, be rhythmically tied to a swinging beat, and provide a link to African American contributions to jazz in its early stages. He has constructed a fortress around mainstream jazz, further dividing fusion, free jazz, and world jazz from the mainstream. Marsalis claims that modern musicians who go outside of the mainstream are, in effect, showing contempt for the basic values of the music and of society, and that the responsibility of all jazz musicians is to define the place of jazz.[85]

The process of manufacturing the musician will not contribute to the continuation of jazz. Are neoclassicists more concerned with manufacturing the next Wynton Marsalis? The question echoed by many critics is, "Why are there no great jazz musicians around today like Monk, Diz, Miles, and 'Trane?" This question often reflects the musical taste of the one asking the question. Jazz critics often cite the flaky marketplace as an excuse for the lack of jazz listeners. Jazz cannot compete with popular music; the pop market will always remain supreme with sales because it is more commercially adept at accommodating the needs of its listeners. Jazz musicians, for the most part, do not want to compromise their art, and remain out of the limelight as a result. This is because the popularity of one type of music is determined by the culture that produces it. For instance, jazz was popular music, while at the same time, Larry Kart says, jazz was "able to address the human condition with a unique intensity and depth."[86] Neoclassicists believe that the market is not only full of adolescents, but of the adolescent- or feeble-minded, those who are weak and subject to the influence of others.

The permanence of the canon causes the stabilization of jazz. However, jazz cannot remain stagnant; it is a music of chance and change, and its very nature is one of extemporaneity. Yet, many seek to define jazz by other musical conventions. What Marsalis seeks to retain in jazz—its traditions, its regularity of rhythm and instruments, its neoclassical rules and regulations, its demand for emphatic allegiance to musical sensibilities of the past—runs counter to the internal core of jazz. Its innovation and irregularity is violated. By this argument, perhaps the old jazz image cannot evolve into a new jazz image.

Often in the Western traditional view of aesthetics, artists only gain recognition if they contribute ideas (viewed as intellectual achievements) that initiate a particular style that blends current social trends of a given era. Ted Gioia states that jazz musicians during and after the bebop era, by taking themselves seriously as artists, "validated the intellectual component of his music" and acknowledged the contribution of earlier players.[87] The style of neoclassicism in jazz is currently based on contributions from bebop players of the 1940s who elevated jazz to an intellectual achievement. At present, no one doubts the status of jazz as sophisticated, intellectual music; however, neoclassicists often worry about the influences that fusion, which includes instruments and techniques from popular "entertainment" music, may have on traditional jazz. Each jazz purist maintains the need to distinguish jazz from pop music and the world of entertainment.[88] The root cause of this splitting of jazz as art can be traced to the furor between jazz musicians themselves during the time their music, as Benny Green says, moved from primitivism to neoclassicism within the space of half a century.[89] In his "Constructing the Jazz Tradition: Jazz Historiography," DeVeaux associates jazz with another type of classical music.

> Marsalis is careful to present jazz as a cultural heritage and, in a sense, a political reality, entirely separate from the European tradition. But his celebrated feat of winning Grammy awards for both jazz and classical recordings underscores the extent to which jazz has become *another kind* of classical music—one indigenous to black culture and reflecting black values, but following the same pattern of institutionalization in conservatories and repertory groups, and demanding of its musicians an empathetic response to aesthetic sensibilities of the past.[90]

Reaffirmation of the value of past musicians helps solidify one's own place in the music of the present. "Like the heroin some bebop musicians took to escape the pain of the present, nostalgia has been a narcotic of choice for people terrified by the unfamiliarity of the ever-changing present."[91] Thus, neoclassical jazz musicians have been able to present a clear identity of themselves by distinguishing their music from previously "failed" music. "Of course," says Gary Giddins, "nothing spurs revival like death, and the passing of Ellington, Mingus, and Monk has encouraged numerous reinvestigations of their music."[92] The death of many instigators of classic jazz allowed the young lions and a new generation of jazz connoisseurs to focus on the contributions of great musicians. One way to pay homage to the innovators of a particular era, such as Monk or Bird, and thereby to reinforce the aesthetics of the past is by reissuing their music in the form of either greatest hits or authentic recording sessions previously unknown to the public. Another way to boost celebrated musical giants is to dedicate an album to a famous artist, thereby promoting the past famous name along with the name of the present performer on the album. For example, "Mingus would listen to *Smith plays Mingus*." "Ellington concurs, *Ellington Ballads by John Smith* is a wonderful album."[93] In fact, sales usually rise if the artist includes the name of a famous musician on front of albums he or she is trying to sell. The name of a well-known artist gives credence to the unknown artist selling the album; similarly, the tribute to a famous artist almost acts as an endorsement of the younger one. The potential buyer of the album becomes a proponent of the jazz canon by recognizing the name of the famous musician and selecting the neoclassical artist whose musical style best complements the jazz great. In addition to the somewhat self-acclaimed authority given to the unknown artist, the known artist receives more exposure as well.

George Bernard Shaw's article about photography, "The Unmechanicalness of Photography," discusses the nature of conservatism as that which consolidates artworks based on the categories created for them:

> This virtuosity in the artist calls for its corresponding connoisseurship in the critic; and the result is that fine art becomes a game of skill in which the original object of the skill is constantly being lost sight of; so that the genuinely original men who recall this object by periodical "returns to nature" are vehemently abused and ridiculed, not because their works are not like nature, but because they are not like pictures.[94]

What is neoclassicism after all but a remolding of old works to make new ones? Shaw indicates that it is academicism, pure and simple. "Mr. Whistler was not academic; but the photographer who aims at producing a Whistleresque print is as academic as Nicolas Poussin."[95]

In theory, the musician who can play tunes from the American songbook is playing tunes written nearly sixty years ago. To Shaw, true art is that which creates new categories. It is the nature of conservatism to consolidate artworks based on the category they fit in; therefore, neoclassicism retains its hegemony by naming the other categories of jazz that have "failed," so to speak, like free jazz and fusion.[96] Neoclassicists love to comment on the failure of the avant-garde because they have "proof" that it is not as stable and popular as neoclassicism. In this same light, one could say that Schoenberg failed in creating the twelve-tone row because it is not in practice by the majority of composers today, or that Wagner's efforts were in vain because composers do not apply his *Gesamtkunstwerk* into every opera. Neoclassicists seem to argue that what is popular is better than what is not. History proves this logic to be incorrect.

In *The Order of Things*, Michel Foucault claims: "In any given culture and at any given time, there is always only one *episteme* that defines the conditions of possibility of all knowledge."[97] The notion of episteme, as used by Foucault, is a basic or fundamental category for the interpretation of history. In our current condition of knowledge, we construct our ideas based on previous reference points that build on one another. The points can be fused into a line, providing the seeker with a foundation for an idea. One line builds on the next, which forms an intricate grid of information to construct the history of something. In postmodern theory, the term "history" contains viable facts only to those who tell it. History, like life, varies according to the one who experiences it. Therefore, history cannot necessarily be agreed upon; it can only be retold through a consensus.

Jazz history seems to focus on that which is told by consensus. Authors like Scott DeVeaux have grappled with how jazz history is depicted. The teaching of jazz usually involves constructing a progressive historical line of development, similar to the way that European classical music or art is taught. Devaux states: "To judge from textbooks aimed at the college market, something like an official history of jazz has taken hold in recent years. On these pages, for all its chaotic diversity of style and expression and for all the complexity of its social origins, jazz is presented as a coherent whole, and its history as a skillfully contrived and easily comprehensible narrative."[98] This progressive line of development becomes the episteme as described by Foucault. From the origins of jazz to bebop in the 1940s and 1950s, there is a straight line, but after bebop, the evolutionary lineage begins to dissolve into the inconclusive coexistence of many different, in some cases hostile styles. Because a linear progression of jazz focuses on the events that lead us to the current style of jazz, much of the significance, especially in its styles and the personal contributions from its artists, is lost. It becomes "the struggle over *possession* of the history, and the legitimacy that it confers."[99] DeVeaux emphasizes the importance of traditions and how it distracts us from the historical surrounding of a style or from the meaning jazz has acquired at a particular time and place.[100] Thus, it is important to recognize the limitations that a narrative history gives to jazz.

The current trend of society is to depict the developments of jazz as something that has been socially determined, a collective representation of art seen through a narrative.[101] Paul Berliner claims that the performer's mastery, the theorist's analysis, the historian's curiosity, and the educator's concern for making musical language accessible to the non-specialist are all struggling with "passing it on," meaning passing on the uniqueness of jazz.[102] There is an urge for all concerned to share the love of the music. But what is the best way to do so? How can jazz be taught, for example, to a college class of freshman students? Can jazz be truncated in order to get through the material in fifteen weeks? Without the sense of progression that a truncated narrative can provide, would jazz be rootless, indistinguishable from any other popular genres that rebel against European classical music? "If we are to understand the canon historically, we must become skeptical of it, and free ourselves from its authority, its ideology, and the whole manner of speech that surrounds it."[103]

Jazz can be defined by its African American roots, but not all African Americans agree on the definition of jazz. The co-founder of the avant-garde group the Association for the Advancement of Creative Musicians, Muhal Richard Abrams, has stated that, just as there are different types of black life, so there are different types of black music.[104] Afropurists, such as Marsalis, Crouch, and Murray, believe that jazz is the intellectual property of African Americans. This is clearly problematic, because other African American musicians choose new forms as representative of jazz music. Avant-garde jazz was initially heralded as the coming of the new black society, and the opinions of white critics were irrelevant. "Racism," states Radano, became the collective cry, the watchword for the avant-garde jazz community that emerged in the 1960s and 1970s. Any type of opposition, whether directed toward a group or an individual, met with the wrath of the jazz avant-garde, who branded the entire jazz establishment as racist.

"Clubs, the traditional showcases for jazz, were now no more than 'crude stables' to Archie Shepp or 'whorehouses' to Ornette Coleman. For these musicians, the clubs were a kid of anachronistic slave market in which the owners were the distributors of the merchandise."[105] Shepp directly confronted the white American populace as the owners of jazz: "By this I mean: you own the music, and we make it." He further claimed avant-garde music in the name of black society.[106] Controversy, says Radano, is the key to any interesting news item; and the colorful, exciting antics of the mostly black members of the avant-garde proved to be a source of entertainment as well as a means for some white readers to deal with their own feelings of guilt.[107] The initial groundwork for racial criticism toward jazz was supplied by the poet and playwright LeRoi Jones (Amiri Baraka). His polemics shared the venom of the avant-garde artists, and his primary concern seemed less the music of jazz than the establishment of a black nation.

The movement from avant-garde artists such as Shepp reflects what Ferdinand Jones calls "the challenge attitude," Adelbert H. Jenkins the "dialectic," and Henry Louis Gates Jr. "counternarrative."[108] All three of these terms refer to the act of substituting another interpretation of the reality often presented to African Americans. Applied to jazz, this means that African Americans must challenge the presentation of jazz in Anglo-American society. The average African American learns to take the reality of white society and search for multiple meanings. One must examine jazz as it is used in contemporary society to determine whether the original African American qualities of the music are being lost.

Consequently, the authentic claim of any type of jazz depends on the one making the claim. Wynton Marsalis believes pure jazz is that which is influenced by the black community, while Archie Shepp and Muhal Richard Abrams set the range for black music beyond neoclassicism, encompassing the avant-garde. One byproduct of marketing a style of music in the name of the black community is that the community itself becomes a label to be placed on jazz.

Jazz, as black music, is often labeled as "other" along with different ethnic and racial groups, women musicians, and folk art.[109] It is too "other" or outside of the Western music tradition to be studied by classical musicians, but not "other" enough to be studied as world music. In fact, one may hypothesize that the Western canon of classical art music acts as a *museum* that houses musical styles like jazz that are tied to classical music but not directed related to it. The canonization by the Western tradition continues to be a process of drawing out the African Americanness of jazz; even our method of evaluating jazz stems from the Western classical tradition. But the musical qualities that one evaluates in jazz are not necessarily found in the canon of art music. Therefore, we are trained to separate those qualities of jazz that demonstrate Euro-classical standardization and those qualities that are African in nature. By using this method of evaluation, are we not casting our own romantic version of racism onto the African American jazz musician?

At least in terms of jazz, it seems that throughout the twentieth century, European musicians may not have gotten the recognition they deserve, and they remain a fringe group in the twenty-first century. Americans, in general, are proud of their independent, strong, boisterous image and wish to keep alive that which made them great. In like manner the jazz image seems equally strong, even masculinized, whether it is in Leonard's photographs or through advertisements featuring Wynton Marsalis. Why is there a lack of criticism about European jazz musicians? Why do jazz critics consistently steer away from reporting on the lesser-known European musician? And more importantly, why have European musicians been left out of the canon of jazz time and time again?[110] E. Taylor Atkins comments on jazz historiography as that which begins and ends in America and has failed to look overseas. Even the Ken Burns documentary virtually omits any mention of relevant developments in other countries and relies too heavily on the ultra-conservative Crouch-Marsalis line for American canonical figures.[111]

One reason is that European jazz musicians do not have the strong image-association relationship maintained by American jazz culture. The jazz musician, in American culture, is almost like an urban version of the cowboy. Just as we cannot imagine a European cowboy, so we cannot imagine a European jazz musician. Several themes within jazz are believed to hold purely American connotations, such as democracy, individualism, social mobility, civil society, free enterprise, ingenuity, inventiveness, and material well-being.[112] These traits are not only understood as a part of jazz culture in the rest of the world, but are also endorsed and practiced along with jazz music. However, the Marsalis-Crouch-Murray line does not think of non-American jazz musicians in the same manner of white musicians playing black music. How could "they" possibly understand the uniqueness of jazz? Jazz has remained an American art form. Of course, jazz is an American invention, and "in no one's mind have the music's ties to its country of origin been severed," yet the practice of the jazz tradition has broadened beyond U.S. boundaries, and this development has remained to a large part unnoticed for decades.[113]

The scholarship of Ekkehard Jost, E. Taylor Atkins, and Stuart Nicholson provides evidence that jazz critics around the globe recognize this problem.[114] The globalization of American music is an issue in any genre, but it seems to be more disturbing with regard to jazz because of the ferocity with which the jazz community clings to America. This is partly due to the fact that the United States, a relatively young country compared to Europe, has not had its own cultural folk music indigenous to this area. Perhaps jazz fills this role. Modernism has also played a role in the development of jazz; however, modernism is considered mostly an American phenomenon. Because of America's victory in two World Wars, capitalism, individualism, social mobility, civil society, ingenuity and inventiveness, material well-being, and ultimately self-indulgence have all fostered modernism as a movement pertinent mainly to American standards.

European jazz musicians represent the diversification of jazz, which, according to jazz traditionalists, weakens its true roots. By expanding jazz qualities to include other musical styles, the purity of the original African American jazz is lost. This same purity is what neoclassicists are fighting so hard to conserve according to Atkins's comments about the Ken Burns's series *Jazz*:

> Burns effaced the contested nature of the jazz idiom itself, by relying too heavily on the ultra-conservative "Crouch-Marsalis line" on canonical figures and developments. However, few of Burns' American critics

objected to the filmmaker's decision to omit virtually all mention of relevant developments in other countries: the setting of the jazz history narrative exclusively within the borders of the United States and the personal experience of American musicians obviously struck most critics as natural and unproblematic.[115]

Surely European musicians contribute to the distribution of jazz beyond its home. Yet, European musicians are seen as the weaker type of musician, not because they lack skill but because they do not fit the jazz image of the strong, masculine, African American male, whom our American society often portrays stereotypically as a sexual predator or a criminal, or as a powerful athlete.[116] Without the image of black masculinity in American jazz, European musicians' lack could be termed a sexual Freudian void, recalling the female body.

The feminist critic Luce Irigaray argues that "sexual difference is intimately connected with vision because it is something that is seen."[117] Her concepts of femininity are based on Freud's traumatizing creation of a castration complex, implying that castration is already complete for girls. The woman's lack of a penis is assumed to be a missing element or flaw in her person. In Irigaray's view this absence of anything to see in female genitalia implies a lack of visualization. A woman exists in terms of a sexual absence as opposed to the visual presence of a penis. This void combined with the perceived physical weakness of the female body suggests a stereotypical intellectual weakness as well. This is precisely why the jazz image contains more visual power if the subject is a black male. The presence of a man in Leonard's photographs symbolizes strength and intelligence, which harkens back to the patriarchal foundation of Western society.

In like manner, the perpetuation of a neoclassical image helps maintain a certain masculinity of jazz. "During the Romantic period, musical and literary genius was attained by incorporating 'feminine imagination with masculine reason.'"[118] In Romantic music, so this argument claims, compositional elements such as excessive ornamentation and chromaticism were used to portray female subjects or femininity. As musical and literary high culture developed in nineteenth-century Europe and the United States in the wake of Romanticism, these elements were combined with the male concept of strength and reason. Consequently, throughout the twentieth century, the gap widened between art music, which contained the masculine characteristics of intellectual reason and integrity, and the more "feminine" mass culture, which does not require the training or technique found with art music. Jazz musicians drew upon this Romantic ethos through its masculine implications as they developed an aesthetic sensibility that favored originality, creativity, and emotional expression. Susan McClary stresses that the gendered meanings in music are not timeless; it is clear that Romantic ideals continue to influence our understanding of music and musicians' ideals about themselves.[119]

The metaphor of viewing musical intellect and strength as masculine compared to the feminine and weaker emotional expression has been used constantly in Western musical analysis.[120] However, Citron reminds us that we are ignoring how the metaphors are used today: "Whether or not we believe in the ideology conveyed in the codes is besides the point. What is important is to understand their implication in the history of ideas and their potential impact on practice."[121] This masculine metaphor seems to be consistent with the treatment of jazz historically. The United States has long led the evolution of jazz into a dominant musical mode; possibly the future of jazz lies in Europe doing its part for the development of jazz worldwide.

The exclusionary property of neoclassicism in jazz, whether intentionally or not, crossed into Europe. Neoclassicism maintains a certain collection of values and intellectual ideas of which musical styles outside of the genre are thought to be lacking the seriousness necessary to be authentic jazz. The principal hierarchy in art has been a division into fine arts (high) and decorative or applied arts, or crafts (low). Paul Whiteman's famous statement "to make a lady out of jazz" grounds his attempt to cultivate the folk music and musicians that jazz came from.[122] However, his gendered sentiment also suggests that the culture surrounding jazz reflects the unethical morals of the red light district, most likely from New Orleans, that gave birth to jazz. As mentioned in chapter 2, the term "jas" or "jass" originally referenced sexual intercourse, and, as its musical characteristics changed over time, jazz could not shake the negative reputation of its illegitimate birth. Jazz, therefore, has been associated with tainted reputation, scandal, amoral lifestyle, prostitution, and so on. Thus, a woman (or man) playing jazz came to be associated with ill repute.

Ironically, these attributes, like Whiteman's statement, are usually in reference to women. Jazz in its early days, according to Whiteman, was a tramp and not part of the civilized lifestyle that a wholesome, educated woman should lead. Some argue that jazz may still be an unethical profession. Much of the creative process takes place in the nightclubs with alcohol, easy women, and a drug culture. In fact, many of our great jazz leaders succumbed to drugs and alcohol while gigging and touring. Much like a rock star (although without a star's budget), many jazz musicians have led a tumultuous life in order to promote their music, and in the process, there has been a strong sense of masculinity among jazz musicians.

Bebop itself grew out of an "all-boy's club" environment in the early 1940s. During the crucial transition years of bebop, male jazz musicians tried to look, act, and perform in a masculine manner while being more sensitive to the harmonies of music. Much of the music of bop is fast-paced, extremely difficult, and depends upon the strength of the frontman to lead the other musicians through his instrument. It was a way of keeping the music pure, intellectually, and thus ideologically, and as a consequence, practically, away from women who could not handle the difficult lifestyle, nor, it was assumed, could they possibly understand the complexity of the music. The most accepted role for women in jazz is as singers who have a strong sense of femininity while on stage. Women playing instruments is much more accepted in pop music than in the jazz community. Of course, there are exceptions, as with Mary Lou Williams, Marian McPartland, and vocalist Carmen McRae, all of whom overcame the obstacles either intentionally or unintentionally placed in front of them.

The reason for such a strong gender bias lies in the performance practice of jazz itself. Any sign of weakness, a stereotype for a woman's physical or intellectual strength, is not accepted on the bandstand. Throughout Western tradition, women are seen not for their individuality, but rather for how their interaction with society determines their moral worth.[123] Women as jazz musicians are not openly discouraged, but they are also not endorsed, recorded, nor do they perform as often as their male counterparts. Women musicians are not as likely to acquire a gig, and when they do are usually seen as a novelty item.[124]

In addition, the image of a female jazz musician does not fit the rugged nature of "the man with the horn" appearance mentioned in chapter 1. The image of jazz musicians, as cultivated in Leonard's photography, reinforces the gender practice of male instrumentalists and female singers, a practice which has held true over the years, with exceptions such as Jane Ira Bloom (soprano saxophone), Lillian Hardin Armstrong (piano), Regina Carter (violin), and Maria Schneider (composer and arranger). The strength that one must possess in order to properly understand and play jazz is still typically found with men.

The absence of European jazz musicians in American neoclassical culture is an extension of the gender-biased hierarchy in jazz history. The European jazz musician is generally perceived as a feminine, non-functioning void that is excluded from the mainstream image of black masculinity.[125] Americans believe Europeans to be more sensitive not only to new music, but also to historical art music, since most of it originated there. Europe already had it own style of music with its own composers, agendas, controversies, and history-making musical accomplishments throughout two thousand years. While there was no malicious intent to reject European musicians, little effort has been made to include European contributions to jazz.

Most applications of aesthetics—the philosophy concerned with general principles of art—consider the worthiness of the art object itself and examine the influences behind its creation. For instance, Immanuel Kant studies the "noumena" of the objects at hand, Heidegger considers the "thingness of the thing," and Plato considers the greatness of art as that which best imitates the Idea of the object. For centuries, in order for someone to analyze art, one had to examine the object that is considered art. Only in the twentieth century did artists reject the requirement of an object and include instead the concept or the idea of the object. Duchamp challenged the artfulness of any object with his "Fountain," James Turrell used light for his object which is arguably not an object at all, and Robert Rauschenberg asked his friend de Kooning to draw a picture on a canvas, which Rauschenberg erased and declared the rubber shaving from the eraser as the artwork instead. In these instances, the creation becomes experience rather than an actual object.

Music, by itself, has always been more difficult to define because it is less tangible and more elusive than other areas of art. Comparatively, it lacks a visual object for analysis. There are instruments and scores present in music, yet these visual occurrences are not the focus. One may hear and understand music, but like algebraic formulas, one cannot visibly see the mathematic calculations. Only on paper does music "exist" tangibly, and it is this piece of paper that has identified classical music throughout the decades. The score allows one to examine the notes, alter the time at which they are heard, and increase the number of instruments playing. After reviewing the score, the conductor can execute the thought behind the composer, and the musicians respond by playing with their scores in front of them.

Music actually occurs from the moment a sound is produced to the moment the sound reaches the ears of the receiver. It exists in time, whereas a painting can hang on a wall as long as one likes. Music cannot be an imitation of the Platonic forms or ideas. Because there is no Idea to replicate, there is no object in nature that music can correctly replicate. And because of this inaccessibility, philosophers such as Martin Heidegger and Arthur Schopenhauer have placed music above visual artworks. Schopenhauer believes that music represents the purest form of emotion or essence. It has the ability to replace the desire for one's own wants and needs with one's original feeling, the source for inspiration or the Will. Other philosophers, such as Eduard Hanslick or Immanuel Kant before him, view music as transitory in nature, because it detracts from the "pure act of contemplation which alone is the true and artistic method of listening."[126]

Unlike classical music, which normally relies on a visual score eliciting what Hanslick calls the "pure act of contemplation," jazz usually has no score, no object. With the improvisatory nature of jazz, the score, containing chord changes, melody, and harmony lines, is less significant. Of course, there are scores used in jazz, especially with big bands, but the score is not the focus of the music. Most of the creative process involves immediate improvisation without much reliance on a written musical score. As Ted Gioia says, "Jazz remains out of place in a culture that places such enormous emphasis on the physical object of art."[127] Whenever these limitations are imposed on the temporal arts like jazz, according to Gioia, the result is to overlook jazz's unpremeditated method of artistic expression.

The artworthy item in jazz, to most aestheticians, is improvisation, which does not require any object. Therefore, when compared to classical music, jazz is lacking the visual object of the score. And part of this assumption underlies current understandings of jazz. Ted Gioia's point is that the lack of an object, such as a score, has hurt the credibility of jazz; and it is this lack of a score that has prevented improvisation from being accepted as legitimate music production. It could mean the jazz musician lacks skill, intelligence, exposure, authenticity, creativity, or acceptance. Such beliefs may not intentionally be harmful. Regardless, there has been an undeniable void for jazz musicians to fill when compared with classical music, and that void has only of late changed as jazz has gained greater acceptance among the rest of the musical community. Perhaps one reason why the jazz image has been repeated is that it helps to fill that void of significance. The photograph is a visual marker of musicians who have proven their worth as artists, thus validating jazz. The image acts as a historical reference of musicians who have brought about a particular change in jazz. Leonard's photographs and the visual work of others establish the significance of jazz, a proof of art's existence.

Jazz remains a debatable topic for those philosophers who place so much emphasis on the physical object. After all, what helps provide us with our own identity are the possessions we own. Karl Marx wrote, "Man is initially posited as a private property owner, i.e., an exclusive owner whose exclusive ownership permits him both to preserve his personality and to distinguish himself from other men, as well as relate to them. . . . Private property is man's personal, distinguishing and hence essential existence."[128]

What one does with one's private property distinguishes one from those who hold the same property. Let us say, for example, that whatever a composer writes is the property of that composer. What he or she decides to do with it—perform it, publish it, or even keep it locked away from prying eyes—exemplifies the personality of the composer. Therefore, what one does with personal property depends on the will of the individual.

For mainstream jazz at least, the private property is the spontaneous creation that comes from a performing musician at one distinguishable moment. Even though the group of musicians contributes to the ownership of one improvised solo, it is the soloist that retains control of the music during his or her solo; thus, whatever direction the soloist takes, the rest of the musicians depend totally on the mood and personality of the soloist. The end result, or the music contained in the solo, is the property of the soloist. The music contained in the solo is the private property of the musician. There is one remaining problem, however, that we cannot erase—the property of music is intangible, as discussed earlier. The physical object remains out of reach for jazz musicians, and again, this proves the necessity of the jazz image to act as the object.

The image of the jazz musician also retains the popularity of jazz, however minute that may be. Krin Gabbard comments on the state of jazz as "*inseparable* from its aura and from displays of race, sexuality, and art,"[129] which is echoed by Larry Kart, Scott DeVeaux, Stuart Nicholson, Peter Townsend, Ted Gioia, and Ingrid Monson. The aura of jazz as depicted in the image of a jazz musician continues to propel jazz into the ears of the public. Compared to other musical styles, jazz has an easy-to-recognize visual image.[130] One cannot recall as well a typical classical musician, except one who wears tails and sits at a piano bench. Even rock or pop music does not have an image that is as ingrained or repeated as jazz, since rock ranges from Marilyn Manson to Flavor Flav or from ZZ Top to Vampire Weekend. Yet, even someone who has no knowledge of jazz history can imagine an African American playing a saxophone.

One reason arises from the recent acceptance of the jazz image by society. In contemporary visual culture, jazz is commodified and played on television commercials to attract the viewer/listener to the smooth ride designed to sell a new car. Jazz is also represented in the commercial venue as a mood setter, creating a romantic moment between characters on a television show.[131] When National Public Radio, the number one major news network for radio broadcasting, plays jazz, it becomes associated with intellectualism and high art. By associating the sound of jazz with news, world events, politics, and the general process of representing the organized thoughts and feelings of our Western society, jazz becomes a sophisticated, intellectual form of composition.

The jazz photographs by Leonard, sold as posters, don the walls of university students. The students who listen to jazz are "hip" to the nature of the music and to jazz culture. These posters are seen in addition to cover art on recordings; even though most music is currently purchased digitally, and programs such as iTunes are now including the cover art with purchased music.

Leonard's photographs have functioned well in this transition period away from CDs and recordings toward digitized music collections. By hanging up a Leonard jazz poster, the owner stamps himself or herself as a rebel, ironically, who will not conform to pop culture; the student declares independence from the "industry" and chooses to follow jazz musicians as artists who must live outside of pop culture. Through more and more college students and educated listeners alike, the posters of Leonard's photos have become part of pop culture. In some cases they allow students to gravitate towards "otherness" as a life or musical choice, or in other cases, they mark the serious work that occurs behind the practice room doors and act as an inspirational image urging complete dedication to improving through practice.

Granted, the jazz image was in full force during the middle of the twentieth century and at that time stood for the same things as it does now. This is partly due to the irrefutable permanence of the jazz image. It has stuck in the minds of musicians for fifty years and continues to do so. However, it is important to recognize the magnitude of this image as it pertains to the shape of jazz to come. As with most musical styles, the pendulum of fashionable music has swung back and forth between the tonal canon and versions of abstraction. Taste in jazz has swung from dance music to serious art music, from cool to free jazz, from the avant-garde to the more formulaic classic jazz. And where is jazz to go from the neoclassical phase? Only the brave can postulate the future of jazz, but for the time being, the jazz community must deal with the "tonal pocket" of neoclassicism.[132]

The image, as with any other stereotype, summarizes the entire history of jazz in one visual picture. Pierre Bourdieu says, "To appropriate a work of art is to assert oneself as the exclusive possessor of the object and of the authentic taste for that object, which is thereby converted into the reified negation of all those who are unworthy of possessing it.. . . What is at stake is indeed 'personality,' i.e., the quality of the person, which is affirmed in the capacity to appropriate an object of quality."[133] Even though Leonard's pictures have become the standard representation of jazz, the identification

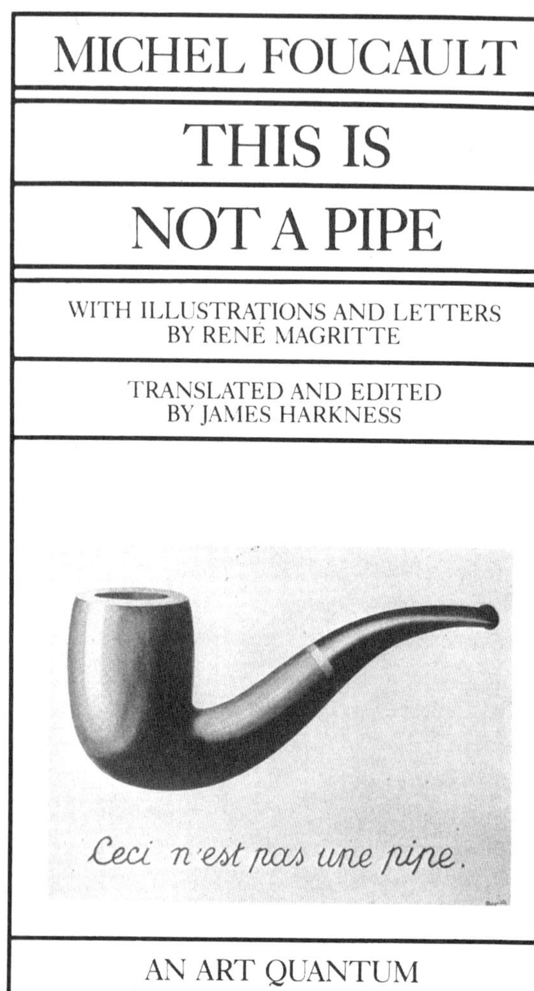

Fig. 3.1. Ceci n'est pas une pipe, appearing on the cover of Michel Foucault's book, *This Is Not a Pipe*, by René Magritte. 1926.

of what jazz is lies in the viewer.[134] If a viewer believes jazz musicians to be alcoholics, then that is what they will see in the photograph. If the viewer knows jazz musicians to be spontaneous, they will see creativity and imagination in the faces of jazz musicians. The viewer relies on his or her own specific social conditioning to interpret the image.

It seems, then, that the jazz image is similar to René Magritte's surrealist painting, *This Is Not a Pipe*. The painting presents an image of what a pipe looks like, but it is merely a painting. Like the title says, it is not a pipe, just a picture of one. The jazz image, as in the photographs by Herman Leonard, represents what is "timeless," "natural," and "authentic" in jazz, but it merely shows a picture of the jazz musicians and cannot adequately present the music itself. Jazz, like the pipe, is not present in the image. Today's jazz musicians are not just black men, but also multicultural individuals. Also, the term "jazz" can be used to refer to a musical style, but instead here refers to "a-style-of-music-which-is-neither-*classical*-nor-*pop*." The image does not refer to itself, just as a word cannot refer to itself. In a Saussurean understanding of language, "dog" is not a real animal, but as James Harkness describes, it has a conceptual signification in that it differs from the idea of a cat.[135]

Much of neoclassicism is based on what it is not: it is not free jazz, nor fusion, nor the avant-garde. To take this a step further, the jazz image no longer refers to jazz's origins at all; the term now refers to the neoclassical image of jazz as that which is a pure aesthetic experience of intellectual music stemming from a black male tradition. But when is jazz removed from its identification as music to a conceptual reference visualized in an image? At some point, we are merely buying into a commercial product. The consumer wants to be hip to whatever the neoclassical image is selling, and responds the way teenagers do to the next boy band. We buy the alternative, marketable image. Even Marsalis himself acknowledged his iconic status: "You have to understand that people who hear about me, they don't listen to the music I play . . . They only know Wynton as an image. Or Wynton, he's on the Grammys, he has a suit on. So their whole thing is media oriented."[136]

Only now, the jazz image is so integrated in films, television commercials, album covers, posters, and National Public Radio that many musicians and scholars have retreated from its permanence. The next chapter will explain how free jazz musicians such as Ornette Coleman, Cecil Taylor, and Don Cherry fought the traditional jazz image through their music in the 1960s. Pat Metheny grew up on a small farm, as a small white child listened to country music, and contributed greatly (along with Herbie Hancock) to the spreading of jazz to other styles in the 1970s and 1980s. In 1985 Miles Davis dedicated to the pop songs of Cyndi Lauper and Michael Jackson an album (*You're Under Arrest*) that challenged the canon as well as the image of jazz. In the twenty-first century, groups such as the Screaming Headless Torsos incorporate hip hop with jazz, while well-known traditional pop artists such as Radiohead, Sting, and the Dave Matthews Band have begun to include a version of jazz in their music. Time and time again, the most noteworthy musicians are those who go against the stereotypical jazz image, but they also have a harder time finding acceptance from the jazz community—not to mention the rest of society.

CHAPTER 4

A "Style Portrait" of the Avant-Garde

The image of jazz today is a complex one that comes from several sources. As we have learned in the previous chapters, Leonard's resurfacing photographs have played a significant role in determining the current composition of the jazz image today. Complementary to Leonard, neoclassicism has blossomed under the support of the jazz community and the general public through endowments, documentaries, commercials, recording contracts, promotions, and the young lions. Both neoclassicism and Leonard's ideal image of jazz has propelled the recent success of jazz, gathering attention from the American and European public.

However, the neoclassical image is not the only stimulant that has transfixed the jazz listeners and general public. Other styles of jazz, such as free jazz, fusion, and the avant-garde, have contributed to experimentation in jazz and to the construction of new images of the jazz musician. Some critics and musicians see these musical styles merely as a stepping stone from the great sounds of bebop, cool, and hard bop of the 1940s and 1950s to the rejuvenation of these styles in the 1980s. But jazz did not die or fade away during this period. Many jazz musicians—including Cecil Taylor, Ornette Coleman, Eric Dolphy, Miles Davis, Herbie Hancock, Pat Metheny, Chick Corea, Don Cherry, Anthony Braxton, John Zorn, and Sun Ra—began to swim against the current, and in so doing not only created other musical styles but spawned different images of what jazz musicians look and sound like.

One such image evolved from the experimentations during the 1950s. Ornette Coleman's album titles, such as *The Shape of Jazz to Come* and *Free Jazz*, announced the solidification of the avant-garde on the music scene. In addition, Coleman's famous statement "Let's play the music, and not the background" reflects the simmering philosophies he and his cohorts used in their attempt to move jazz to the forefront of musical and artistic expression.[1] But the stylistic shift in jazz was anticipated somewhat by the transition from traditional to experimental often made in the arts. The pendulum of most art forms swings from that which inspires to that which challenges. This is not to say that jazz is necessarily composed of binary principles based on what fits with common practice and what lies outside. Rather, it is the purpose of this chapter to present other ideas, sounds, and identities of jazz that exist in contrast to the neoclassical figure that has gained so much popularity as a icon in photography. In this manner, the striking figures of the budding avant-garde movement in jazz represent an alternative jazz image. Jazz musicians who go against the canon and fight their way to success eventually become canonized themselves, as revolutionaries. But in so doing, they create an image of opposition to the more accepted means of expressing art.

Experimental musicians are expected to behave, perform, and function differently from the mainstream because, in order to be classified as avant-garde, they must deviate drastically from the norm. They want to stand out from the traditional methods of performing jazz, and will shy away from the commercialization of their music. However, most members of the avant-garde, regardless of their eventual classification, have preconceived stipulations imposed on them by society to act or perform a certain way. Therefore, even though many musicians fight to withstand having their music pigeonholed, such a fight becomes a classification in itself. Their opposition to categorization and to using previous musical styles is perceived as typical for an avant-garde artist. Thus an image is imposed on them that fits their style of music accordingly.

So, how does one create, or attempt to create, an image that differs from the mainstream? And if the neoclassical image of jazz was indeed enhanced with the aid of Leonard's camera, which elements helped create other images in jazz? While there are numerous profiles of jazz musicians throughout history that would initiate fodder for discussion on the evolution of the jazz image, two emblem-crafting personalities lend themselves to epic battles on the true form of jazz: the free jazz of Ornette Coleman and the avant-garde music of Muhal Richard Abrams via the Association for the Advancement of Creative Musicians (AACM.) There are specific factors found in the music and personalities of Coleman and Abrams that spark curiosity in their audience; this, in turn, lays the foundation for a new face for the jazz image. The images of these musicians are not necessarily omitted in the jazz community, but because of their affiliation with music that lies outside the mainstream, their image also plays a smaller role in jazz's visual culture. As a part of this discussion, one must grapple with the definitions of "free jazz" and "avant-garde"; seek to determine whether these terms are appropriate to apply to the music of Coleman and Abrams; and examine what free jazz critic Ekkehard Jost calls the "style portrait" of each musician as an innovator in the field of music.

Abrams and Coleman have created their own image, not only by visual association but also by the creative techniques they bring to the jazz scene. For instance, the exploration of "original music" initiated by the AACM is just one method that separated them from the mainstream. Other aspects were to tease the relationship between music and text, encourage dissociation from other types of music in their formalistic properties, and bring in nonmusical items such as masks, Raggedy Ann dolls, paintings, and costumes. By sprinkling their performances with stage movements and costumes, as seen with the AACM-inspired Chicago Art Ensemble and the Anthony Braxton Trio, many jazz musicians sought original music that also restructured the jazz image in the process. The result is what one might call a style portrait of the avant-garde. Just as their musical initiatives lie outside traditional music production, so, too, is their visual presence and identity defined by nonvisual characteristics such as attitude, philosophy, or religious affiliation. The images of Coleman and Abrams capture musical styles that embrace the nonmusical characteristics of philosophy, visual art, and poetry.[2] If we explore their music and practice using traditional analytical methods of classification, we obtain greater depth concerning the jazz image—and ultimately the music itself.

In order for a work to be considered avant-garde, it must be different from the norm; adjectives typically associated with the avant-garde are experimental, difficult, reactionary, forward-looking, modern, cutting-edge, groundbreaking, progressive, advanced. Avant-garde work of any kind refers to ideas, projects, or art that is ahead of its time and often unconventional. Art would not be placed into this category if it were not unique or drastically different in comparison to the Western canon of the arts. Painting, sculpture, theater, and film, and especially performance art all have artworks that are considered difficult for the viewer or listener to accept, and occasionally such artworks antagonize the audience and cause some form of hostility. Parameters that are direct results of controversial work include the addition of the Decency Clause to the National Endowment for the Arts as a reaction to the NEA Four[3] and former mayor Rudolph Giuliani's attempted lawsuit against the Brooklyn Museum of Art in response to Chris Ofili's *Madonna* and Renée Cox's *Yo Mama's Last Supper*.[4]

Difficult art, often appearing on the creative edge of artistic production, poses objectionable reactions and is meant to challenge not only our moral boundaries but also our concept of art. For example, the Society of Independent Artists rejected Marcel Duchamp's urinal, *Fountain*, in 1917 as a legitimate work of art, and many consider Piero Manzoni "difficult" in his creation of ninety cans contenting thirty grams of his freshly preserved feces, produced and tinned in May 1961.[5] But not until an avant-garde work causes a public sensation and is seen as an interruption to the quiet progression of the canon are specific categories (Futurism, Post-Modernism, Nouveau Réalisme, Fluxus, Dada, and so on) assigned to previously uncategorized works. While not all pieces gain classification in this way, works that are not initially understood or that fiercely reject labeling are often put into the broader category of avant-garde.

The avant-garde in relation to music is difficult to define because the rules used in composing, arranging, and performing are needed in order to assess the differences between musics. Intimate knowledge of scales, chord changes, instrumentation, harmony, and rhythm found in music theory, not to mention music development for over two thousand years, is a staple for any professional classical or jazz musician.[6] Again, one assumes that an avant-garde musician will deviate from the typical methods of performing, arranging, and recording music and will experiment with sound production itself. Max Neuhaus is a good example: his computer-generated piece called *Times Square* features sounds emitting from beneath the sidewalk of a pedestrian island in Times Square and is noticeable only when someone stands over the vent.[7] But is this music or is this noise? Where does one draw the line when it comes to definitions of music? One may claim that the permanence and lack of structured organization declassifies Neuhaus's work as actual music, or one could merely focus on the experience of music that imitates the soundscape of New York City through the isolation of one chord indefinitely.

As far as the avant-garde is concerned, the labeling, categorization, and discussion of terms surrounding experimental jazz are supposed to be controversial. Several critics have become aware of the diatribe between the two jazz "camps" of the traditional and the avant-garde. Ronald Radano has proposed that the jazz avant-garde (the marginalized) and the jazz mainstream (the dominant) are two subgroups interacting within the same community. But, he adds, "While the avant-garde musicians identified with jazz and the jazz community, they themselves remained a separate community."[8] Rudolf Stephan describes the tension between the avant-garde and the jazz community as an interaction between the norm (identified as the "musically universal") and the experimental or avant-garde (the "musically particular"). Stephan sees the "musically universal" as the Westernized arrangement of music and style of playing that has remained constant throughout the years of jazz evolution, while the "musically particular," with its innovative music like fusion, free jazz, and other avant-garde, has changed in reaction to the musically universal.[9] Although it might be unfair to assume the set of song standards and combo setting of mainstream jazz is universal, Stephan correctly points out that new ideas, regardless of which era they appear as new, have always faced adversity in relation to the musically universal. And, as previously mentioned, there is much more to the history of jazz than a series of truncated episodes between two camps: the ins and the outs.

Regardless of its evolving role, avant-garde music will continue to have a presence throughout history, because without it any style is in danger of simply becoming repetitive. But what is it about the avant-garde musician that continuously seeks to challenge established musical conventions? What characteristics do we use to separate avant-garde music from other musical styles? Part of the answer lies in the personality of the musician. We expect avant-garde musicians to act in accordance to our understanding of their music. For instance, the notable avant-garde musician, Frank Zappa, was known for his zany antics on stage, while John Zorn and non-jazz musician Laurie Anderson include visual aspects in their musical compositions. We assume that the avant-garde jazz musician (1) is free to choose a musical style outside the mainstream, (2) creates music for the sake of originality and not for popular taste, (3) possesses the vision necessary to organize music outside traditional methods, (4) possesses an identity not obtainable within the mainstream jazz community, and (5) incorporates the metaphysical into his or her style, which reflects the education and political leanings of the artist.[10]

As previously discussed, music in our current society is extremely dependent on the visual image. Clearly this is also true for the avant-garde. Musicians who portray a successful visual image gain the greatest notoriety. Often, their visual representation is based on their own identification and appearance as avant-garde musicians, or they are associated in conjunction with nonmusical characteristics such as philosophy, religion, or political ideas or the more tangible disciplines of poetry, literature, theater, cover art, or fashion. Regardless of association, avant-garde musicians find themselves at a disadvantage when it comes to album sales and marketing because, as avant-garde artists, their music may not be accessible to the general public for mass consumption. Instead, their work will be sold to a select few. Of the small number of people who actually purchase jazz recordings, even fewer purchase avant-garde jazz. Often, it is a lack of understanding such musicians that leads to poor sales.

So part of the process of understanding "difficult" music is to assign presuppositions onto an image. As mentioned earlier, the image of an avant-garde musician assumes that one has the freedom to choose a musical style outside the mainstream, that music is written for the sake of originality and not to appease society at large, that one possesses the vision necessary to organize music outside traditional methods, that one maintains an identity not obtainable within the mainstream jazz community, and that one has the education to know what type of music has come before him or her.[11] The burden of creating a different image from what is already deemed "avant-garde" by society, then, falls on the artist. The audience, in turn, can focus on the contribution of the musician as creating something entirely new. One would think, therefore, that avant-garde artists have an advantage: they can offer a new image to society, one that they can create and facilitate according to their own needs as artists. As in art, one must compare the avant-garde to something found within the canon or the mainstream in order to develop a common language to appreciate form; and by examining the image of musicians that lie outside of the canon, one can also begin to understand how they relate to society.

Certain principles found within the avant-garde movement of the 1950s and 1960s jazz culture have coalesced into a visual image of the avant-garde musician. The classifications "avant-garde" and "free jazz" are similar in nature. Both subscribe to the idea of "art for art's sake," inferring that the purpose of art is not to fulfill particular social functions, but rather that art exists for the purpose of art, as an end in itself. The musician is often isolated from society. Each term refers to a style of music that is outside of the mainstream, yet established enough to contain its own canon of musicians. However, despite the similarities found between the terms, they have come to indicate different streams of jazz history.

> In the 1970s and 1980s many musicians preferred the label "avant-garde," since the word "free" is misleading: in many instances their music is highly organized. As free jazz became more familiar and was absorbed into the standard repertory, however, the term "avant-garde" ceased to describe the genre accurately; moreover, the use of an alternative term obscures the many streams linking the free-jazz musicians of later decades with the pioneers Ornette Coleman, Cecil Taylor, Albert Ayler, and John Coltrane.[12]

Once associated entirely with the avant-garde, free jazz is now considered more of a sub-category of the broader genre—specifically, a particular group of musicians who in the 1960s experimented with sound production and improvisation. It also refers to a precise sound, one that does not often contain tonal harmonies that are essential elements that most musicians use. This unique factor, along with collective improvisation, unusual instrumentation, and freedom from traditional music practices, has come to identify the sound of the music as "free." But not all musicians want to be associated with free jazz. Some consider the term misleading; and much of the music out of the avant-garde scene is highly organized.

As J. Bradford Robinson says in *Grove's Dictionary of Music*, free jazz is probably best defined by such negative features as "the absence of tonality and predetermined chord sequences; the abandonment of the jazz chorus structure . . . ; an avoidance of "cool" instrumental timbres in favor of more "voice-like" sounds; and the suspension of standard time keeping patterns for a free rubato."[13] These absences are associated with the term whenever it is used. The idea of negation presupposes the music of free jazz. Free jazz is quite often defined by what it is not: it is not danceable, it is not traditional, usually it is not tonal, and it is not singable. Sound qualities and instrumentation are not used in the same manner as mainstream jazz or other forms of music. We mentally picture one who composes music that is not normal, not traditional, and not pretty; who directly reflects the music he or she represents through garish clothing and zany behavior; or who physically turns his/her back on popular taste. We picture the weird, the outlandish, and the unordinary, and our minds, stirred with curiosity, imagine what key-less suffering these musicians could impose on the listener.

The negativity found within the definition of free jazz itself is one more reason why AACM members avoid any association with the term, claiming originality as their only requirement. Gene Easton explains:

> "Original," in one sense, means something you write in the particular system that we're locked up with now in this society. We express ourselves in this system because it's what we learned, and if you don't express in the system that is known, you're ostracized. But as we learn more of other systems of music around the world we're getting closer to the music that our ancestors played—sound-conscious musicians, finding a complete new system that expresses *us*. Because there are far better systems, and I feel that we will be locked up for the rest of our days in this system unless we can get out of it through some means such as this.[14]

Upon reading Easton's explanation on "original" music systems, we may conclude that the term "free jazz" restricts the system of sound he wants to express. Musicians such as Ornette Coleman and Muhal Richard Abrams, who have changed the face of jazz as we know it today through their experimentation with various systems, reject "free jazz" as a categorization. Both musicians are considered musical giants in their fields and appear in the jazz canon, although neither Coleman nor Abrams seem to fit the model/image of the jazz musician as discussed in this book. Nor do they desire to be categorized as "difficult" artists, nor approve of any label placed upon them by others. Abrams does not even consider himself a jazz musician at all.[15] However, in order to understand or analyze Coleman or Abram's music, we must use the vocabulary that is already in practice such as "free jazz" or "avant-garde," even though they are inadequate.

For the purposes of this book, the negation already stipulated will be applied in a manner much like Derrida's *erasure*, by using "~~free jazz.~~"[16] By putting a line directly through a term, Derrida simultaneously embraces and rejects its literal meaning. Since ~~free jazz~~ is associated with what it is not, the strikethrough will act as a visual reference that exposes the negation associated with the literal definition while enforcing the inadequacy of language to define an artistic movement. While the strikethrough attaches the word to its meaning, it also conceals other meanings, styles, musicians, recordings, time periods, and yes, images, that are attached to this term but do not always fit its description. And as we will see, Coleman and Abrams simultaneously comply with and reject the categorizations given to them by critics and the jazz community, yet maintain a central objective: to create their own musical paths outside of traditional musical standards.

Additionally, ~~free jazz~~ is often associated with "freedom" from traditional musical harmony, melody, and tonal organization, and as Ekkehard Jost claims, it is "independent of pre-set patterns."[17] Literally, it is the freedom *not* to apply the constraints of a particular musical practice on melody, harmony, or rhythm. Later, ~~free jazz~~ musicians began to widen this concept to any means by which musicians can achieve freedom in their music, based on what, in their minds, needs to be freed. Trumpeter Lester Bowie stated, "We're free to express ourselves in any so-called idiom, to draw from any source, to deny any limitation. We weren't restricted to bebop, free jazz, Dixieland, theater or poetry. We could put it all together. We could sequence it any way we felt like it. It was entirely up to us."[18] The "freedom" principle began as a specific and narrow reference to the rejection of any allegiance to traditional music. This principle also included the freedom to include nonmusical practices such as philosophy, religion, and other disciplines in a musical environment.

For musicians such as William Parker, ~~free jazz~~ was akin to a spiritual journey or life experience: "However, for free music to succeed, it must grow into free spiritual music which is not . . . a musical form; it should be based off of a life form. It is emptying oneself and being."[19] Muhal Richard Abrams and Roscoe Mitchell of the Association for the Advancement of Creative Musicians explained further: "Cats that play bop are more concerned with things like chords and changes rather than spirits . . . in free music you are dependent on the spirits because you don't want to fool with those chords."[20] According to Abrams and Mitchell, harmony acted as an aesthetic barrier that restrained black musicians from their journey towards spiritual unity. And it is the same harmony in ~~free jazz~~ that similarly represented white cultural dominance, "harmony was a sonic reconstruction of the chains that had bridled blacks, of the rationalism that had stifled African spiritualism."[21] Thus the spiritual unity in ~~free jazz~~ is found by resisting traditional uses of harmony and melody.

The freedom principle in jazz allocates to the freedom experienced in improvisation as a musical association, but it can also reference the social, political freedom of the individual as with African Americans. ~~Free jazz~~ for European musicians, for example, brought them the freedom not only from traditional jazz standards, but also freedom from the traditional American claim on jazz.[22] Another extramusical association of ~~free jazz~~ is to the Black Power movement, a subject on which many scholars, including George Lewis and Ronald Radano, have written extensively.[23] Rhythm and melody, according to Radano, served as a formal component shared between musicians stressing the communal and original sounds of West African music and traditional African American styles.[24] In addition, as mentioned in chapter 3, several connections have been made between the cultural products or art forms made by black Americans and the Black Nationalist movement, also called the Second Black Renaissance or the Black Revolution.[25]

From 1965 to 1975 a number of new collectives appeared on the scene along with the AACM, including the Black Artists Group (BAG), the Aboriginal Music Society, the Revolutionary Ensemble, the Human Arts Association, the Jazz and People's Movement, Collective Black Artists, and the Jazz Composers Orchestra Association (JCOA). Some groups, like the AACM, BAG, the Jazz and People's Movement, Collective Black Artists, and the Human Arts Association, cultivated ties with other black cultural nationalist groups and artists as well as with black communities. These affiliations often reflected developments in black ideology at the same time when two leading figures of black cultural nationalism in the U.S., Amiri Baraka and Maulana Ron Karenga, developed a "Black Value System" based on what they considered "primordial African values, customs, and codes of morality."[26] Several artists, some from the jazz community, identified with the cultural revitalization of African or African Americans found in the Black Aesthetic Movement.[27] The black aesthetic was that "black cultural products or art forms should promote black life, unity, history, and experience," and the formation of ~~free jazz~~ represented this catalyst for change in musical terms.[28]

But the intense political action associated with Black Nationalism caused some musicians to differ in their interpretation of the black aesthetic. Musicians like avant-garde saxophonist Archie Shepp strengthened the ties between the avant-garde and the ideologies of Black Nationalism. However, the principles that drive the avant-garde African American pianist Sun Ra vary greatly from the principles that drive Archie Shepp. For instance, Archie Shepp took offense at being labeled as a "jazz" musician completely and opted for the generic "black music." Sun Ra chose to represent his thoughts in poetry as well as directly through his music. In one poem entitled "Black Man," Sun Ra addresses the perception of blackness in society, "Such tales and tales that are told / Are not my myths / But other myths of black mythology," and Ra denounces these presuppositions as not being his own.[29]

Some ~~free jazz~~ musicians, like Ornette Coleman, felt that their role was minimized in music. As Coleman explains, "I still have that 'black jazz' image; I'm an entertainer who's suppose to exist on a certain level and that's it."[30] As he noted, a singularly "black jazz" image assumes a monolithic treatment of the black aesthetic. Along those lines, it is interesting to note that ~~free jazz~~, as a black art, has been used to expose the repression of African Americans while, at the same time, representing the rise of avant-garde musicians supported by white critics and listeners. For example, critic and historian Gunther Schuller asked Ornette Coleman to perform at the Tanglewood Music Festival, which led to Coleman's job at the Five Spot in New York City. This connection instantly propelled Coleman to recognition and allowed him to bypass the arduous years of climbing the musical ladder from the bottom up. It is worth noting that many musicians who were racially discriminated against were endorsed by certain sectors of white society.

However, Coleman's music is not considered mainstream jazz at all by some audiences, and is therefore not fully accepted by the jazz community. One could say that ~~free jazz~~ was ostracized by mainstream jazz musicians, just as African Americans were (and continue to be) ostracized by the dominant society. At any rate, the concept of freedom outside of jazz has become an organizational, symbolic, spiritual, racial, and political device within this music; all musicians are free to explore jazz outside any confining limits of society, politics, and artistry. Often the abstraction of sound in ~~free jazz~~ becomes the focus for critics and listeners, not the underlying values that construct a new image of the musician.

There was a great deal of history about ~~free jazz~~ before Coleman became one of its primary leaders. As a musical style, ~~free jazz~~ grew out of the bebop era and post–World War II era in the late 1950s. The bop combo setting, consisting of a rhythm section and soloist, became the pervasive manner of playing, while bop phrasing and chord progressions steadily progressed into more dissonant music. Much of the ~~free jazz~~ sound of collective improvisation and experimental tonality stemmed from the combo instrumentation and chromatic movement of bop. Several bop musicians exhibited some of the qualities of ~~free jazz~~ before the term was being used, include Charlie Parker, Charles Mingus, John Coltrane, and Thelonious Monk.[31] Yet, it is Ornette Coleman, along with Archie Shepp, Pharoah Sanders, Cecil Taylor, and Don Cherry, who sits atop the ~~free jazz~~ canon. Coleman expedited his philosophy of music and transferred it to jazz, thereby creating the sound that we most identify as ~~free jazz~~. His album *Free Jazz: A Collective Improvisation* was the first to designate this term for the new movement of music, just as the previous album, *The Shape of Jazz to Come*, had posed a fundamental question for the jazz world: what is the future of jazz?

Coleman's answer was his exploration into a musical style that explored creativity outside of previously established barriers. *Free Jazz* allowed Coleman to reiterate his thoughts on the improvisatory nature of jazz. By the age of twenty-nine he had established his own philosophy of music and had succeeded in creating a new style of composition. His philosophy centered on jazz as a process rather than as a performance, thereby complementing his musical style of playing. Coleman's approach to jazz and his constant reinvention of himself kept him in the forefront of new music.

Influenced by Charlie Parker, Coleman gradually pieced together his own musical style from a combination of sheer intuition and his interpretation of harmony and theory textbooks. Early in his career, Coleman moved to Los Angeles and mingled with other musicians who possessed an equally creative spark. He met Red Mitchell and Percy Heath of the Modern Jazz Quartet and recorded his first album for Contemporary Records in 1958. Around this point, he met the musicians who would shape his career: trumpeter Don Cherry, bassist Charlie Haden, and drummers Ed Blackwell and Billy Higgins. The energy and electricity that had been building around Ornette and his players suddenly exploded during a now legendary engagement in November 1959, at the Five Spot in New York. Coleman's instant popularity was also sparked by Cecil Taylor's appearance in the New York avant-garde jazz scene some two years earlier.[32] At first, Coleman won acclaim from the jazz community: members of the Modern Jazz Quartet supported him, Leonard Bernstein called him "the greatest innovator in jazz since Charlie Parker," and writers for *Down Beat*, the most popular journal of mainstream jazz, supported him by proclaiming that "Ornette is heart and soul an artist following the star of his own musical and esthetic convictions."[33]

Shortly afterward, Coleman tackled the studio and recorded *The Shape of Jazz to Come* in which he used a novel performance technique that included introducing a theme; however, he and the rest of the band would improvise *without* following the predetermined melodic and harmonic progression heard during the theme. His next album *Free Jazz* featured a double quartet, including Cherry and Freddie Hubbard on trumpet, Eric Dolphy on bass clarinet, Haden and LaFaro on bass, and both Higgins and Blackwell on drums. The session is recorded in stereo with a reed/brass/bass/drums quartet, isolated in each stereo channel and heard on opposite sides. The title track lasted around forty minutes, which was the longest jazz recording at this point in history and was instantly one of Coleman's most controversial albums. Each group of musicians tackles improvisation in a distinctively individual way, yet they still play together as a unit. One drummer plays according to the rhythm of the musicians, while the other drummer plays twice as fast or double time. During the solo sections, one musician is the focus, but all are encouraged to accompany the solo. At times, all musicians are performing the namesake of the title, a *collective improvisation*. Also, abstraction in the cover art of the album, Jackson Pollock's painting entitled *White Light*, conveys the unity found in color, shape, and the flatness of space in Coleman's freedom principle. As in two-dimensional work without perspective, no one line remains more important than the other.

Coleman's approach to music differed greatly from bebop in choosing not to use harmony and chord progressions in the traditional sense, and to confirm this point, he declined to use a piano in his rhythm section. As one listens to "Lonely Woman" on *The Shape of Jazz To Come*, one can hear Coleman playing somewhat out of tune. However, as Jost sees it, playing out of tune is relative, depending on the musical temperament. To European ears trained in equal temperament, "wrong" notes clash with the ensemble; but they may be perfectly right in another musical context, culture, or tuning system.[34] Jazz is full of bent notes, slides, and alterations

Fig. 4.1. *Free Jazz: A Collective Improvisation* by the Ornette Coleman Double Quartet, 1960.

to pitch, as with bent thirds and sevenths; Coleman just decides to interpret many of these traditional jazz idiosyncrasies in his playing. Just as abstract artists of the twentieth century chose not to represent traditional objects in the manner we are used to seeing them, so does Coleman choose not to represent music as we are used to hearing it.

Following his epic recording of *Free Jazz*, Coleman used a Guggenheim Foundation grant to write a twenty-one-movement composition for orchestra called *Skies of America*, and then in 1962, briefly turned away from performing to teach himself the violin and trumpet. In 1963, his travels to Morocco and Nigeria helped stimulate his metaphysical explorations into the equality between harmony and melody. He received acclaim when he recorded again in 1965, and found himself seized this time by the European avant-garde movement. In 1975, he founded the electronic fusion ensemble Prime Time, which incorporated as many different musical styles as

Coleman could maintain. In 1994 he won a MacArthur Foundation grant, which he used to perform large concerts intended for several nights of production.[35]

In contrast to Coleman's popularity, the introduction of free jazz into the jazz community caused alarm, especially when his recordings made in the 1950s and 1960s, that featured Charlie Haden on bass, Don Cherry on cornet or pocket trumpet, and Billy Higgins or Ed Blackwell on drums, began to circulate. Reluctance to accept Coleman's style and philosophy in jazz, apart from his music being avant-garde, was based on other musicians feeling that (1) he had not "paid his dues" (the unspoken stipulation that a musician must learn the playing techniques of those before him or her, imitate their sound as closely as possible, and struggle as an artist financially for years); (2) he disrespected the harmonic framework that became standardized in the 1950s; and (3) he could not follow the bebop approach of jazz because he rarely performed well in jam sessions that relied on technical skill and accomplishment.

Critics whose tastes were founded on mainstream jazz thought Coleman was subverting the technique necessary to become a part of the jazz community. The same John Tynan who first classified Coleman's sound as "neo-bop" after his thorough imitation of Charlie Parker[36] and in *Down Beat* hailed Coleman as a "star of his own musical and esthetic convictions," a mere ten months later wrote the following in a review of Coleman's *Free Jazz*: "Where does neurosis and psychosis begin? The answer must lie somewhere within this maelstrom of Coleman's music. . . . Collective improvisation? Nonsense. The only semblance of collectivity lies in the fact that these eight nihilists were collected together in one studio at one time and with one common cause: to destroy the music that gave them birth."[37]

This type of critical response of Coleman is typical; his experimental music remains controversial and lies outside the canon of jazz. Even today, members of the jazz community do not approve of Coleman's approach to jazz. But the transition from John Tynan's first comment to the second marks Coleman's drastic crossover from mainstream jazz to more "difficult" performances.

This transition caused many in the jazz community to reject Coleman because he seemed to be rejecting his roots both as an African American and as a jazz musician. Coleman's stance on free jazz disturbed the image of the mainstream musician of the 1950s, while at the same time reinitiating the primitivist myth of the intuitive black genius who maintains some kind of organic relationship between the production of art and himself. "If ever a modernist in jazz could be called a primitive," says Gioia, "Ornette would seem to be one."[38] He seemed to come out of nowhere and use untutored, natural skills to create a new kind of music without the traditional forms found in classical music or jazz. Even James Lincoln Collier said that Coleman "must be seen as a primitive artist."[39] Since he did not pay his dues by struggling from gig to gig for recognition, Coleman seemed to spring from outside of the jazz community, carrying with him a mystique of primitive genius that, in fact, helped him achieve his fame.

Whether consciously or not, Coleman did not reject his newfound image of jazz primitive. Instead, he summoned other musicians who shared his ideology, like Don Cherry (who used curious instruments such as a white plastic alto saxophone and toy trumpet), designed waistcoats for members of his band to wear during performances,[40] marketed himself through recordings and additional performances, and created a revolutionary philosophy to accompany his approach to music. Coleman maintained his status as the primitive, but successful, artist—or perhaps, as Gioia surmises, he owned his image as a way to separate his work from the "seriousness" of traditional Western music.[41]

Coleman's approach to jazz was unique and controversial, but his true contribution lies in his method of performance. Coleman revolutionized improvisation. Perhaps we can define his music as Leo Tolstoy defines art: it is the process of communicating an idea and stimulating a relationship between the viewer and the work of art, or in this case, the listener and the music.[42] It is this relationship, not the actual music, that frustrates, inspires, or enlivens the listener and this interaction itself becomes the work of art. The *idea* of creating anew by breaking down traditional barriers becomes the art in as much as the music itself. The moment Ornette Coleman and Charlie Haden left behind the method of organizing notes into a system of scales, modes, and harmonies that they were taught their entire life is the moment identified as the beginning of ~~free jazz~~.

The sound of ~~free jazz~~ recalls music that lacks traditional tonality, just like Schoenberg's twelve-tone row, which lacks tonality but leads to a new system of organized music: serialism. The listener, in turn, tends to focus on the contribution of the avant-garde musician rather than the recordings themselves. Within the sound of ~~free jazz~~, an image appears in our mind of Coleman and the gradual process he undertook to leaving the traditional organization of music. It is this moment that we associate with the style of ~~free jazz~~; and simultaneously following Coleman's principles, it is this moment that represents all of ~~free jazz~~.

Throughout his career, Coleman has been able to continually span different musical styles, including ~~free jazz~~, fusion, jazz-rock, and avant-garde. What made Coleman such an innovative musician were his instructions to the musicians in his band to play in a way that contributed to, or deepened, the mood of the piece. The emphasis of his music was not on the head or lyricism of the melody as a lounge singer would portray it in a hotel bar, but instead on the shift away from the standard format to a spontaneous collaboration between people. What unfolds becomes the music. As Pete Welding says, "it does not break with jazz tradition; rather, it restores to currency an element that has been absent in most jazz since the onset of the swing orchestra—spontaneous group improvisation."[43]

The texture of Coleman's playing does not sound very different from that of a standard bebop combo, but as soon as the solo begins in each tune, it becomes evident that the chord changes are no longer the foundation for the improvised section. The bending of tonality, the unified presence of each musician, and the democratic treatment of each instrument are the main differences between an improvised bebop solo and Coleman's ~~free jazz~~. Standardized improvisation, as in bebop, endangered the progression of Coleman's performance. Thus, he had to find another way to unify his music once he left the traditional methods of theme and harmonic progression. Typically, a theme introduces a predetermined set of chord sequences which then follow a pattern, but in ~~free jazz~~ "the theme very often functions merely as the purveyor of chord progressions or scales."[44]

Coleman's music goes beyond creating a new system of technique; part of the process is to interpret the emotional content of a theme. He could foster the energy of each musician to inspire further activity and create music through the collective experience of music-making. This process of "compositional improvisation," according to Coleman, actually removes "the caste system from sound."[45] No one person is more important than the other; there is no front man; everyone plays the melody and everyone can improvise at any time. Robert Palmer says in the liner notes of Ornette Coleman, *Beauty Is a Rare Thing: The Complete Atlantic Recordings:*

> Coleman is a painter as well as a musician. . . . Sometime it's more like he is visualizing a note or phrase as a three-dimensional construct . . . examined from a variety of angles. This effect is intensified when the music involves a group of players improvising collectively. Each musician is relating to and drawing from a theme Coleman has written out in advance, but each individual hears it, and plays it somewhat differently.

> And from Ornette's point of view, each contribution is equally essential to the whole.[46]

Again, the strength of his music lies not just in himself, but also in the agreed placement of the improvisation between all the musicians. He deliberately coaches each player to bring out his or her own style to achieve a total effect.

This democratic, almost utopian, method of performing is also transferred into Coleman's metaphysical quest, which he would later call the theory of *harmolodics*.

> What is harmolodics? Harmolodics is the use of the physical and mental of one's own logic made into an expression of sound to bring about the musical sensation of unison executed by a single person or with a group. Harmony, melody, speed, rhythm, time, and phrases all have equal portion in the results that come from the placing and spacing of ideas. This is the motive and action of harmolodics.[47]

Although his statements on harmolodics remain intentionally vague—so as not to limit the various interpretations discovered in the term—for the most part Coleman seems to imply that the word has three qualities. First, the philosophy of equal treatment of music should apply to each musician.[48] For example, a "harmolodic" person is someone who can adapt to all kinds of different situations, as in a musical ensemble. Second, according to Coleman's website, harmolodic music should also appeal to a combination of the senses of sight, sound, taste, touch, and smell. Third, says Coleman, it is a philosophy of music, words, colors, shapes, and dimensions, thus employing an interdisciplinary approach. Vivien Goldman adds a fourth element when she explains harmolodic musicians as those who improvise equally together, while always keeping deeply in tune with the flow, direction, and needs of their fellow players.[49] Goldman continues, "On a broader level, harmolodics equates with the freedom to be as you please, as long as you listen to others and work with them to develop your own individual harmony."[50] Even as Coleman and Don Cherry play the same theme and the same notes to "Lonely Woman" on *The Shape of Jazz to Come* album, they play it as individuals.[51] In what one might call "unified diversity," the listener can hear distinct differences in their style of playing, while at the same time noting a unified musical flow.

Ted Gioia implies that Coleman's creation of his harmolodic theory is, in part, a response to his label as a primitive artist. Coleman includes

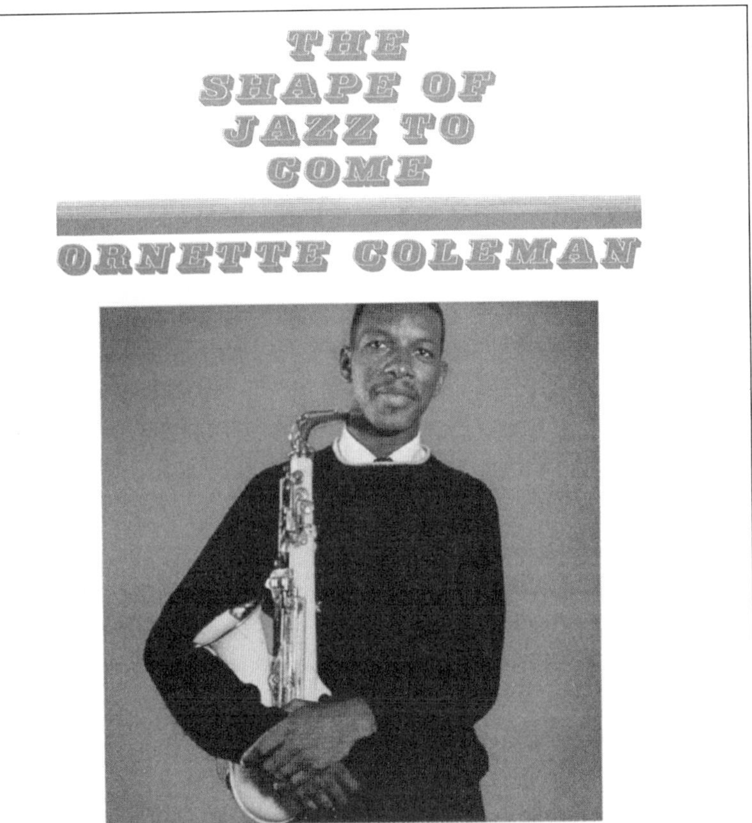

Fig. 4.2. Ornette Coleman cover art for *The Shape of Jazz to Come.*

"technical-sounding jargon" in his harmolodic theory, "which resembled, in form if not in content, the theoretical underpinnings of 'serious' art."[52] The purpose, then, could be to add another dimension to his image of the African American genius by choosing some aspects of "serious" art to include in his harmolodic theory, but leaving out aspects of the Western tradition in his music.

As another means to broaden the depth of his image, Coleman uses his idealized vision of collective happening, improvisation, and experience in his life as well as in his music, putting him in line with other metaphysical thinkers such as Coltrane and Mingus. Although we often think of the improvisatory nature of jazz as being an analogy to living life, few musicians actually establish a method of living life in order to apply it to their musical technique. Coleman said, "Let's play the music, and not the background," expressing his desire to create something art-worthy instead of a "general framework of jazz improvisation which had established itself soon after the birth of jazz as more or less the incontestable norm."[53] His application of harmolodics in other realms of his life suggests that his listeners should allow for music to be heard in other venues besides a bar or background setting. Music is no longer a method to organize sound in time; it is now a way of life. The way we play music or create art should be the way we live. Therefore, contends Coleman, his creation has proven that ~~free jazz~~/harmolodics is a combination of art and life experiences, an artistic approach to life through nonmusical effects such as philosophy, poetry, and artwork.

One of the most famous pictures of Ornette Coleman is on his album cover to *The Shape of Jazz To Come*, a photo of Coleman holding his saxophone in front of a red background. Even though this picture was included on a 1959 album, Coleman's other photographs have changed little. Most of them show him standing with a friendly demeanor for the camera with his arms relaxed by his side, or holding the saxophone in his hands, or playing his saxophone. In contrast to the images presented by Leonard's black and white photographs containing artfully posed and compositionally balanced portraits, one is forced to conclude that Coleman's picture is not presented in the same artistic manner that Leonard presents his. Coleman's photograph is not in black and white, nor is there any indication of the setting. He is not symbolizing anything other than himself, nor does the picture indicate the nature of his music or personality. It is uneventful, unenlightening, and offers little visual pleasure or visual stimulation that would lead one to examine Coleman or his music further. And in this case, the visual depiction of the jazz musician indicates little if anything of the avant-garde.

On the other hand, what Coleman's image does provide is an honest look into the man who made such a huge contribution to the music world. He stands unassumingly and appears frail and thin, and the photograph is not doctored in any way to enhance his frame. His appearance does not present him as an artist, and the only indications given that determines his occupation are his saxophone and the fact that he is on the cover of his own album of musical recordings.

In examining Coleman's photograph, it becomes clear that the visual image of avant-garde musicians is not as noteworthy, nor are they marketed in the same manner as the black and white photographs of mainstream players. No "great" jazz photographs of avant-garde musicians stand out in the mainstream media, which is rather ironic, since ~~free jazz~~ succeeded bebop quickly in the late 1950s. So is the lack of a standardized photograph because there are no great photographs of avant-garde musicians, or is it simply easier to market the image as well as the music of more mainstream

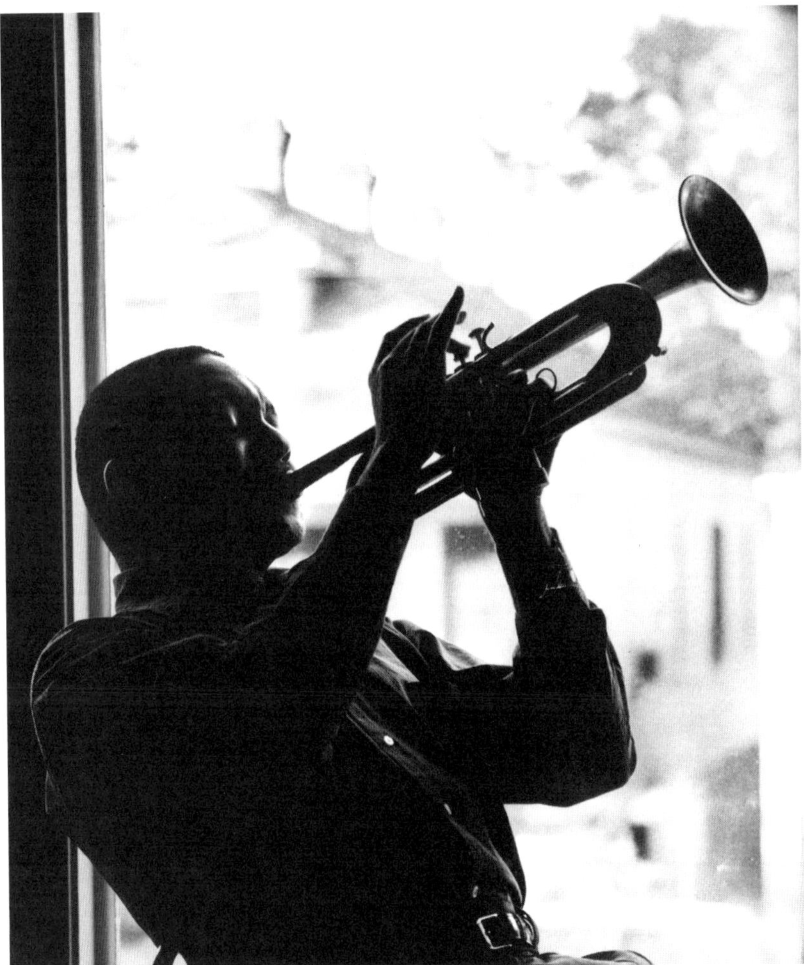

Fig. 4.3. Wynton Marsalis, New Orleans 1993, code #WYM02, by Herman Leonard. © Herman Leonard Photography LLC/CTSIMAGES.COM.

players? Perhaps the timing of photography and the ever-broadening range of jazz styles do not coincide with those musicians who emerged during the avant-garde period. Leonard turned to commercial photography, because it was impossible to make a living as a jazz photographer, although many of his contemporaries kept flashing away. Leonard did, however, photograph jazz musicians when they were on tour in Europe and when he could break from his commercial schedule to hear them. When he returned to New Orleans decades later, he continued where he left off although his recent photographs have not yet achieved the same notoriety as those he took in New York City during the 1940s and 1950s.

So why are the visual images of avant-garde players not as stimulating or profitable as their more tonal-sounding contemporaries? Does this mean that photographers like Herman Leonard and Ole Brask did not consider free jazz as important as bop? Or was the idea of Coleman (as with other free jazz musicians, such as Cecil Taylor and Eric Dolphy) becoming part of jazz history so far beyond the comprehension of the community at the time that their pictures were not considered valuable? Part of the answer may lie in the section already discussed on the reception of Coleman's music. He seemed to have waltzed into the spotlight while many hard-working traditional musicians scrambled to make ends meet. The fact that he did not "pay his dues" or have to struggle financially devalued his legitimacy in the eyes of jazz purists, not to mention the fact that his music never followed the traditional practice of jazz.

By no means does Coleman's visual image indicate the way avant-garde musicians want to be represented. As seen in Jan Persson's photograph (see Fig. 4.4) of ~~free jazz~~ and experimental musician Sun Ra, other avant-garde musicians do wear their musical image on their sleeve. By comparing neo-classicist Wynton Marsalis's photograph (see Fig. 4.3) to Sun Ra's, one can uncover a purposeful distinction between the two artists. Marsalis plays his trumpet in front of a brightly lit window. Dressed in a button-up shirt, his face is only partially lit by light that cascades down onto his face from what appears to be a window. Triumphantly, the bell of the trumpet points upward in a diagonal line, out into the world, as if his music is being given to the audience of his own free will. Confident, poised, with no other visual stimulation to detract from his playing, or the trumpet, or himself, his eyes are closed in concentration in order to put all visual distractions away. The play of light upon dark, brightness upon shadow, creates an image of him as a beacon of music, beaming the sound out into the air just as a lighthouse beams its own light to a wandering ship. The house, lit by the afternoon sun in the background, is reminiscent of New Orleans, which reminds the viewer of the economic oppression and struggling community that birthed jazz. The photograph was taken before the effects of Hurricane Katrina; but even so Marsalis, poses as the leader of victory and truth, before the storm as well as after. His presence is classical, like a Greek statue, perpetuating his talent as a musician by having the viewer watch him play his trumpet.

In vivid contrast, Sun Ra glows with shimmering light that radiates from his head to his face. The background gives no indication of location; therefore, we are forced to focus entirely on his head. The metallic cap, often worn by Sun Ra on stage, strikes us as a pulsating crown of light. Plastic

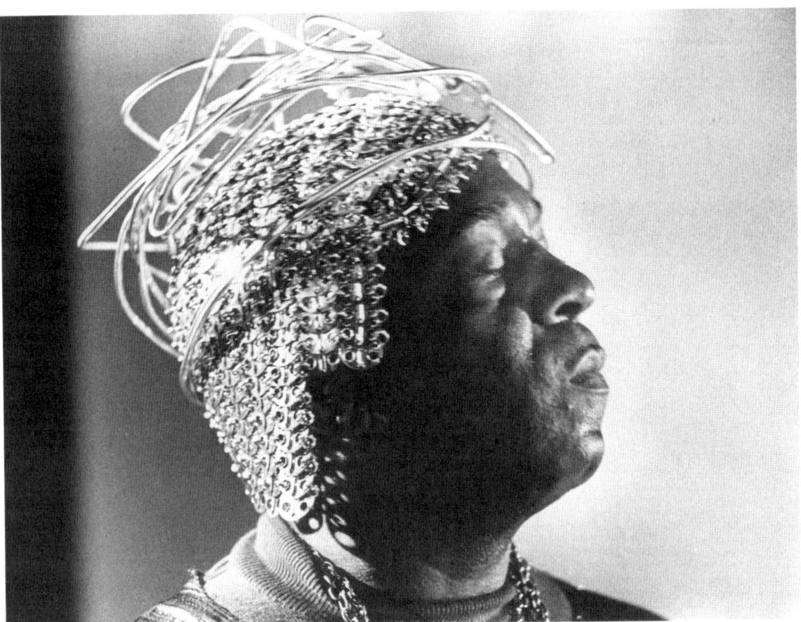

Fig. 4.4. Sun Ra, Berlin Jazz Tage, October 1970, by Jan Persson. © Jan Persson/CTSIMAGES.COM

tubes circle around his head like Medusa's serpents, while our eyes follow the lines down to his face. A strong light source shines directly onto his hat, casting a shadow on the side of his face. He sits in meditative thought, calling forth some muse of artistic creation; his thinking cap of metallic material balances on his large head like a bird's nest on a limb.

His pursed lips recall the embouchure of a horn player, as if the photo was taken a moment before Ra blows a trumpet to herald soldiers in an army. Similarly, the chain links in the hat resemble armor from medieval knights riding on horseback. The jutted posture of his neck and shoulders establish a feeling that we are in the presence of a champion, one who commands honor and respect. Whereas Marsalis is projecting the sound from his horn, Sun Ra is beaming the sound out of his head with his eyes closed in cosmic reflection. Light that baths his face and head in serenity symbolizes Ra's creativity. We assume he is contemplating about music, although there is no indication that that is the case. Metaphorically, he is channeling his music from its source of inspiration: his head. Neither his hands nor his body are in the picture. There is no sign of the instrument he plays, the piano, nor is there a hint of sternness in his face.

Sun Ra lives up to his name comically, indicating that the viewer should enjoy his theatricality, as in the album *Space Is the Place*, and his outrageous musical antics in ~~free jazz~~, fusion, Latin, rock, and mainstream jazz. When comparing these photographs, it becomes clear that avant-garde musicians like Sun Ra want to be seen as different from the norm; they prefer to be racy and imaginative. Their image may represent their music as nontraditional. As seen in the example of Sun Ra, some musicians allow their image to express any component that makes them unique in order to create a lasting memory, even a comical or provocative one.

Although these two pictures are by different photographers with very different styles, they do have some things in common. First, both are black and white images of musical figures; second, both seem to focus on light and dark, although in different modes; third, both emphasize a single human musical figure in the foreground; and fourth both are seen in vertical profile. As the three previous chapters have emphasized, black and white photographs of bop musicians are a stable component of the jazz community. They represent the truest sense of jazz where the general public is concerned. But one may conclude that the image of avant-garde musicians, like those of Coleman and Sun Ra, are characterized by their nontraditional contributions to jazz. Like their music, they are defined by what they are not. And they are not mainstream; therefore, their images cannot be equated with images of mainstream jazz. Their image relies more on the qualities that are exclusively avant-garde. They must create their own image, and the means by which they do so anticipates the jazz community's concept of the avant-garde. We expect them to behave uniquely, which forces them to satiate our appetite for difference. In some instances, shock appeal is an attractive way to gain attention, but it runs the risk of falling into the realm of popular music. Avant-garde musicians must remain different, but artful, in order to gain any credibility among critics and supporters.

It is well known that establishment of the Association for the Advancement of Creative Musicians (AACM) in Chicago in 1965 strove to inspire originality among their contemporaries. The first generation of these musicians including Anthony Braxton, Joseph Jarman, Kalaparush(a) Maurice McIntyre, Muhal Richard Abrams, and Lester Bowie experimented with layers of sound, especially with the treatment of aural space and rhythm in music. In the minds of these artists, music is found in the distribution of tension and the release of sound—which assumes that any style of music, including jazz, contains the potential for new expressions outside the traditional methods of performance. In fact, members of the AACM began their own revolution of performance practice by performing without the constraints of time or tonality. Thus through experimentation, these Chicago musicians were able to advance music to a different plane, while at the same time, broaden their realm of creativity in the arts outside of music.[54] For example, Muhal Richard Abram, Joseph Jarman, and Roscoe Mitchell wrote spoken text and often performed songs that included the sound of the human voice as an instrument; Jarman is known for incorporating theatrical settings to go along with his improvisations. In their group dynamic, music composition becomes a multidimensional activity by injecting other art forms into recordings and performances. In this manner, the AACM not only becomes a vehicle for further forms of expression in the arts, but also creates new versions of the jazz image, as we will see shortly in the combination of music and poetry in Muhal Richard Abrams's *Levels and Degrees of Light*.

Musicians of the first generation of the AACM, such as Braxton, Jarman, McIntyre, Abrams, and Bowie, lived in the South Side community of Chicago where most had worked with Abrams in his Experimental Band. The formation of the AACM in 1965 into a nonprofit organization chartered by the State of Illinois uncovered the desire to unify, to expose, and to showcase their original music. Consequently, the emphasis was not on jazz per se, but on the freedom to create different kinds of original music sponsored by the group. Now, as a unified whole, the AACM organization could proceed with its own endeavors.[55] In an interview with John Litweiler in 1975 Muhal Richard Abrams, the co-founder of the AACM, said:

> The AACM inspires musicians to band together to do what they do, because otherwise it wouldn't be done. . . . From what they've told us, we've commanded the respect of musicians all over the world . . . not so much because of the music itself, but the idea. It's not so much what is or isn't done; it's the idea and what it could mean to different groups, depending on their energy. The idea: to pool our energies together to a common cause.[56]

Although many other groups of jazz musicians were forming all over the world in the 1960s, the establishment of a nonprofit organization for the performance, cultivation, and production of original music set the AACM apart from others. The AACM members see themselves as having been transformed into "new, community stars who reaffirm the essence of 'the art of jazz[.]' . . . The legacy of the AACM and its finest musicians has ultimately become a metaphor for the durability of jazz as a whole, even as the artists themselves challenge, both rhetorically and artistically, classicist labels and style-specific categorization."[57]

By establishing their own set of values as a part of their approach to music, the AACM members set an agenda, based on the social and musical conditions of the time, and emerged to represent "a legitimate challenge to mainstream conceptions of artistic value and stylistic continuity."[58] It is this collective agreement to establish an organization whose main purpose is to promote creative/original music that gives the AACM its memorable power. AACM members have grown beyond their Chicago South Side grass roots project. These musicians offer their music as a gift to the public, and their effort comes across as noble and sympathetic. Ekkehard Jost comments that

> What is revolutionary about this program is not only what it sets out to do, but also the fact that it was created by jazz musicians, particularly by a group which had always thought of itself as a fringe group of society (society itself thought so too). For jazzmen, any organization beyond what was absolutely essential for playing in an orchestra or a combo, was normally a concession to a bourgeois style of behavior, and that they did their best to avoid by non-conformity.[59]

In the acclaimed book *Free Jazz*, Jost correctly suggests that the establishment of Chicago as the hotbed for experimental jazz was not based on its geographical location alone, especially since the Art Ensemble of Chicago, with its members from the AACM, grew to fruition in Paris and found more accepting listeners in Europe.[60] Instead, as Jost notes, the roots of jazz stemmed from the reaction of the New York scene, which was and continues to be a competitive scenario for musicians. "There was a unifying bond from the outset, in that the musicians were members of a larger organization and renounced all claims to individual fame."[61]

As Jost says, the image found within the collective unit of the AACM does not necessarily consist of one individual. Since the group identifies itself according to the contribution of all members, the type of jazz image found in the photographs of Herman Leonard does not fit the multidimensional components of the AACM. Their title contains no mention of "jazz." Initially the AACM adopted the motto "Great Black Music: Ancient to the Future." This emphasized their connection to ancient African music, the root of jazz. Another reason in organizing the AACM—besides establishing a healthy environment for creative musicians to compose and perform and a social environment to teach music to others—was an attempt to escape traditional means of categorization. Even though many of them were trained in the field of jazz, they preferred not to be confined solely within that genre. They exist as a collective unit rather than as a group who performs a similar style of music. Thus, they leave behind not only the traditional sound of jazz, but the traditional image as well.

As we have seen earlier in this book, most visual images of jazz focus on one musician. There may be other musicians in the picture (as with Leonard's photos of Dexter Gordon and Max Roach), but the scope of the photograph concentrates on the individual. The talent and visual appeal of Gordon, Gillespie, Sinatra, Ellington, and the elusive Lester Young are solely attributed to their personal innovation and technique. By contrast, those aspects of the AACM that make them extraordinary are what unite them together as a cohesive unit. There is no single director, no individual who leads by example. There are those who organized the group such as Abrams; but once he gathered other interested musicians into his collective, Abrams stepped back from any executive title with the organization and encouraged collaborative musical happenings to take place among its members. This distribution of power to all members of the AACM cannot compete with the hero worship much associated with jazz and other musical styles. The image of the solitary jazz musician cannot be spliced into sections. Thus, visualization of the AACM, as an avant-garde group, requires one to include their multifaceted identification.

The sound of jazz is often simplified into a traditional blurb or blip over the radio or television. The average person, familiar enough with the sound of jazz as a musical style, may be able to recognize some musical qualities that are discernable as jazz. These qualities are distinguishable according to two groups: big band swing music, or smaller bebop combo consisting of rhythm section (drums, bass, piano or guitar) and soloist (saxophone, trumpet, clarinet, or trombone). But the avant-garde does not use the traditional instrumentation found in jazz. Like Don Cherry's toy trumpet and Ornette Coleman's plastic alto saxophone, AACM musicians include small, often African instruments into their playing. Plus, they often dress in African clothing when performing, emphasizing their ties as African Americans to Africa. Members did not ignore instruments associated with jazz like the saxophone, trumpet, drums, and piano, but played them in a way not reminiscent of the traditional sounds of jazz—thereby detaching themselves from the image of the black man playing the saxophone, piano, or trumpet.

Because of their need to reject categorization and traditional jazz instrumentation, the AACM purposefully severed their ties with the jazz image. But, as mentioned before, their need to exist independently from the jazz image merely thrust another preconceived image upon them: that of avant-garde artists. If they experiment with musical production, we, as an audience, expect their behavior to be as different as their music. We anticipate pocket trumpets, small drums, and such from them, and, as a result, they remain attached to our conception of the avant-garde.

The music that came from the AACM is identifiably different from all other forms of music in its formalist properties. Of all the arbitrary terms used to describe the musical style of the AACM, the ones that have stuck in the minds of the scholarly community are avant-garde and ~~free jazz~~. But the music of the AACM has in the past been incorrectly labeled as ~~free jazz~~. AACM members do not designate their music as such, primarily because most artists do not want to be identified with just one style, and as Lester Bowie says, "Our shit is beyond the people who are trying to define it."[62] However, the ~~free jazz~~ designation is frequently associated with the music of the AACM because of their experimentation with improvisation, lack of traditional composition methods, the absence of tonality, and collective improvisation. These same qualities are found in Ornette Coleman's style of ~~free jazz~~ discussed in the previous section.

The first recording by the AACM was significant, an album entitled *Sound* featuring Roscoe Mitchell, Lester Bowie, and Malachi Favors, with drummer Robert Wilson. Their first album drew from the influential "energy music" of Cecil Taylor, Albert Ayler, and John Coltrane, who sought release from rhythmic and harmonic constraints.[63] These musicians distorted the sounds produced by traditional instruments and then totally reinvented the function of sound through the kinetic and psychological energy felt between the musicians at the moment of its creation. In free improvisation, musicians work collaboratively, similar to any other musical group, by playing off one another's sound. For instance, Mitchell might produce a large burst of energy through his horn, which might be imitated by Bowie, but Bowie will not play the same passage in the same key. The energy is intuitive rather than audible, and the energy is communicated to other band members as well as to the audience.

For Mitchell and the other Chicago musicians, kinetic energy is a way of achieving new forms of organization; yet they pursue several innovative possibilities, one of which is the exploration of temporal time and aural space to create an atmosphere of sound rather than structured music. For instance, instead of using traditional forms of composition such as meter, beats, and time signature, they choose to improvise their own rhythm that follow the natural and suggestive rhythmical energy radiating from one to another. Abrams phrased it well in response to a question on his 1995 release entitled *Song for All*:

NATE CHINEN: One of the most striking things about *Song for All* is the way in which each song adheres to a single compositional voice.

ABRAMS: It's like riding on a train, I guess. If you're on Train Z, then you're on Train Z. It has its pace, and its atmosphere. . . . If I played Body and Soul, I would play the atmosphere of Body and Soul. Now, it goes further than that, because, doing improvisation, it introduces new types of space within the space. But I think you're referring to the overall flavor. It's simply that you try to adhere to the vehicle that you're dealing with. Otherwise everything would sound the same.[64]

The musicians who perform *Sound* emphasize the coordination and synthesis of spatial events, time, and sound, all of which create a principal unifying device for the musicians to follow. In fact, the innovative and radical Mitchell quartet sought other ways to unify their music. During some performances poets read aloud or a player dressed up and acted dramatic roles on stage. John Litweiler recalls how "a player in a Lyndon Johnson mask would appear, bowing and gesturing grandiosely—Mitchell would demolish him with a custard pie. One concert opened with Favors playing a banjo, while drummer Abdullah Yakub (Leonard Smith) danced with a huge Raggedy Ann doll, and Wilson stalked him with a shotgun. . . ."[65] In pre–Frank Zappa fashion, the Mitchell quartet accentuated the visual spontaneity of their music. Their play on color—both visually with staged movements and costumes for the players and audibly with provocative improvisation and experimentations with rhythm—encouraged other musicians to follow this creative path, as seen with the Art Ensemble of Chicago and the Anthony Braxton Trio.

One very important addition to the music of the AACM was its treatment of poetry. Similar to how music is used, their handling of text is broadened beyond its typical role as the narrative of the song. For instance, the marriage between poetry and music is now a cliché, with a vocalist singing the written text and the instruments in the background, but members of the AACM placed their chosen text side by side with the other instruments. Typically, words appear at the forefront of the band, both visually with the singer in front of the instrumentalists and figuratively with the text dictating the "verse-chorus-verse-solo-chorus" order of the song.[66] However, members of the AACM treated the text as a separate unit in conjunction with the music.

For instance, Muhal Richard Abrams recruited Thurman Baker, Anthony Braxton, Charles Clark, Gordon Emmanuel, Leroy Jenkins, Leonard Jones, and Kalaparush(a) Maurice McIntyre to perform on the 1967 release *Levels and Degrees of Light* on the Delmark label. Although Abrams is often reticent about his own music, this album purposefully places the experience of the album as created by Abrams in its totality well above appreciating the actual recorded sound.[67] He introduces the album by writing his own text punctuated with ellipses that create breaks between words that recall each song in the album: "My Thoughts Are My Future—Now and Forever," "The Bird Song," and "Levels and Degrees of Light." Much like e. e. cummings's word placement, the spacing between words in the liner notes simultaneously disrupts and connects the flow of thoughts of the reader, and forces one to pause and become actively engaged in connecting the previous word to the next, thereby inviting various interpretations of the phrases. Such phrasing has the added advantage of creating a repeated rhythmic effect. At the onset, the reader is unsure of the poem's relation to the album other than the inclusion of the title, but the purpose clearly is to enhance the experience of the album. Thus it becomes a statement by Abrams which introduces the album, while simultaneously existing as a separate art form independent of the music. There is no other reference to Abrams's statement in the music or in the liner notes.

The second track, entitled "The Bird Song," is a wonderfully complicated work of art. A series of sounds and "ornithological allusions" are created, recalling an abundance of composers such as Charlie Parker (whose nickname "bird" reflected his playing style that simulated a bird in flight and his composition "Yardbird"), Eric Dolphy (who also simulates the flight of a bird), and Oliver Messiaen (who transcribed many bird chirpings to include in his modern classical compositions).[68] After a minute of free improvisation, the music stops and the words "Birds and prophecy" begin what appears to be a spoken poem by Amus Mor (David Moore). Although the poem is meant to be heard in relation to the song (and credit is given on the album to the "poet" David Moore), it is not referenced or written out in the liner notes of the album. Why not? After looking for the additional meanings often sought within traditional forms of art, one must conclude that this is not meant to be poetry after all. The voice proceeds through time along with the other instruments and is utilized as another instrument. But the words do not rhyme, nor does the sentence structure represent a traditional narrative, nor is the text spoken in stanzas, but rather, the poem contains its own space and timing, having been chosen for its own timbre and sound production independent from the rest of the music.

As cummings rearranges syllables and letters to form new meanings in poetry, so do Moore and Abrams rearrange words and notes to create new meanings in music. In this manner, the text peppers the soundscape, as alliteration found in literature, while functioning as a single unit with the music. Word and note are both prominent in the creative effort and separate in their purpose. Moore's voice and words on the recording create another sonority in the music, just as one experiences a different perception by viewing the artwork found on the cover of the album.

Abrams includes his own visual reference with abstract paintings (see Fig. 4.5). In a rare interview with Abrams, Nate Chinen asked, "Your paintings have appeared on the covers of many of your albums. To what extent do tonal colors figure into your compositions? I often find myself using that metaphor with your music." Abrams responded with a brief glimpse into his thoughts:

> Well, that's fine, because I don't think there's a real difference except in how each medium is administered. There's color in painting, there's rhythm in painting, and tone, and it parallels the same situation in music. So the correlation or the use of the same parameters or properties in both media is a natural phenomenon. And I think that's more or less where everything comes from—it's a natural situation. I paint because I love to paint. I play music because I love to play music. So it all is coming from an individual creative action.[69]

Chinen's question on visual and aural media, an artistic version of synesthesia, echoes the broader theory of harmolodics by Ornette Coleman. As mentioned earlier, Abrams and other members of the AACM do not see a difference in word, note, line, or color; each can be used democratically to express something since "the use of the same parameters or properties," says Abrams, "is a natural phenomenon."

While words, music, and cover art function together as one final product, they also establish three different experiences of art. The album acts as a prism refracting various exposures of aural and visual elements into a unified goal: the production of original art. *Levels and Degrees of Light* is treated similarly to light itself; it is reflected, refracted, bent, and arrayed. Of course, the album does not spell out the intentions of the musicians, poet, or Abrams; it is left to the listener to find his or her own meaning. Abrams and other ~~free jazz~~ musicians present various "levels and degrees" of art through sound, image, and/or word, yet it is not their purpose to indicate how to interpret them. The lack of direction may frustrate a listener; yet this frustration is a valid reaction precisely because it is one type of reaction. Again in reference to Tolstoy's definition of art, even the lack of a reaction

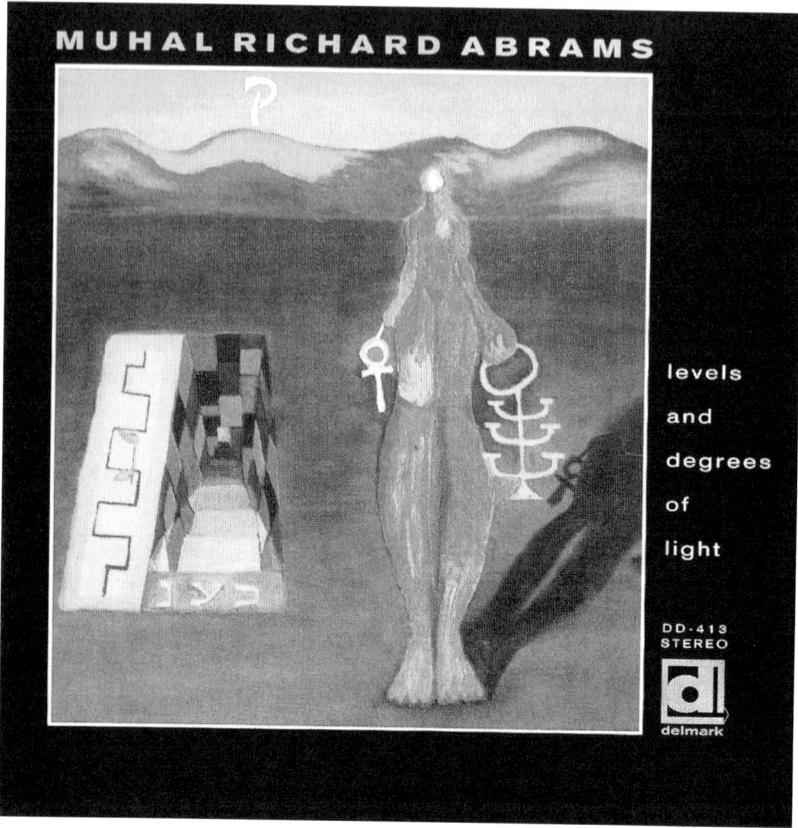

Fig. 4.5. Cover art of *Levels and Degrees of Light* by Muhal Richard Abrams.

is, nonetheless, a reaction, and any meaning achieved by the listener is a self-imposed meaning inspired by the album. Music is the impetus, but the listener is the creator.

The more common way of utilizing text with typical instrumental music would be to have each art form function together to create an artful product. So we observe that Charles Mingus wrote *Scenes in the City*, which contains both poetic story line and music, to depict a musician's life in New York City. Previous uses of a text in music or associations with a certain idea for jazz, as with Langston Hughes's *Weary Blues* or Coltrane's *A Love Supreme*, bring to mind the elaborate program music of the Romantic era. With this concept, musicians provide the listener with an extra-musical image that accompanies the music. In *Levels and Degrees of Light*, both text and sound are used as abstractions. The combination of words is abstract, and they create illogical, disjointed abstract images in the mind; the music, also abstract in sound, similarly creates a connection between space and the production of sound. The inclusion of a text in music does not have to present a specific meaning even though some may interpret its inclusion as doing so. "Blending references to ancient Africa with poetic images of life on the South Side, Moore's reading transcends the isolation of history to promote an exalted sense of blackness."[70] One hears the words as they are read, just as one hears the notes as they are played. The incorporation of this verbal sound, even if abstract, is an important creative element in Abrams's music. His work, along with that of the AACM, explores a broader spectrum of meaning by presenting three narratives—music, art, and poetry—without instruction. The liner notes do not have to be an instruction booklet, holding the listener's hand through each track. Instead, the art cover, text, and sound coalesce into a totally new, multidimensional artistic experience for the listener.

Indeed, other forms of text with music can be seen in the AACM-influenced Art Ensemble of Chicago's *Bap-Tisum*, in the spoken grunts and growls of the musicians recorded on stage at the Ann Arbor Blues and Jazz festival in 1972. It is a conflation of Lester Bowie's poetry, speech, preaching, smears, stabs, and vocalisms of all sorts, says Steven Smith after the re-release of the album in 1998.[71] Lester Bowie literally leads the call to sound with African drumming, setting a pace for the rest of the music. The third track, entitled "Immm," begins with bleatings and guttural noises that imitate the percussive gestures heard before. Then, incited by a rattle or drum roll, the musicians imitate a call and response based on syllabic humming "ummmm, ummmm, ummmm; the moon says, the flowers they cry all day." Here, the words are as abstract as the sounds of the instruments that lead the other musicians through the energy of the human voice, as seen when Bowie howls into the air and spurs greater response from the musicians. Then, he barks and yips like a dog, punctuating the air with dotted rhythms. The slower groaning of "ummmm," brings to mind the painful moans of African slaves working in the heat of the American sun. The great mixture of timbres and colors create an amazing array of sounds in five minutes. But one must be careful not to view such innovations as shock for the sake of shock value; the goal is a rejection of the rules for the sake of unrestricted music, not for the sake of sensationalism (although it helps).

With musicians such as Charles Mingus, poetry is used in the form of storytelling to reflect African American customs often associated with characteristics of jazz. But with members and followers of the AACM, the search for originality and the creation of an atmosphere in music becomes the primary goal over the formation of a narrative. Poetry may maintain its role as poetry, but without a traditional sequence of introduction, event, place, meaning, and ending. With Abrams's *Levels and Degrees of Light*, the addition of text to music is taken to a new level. Now, the listener must focus on the sound of the word as an instrument woven into the musical fabric, enhancing the artistic experience completely, instead of the traditional use of language as an organized system of words to form a coherent thought. It is the pursuit of creative, original art that demands our attention. Words are independent forces, similar to the way Anton Webern uses each individual note in a twelve-tone sequence. Each musical note, then, acts as an exclamation mark, punctuating our ears with a dramatic expression of artistic imagery. Abrams wants the listener to create his or her own meaning without the composer assigning meaning to the music.

A recording of taped or digitized music projects only one side of the musician's talents and personality. The musician in a recording has a fixed authorship, and like the author of a book, the musician continues to live, thrive, and authorize other documented media long after the recording is finalized. Roland Barthes labels this fixed authorship the "death of the author."[72] Even though the author is the primary voice of the written material, the author cannot respond to any thoughts or comments by the reader. Similarly in jazz, the recording acts as an authorized document, encapsulating the events that occur at a certain time in a certain place. Whatever is captured in the music becomes associated with the musician, and it is the receptor that determines the credibility of the recording, not the creator. In addition, the recording allows the listener to project his or her own thoughts and opinions onto the artist.

But the best way to experience avant-garde music (or any music, for that matter) is live performance, which produces a total involvement and, in effect, changes the entire reception for the listener. The listener plays more of an active role in the performance just by being there and absorbing the sound waves. A recording cannot capture the tense air between performer and audience, nor can it capture the effect the performance has on either as they mentally search for meaning in the music. As David Borgo says in his study on free jazz: "These artists and authors seem to agree on two points: (1) an audio recording, no matter its fidelity, necessarily reproduces only a limited spectrum of the performance experience, and (2) the act of listening to improvised music away from its initial performance context and on several occasions forever alters its meaning and impact."[73] A recording cannot re-create the atmosphere in which it was produced. And Gunther Schuller correctly indicates that a recording of a jazz improvisation is not meant to be definitive.[74] Yet in order for the recording to be marketed, music critics and aficionados must prescribe labels to the music on the recording—labels like avant-garde and ~~free jazz~~.

The author had the chance to see several avant-garde concerts featuring Anthony Braxton, Oliver Lake, and Ornette Coleman. One in particular stood out from the rest: AACM members Muhal Richard Abrams and George Lewis performing in Chicago in March 2006. The concert was over an hour long and consisted of one piece. Abrams sat behind a bright grand piano. Lewis resembled a helmsman conducting flight patterns at mission control, with an electrical board full of computer equipment and his trombone by his side. Attached to his trombone was an electronic device that created supersonic effects to any sound that came out of his instrument. In addition to a host of echo, reverb, distortion, chorus, harmony, and other musical effects made to enhance the timbre of his trombone, he also created sounds, with the aid of his computer, completely different from that of a brass instrument, such as swoops, swirls, cackles, and shrieking sounds that others would typify as noise. However, the "noise" did not fully consist of harsh, piercing sounds normally associated with the mechanical racket coming from a motorcycle engine, trash compactor, or vacuum cleaner. Instead, Lewis created an array of enchanting noises, ranging from a whale, calling from the depths of the ocean, to a thunderous growl heard in a heavy cloud. The sounds were not meant to resemble anything intentionally; it was up to the listener to associate meaning to the sounds being played.

The atmosphere of the performance changed after about twenty minutes; even the more patient listeners gradually began to squirm in their seats. The educated but slightly confused audience (at an Association of African American History, Research, and Preservation conference) seemed to be waiting for a pause in the music to clap in response, as is typical for any other concert setting. Rumblings and whisperings were heard, women crossed and uncrossed their legs, and men shuffled their feet and began to look at their watches. At this moment, they were lost. They found the continuous stream of sound to be awkward but were polite enough to wait for an ending. Some audience members were found closing their eyes to block out any visual simulation. They listened without looking, which one would not expect to do at a live performance.

The sound, either interpreted as noise or music, was the focus here, and the journey created by Abrams and Lewis was not meant to have a particular narrative in the sense of a beginning, middle, and end. Instead the music was presented as a continuous wave of give-and-take. The listener rode along to see where it would go. The music was unapologetic and, to most ears, agreeable. There were no harsh sounds or piercing timbres that caused a listener to wince in discomfort. Each eruption of noise carried into the next and was fed by a computer and nimble fingers on a piano. One could catch how Abrams and Lewis allotted space for each other and were careful not to overplay. The manner in which they listened to each other became an instruction to the audience on how to receive original music. Dave Liebman agrees: "In any serious art, the level of the audience's sophistication and the depth of the work presented, should be equal for maximum effect. It isn't fair to place serious, complex and abstract art in front of people who are not educated in how or what to feel."[75] Even when played in front of an informed or trained audience, "serious, complex, and abstract art" is often not enjoyed. Regardless of his/her status of education, the general listener wants to connect with the music; if it contains few possibilities of connection through traditional means, the result is a restless audience.

An audience member is conditioned to hear music as an unspoken understanding between the performer and the listener, and relate to it by aural association. In jazz, this association takes various forms such as quoting, melody, rhythm, and so forth. For example, jazz players will sometimes quote the *Flintstones* theme song over the rhythm changes if the melody complements the chord progressions of the song. In this manner, the audience can hear the quote and recognize it because they are familiar with the cartoon on television. In more avant-garde music, the listener wants desperately to find something to connect to in the music, and they will most likely have a harder time relating to it since the music is not based on familiarity of melody or tonality. Some audience members, including jazz critics, attempt to understand experimental music by comparing it to other nonconformist musical styles such as fusion, new age, or world music. Even this is an unfair comparison since both free jazz and avant-garde musicians experiment with sounds outside typical musical production. One wonders why the attempt is made to find tonal associations in a work that does not have the associations to begin with.

Further examples of society's difficulty in understanding the avant-garde or adjusting to the newness of free music lie in our conditioned ears. Tonal music is more accessible and so much a part of the norm that anything heard, played, or performed outside of what Henry Cowell calls "the black and white prison bars of the piano" is difficult to accept as music. Just as avant-garde or free jazz musicians label themselves as artists, so must the public give them license to act as artists, accepting dissonance and chaos, grunts and groans, nontraditional or modern technique—all the while fully expecting, even demanding, creative or abstract compositions for the sake of exploring new ground. If one can anticipate the lack of traditional means of expression, then it is possible to relate and react to their music.

As stated in Robinson's definition of ~~free jazz~~, lack of tonality makes this music difficult to listen to for even the most open-eared and patient listeners. In free improvisation, when a tonal moment occurs it is not necessarily intended, but it is received as a moment shared between performers. Similarly, Abrams's music, as we have examined, also lacks the tonality found in mainstream music; however, applying the term ~~free jazz~~ to the music of the AACM and the Art Ensemble of Chicago is misleading, because, by definition, the term refers only to music. The music is only one component of an album like *Levels and Degrees of Light.* The synthesis of events complete the album, but neither the AACM nor Abrams declares a correct interpretation of any of their music, except to say, "it is not music at all, it's art."[76]

In an interview with the author, Abrams declared that his music, at least, exists beyond the boundaries of traditional music, whether that is mainstream jazz or a Bach cantata. By insisting that his creations be seen as art instead of music, he can make a more aesthetic and philosophical contribution to society than merely by producing a musical recording. By pronouncing his own work as art, Abrams gives more power to the product; he includes the visual, philosophical, verbal, and spiritual components as well as the corporeal experience of the album—the mental stimulation, the physical motions of the body, and the reaction of each individual as the music is being heard.

Because Abrams's statement "it is not music at all, it's art" carries with it the broader implications of art in general, it has a much more significant impact on the history of jazz even while he tries to detach himself completely from the classification of jazz musician. This marks a trend by current musicians away from any category or movement, all the while edging toward a postmodern prospect of art.[77] Postmodernity is a relatively recent philosophical approach toward creating art that challenges assumed meanings found in everyday life and acknowledges the constant need for change. Postmodernism rejects formal properties and principles associated with creating any type of art and discounts many assumed meanings in our language, such as the terms "history," "art," and "truth."[78] No doubt the reader will notice that the postmodern argument, as so far indicated, resembles the modernist agreement as mentioned in the third chapter.

When Abrams insists on not being compared with other musicians who rely on formal technique in their music, he is exhibiting the standards of a postmodern artist, whether or not this is his intention. Postmodernists define their own identity, constructed by the intersection of gender, sex, race, and so on. They acknowledge that we all have roots, but focus on a constantly shifting sense of self which adapts to various roles that each individual plays in society. This means that one can self-proclaim their heritage and background while simultaneously stating that their heritage does not identify who they are as a person. Postmodern artists exist autonomously: they are influenced by their history and current surroundings but not necessarily joined to them. Abrams, as co-founder of the AACM, was influenced by the unity of the group and shared goals among musicians, yet the establishment of this group does not identify who he is as an artist. He exists within the group while functioning independently at the same time. Without meaning to, Ornette Coleman utilizes the same methodology. His concept of harmolodics, as an unidentifiable philosophy but one that may somehow be practiced, potentially qualifies him as a postmodern artist as well. Harmolodics in music maintains the individual contribution to a group that shares the responsibility of creating a product.

In addition, Abrams moves away from declaring a musical style and toward what Jonathan Kramer calls "a postmodern attitude."[79] Abrams does not analyze his music according to characteristics established by other players, and even seeks to separate it from other styles and to place it beyond the limitations of music itself. This act represents a change in attitude by staking a claim on one's style that exists outside of boundaries and qualifications of music. Abrams succeeds in setting himself apart as an individual and as an artist, whether or not he intends his statement to be postmodern or to make a statement with postmodern tendencies.

It is the nature of most artists to strive to venture beyond the limits placed before them; similarly, experimental and ~~free jazz~~ musicians sought to enhance certain characteristics of jazz, such as improvisation, in order to carry jazz past its tonal and stylistic boundaries. But the rejection of many listeners successfully established boundaries within the jazz tradition. In this manner, music of the 1960s and 1970s played a large role in the transitioning of jazz to its current state.

Many critics would argue that avant-garde jazz actually devalued the artful qualities of jazz that bop musicians fought so hard to establish. Without the traditional sense of tonality or melody, as found in the ~~free jazz~~ of Ornette Coleman, the jazz community claimed this sound cheapened the difficult chord progressions and theoretical puzzles that were meticulously practiced and performed by boppers at blazing speeds. Beginning with Miles Davis's *Bitches Brew* in 1969 and the fusion electronic sounds of fusion with Chick Corea and Pat Metheny in the 1970s, many jazz aficionados rejected the infusion of funk, rock, and now ethno-pop and hip-hop into mainstream jazz for the sake of preserving its status as "high art" music. Jazz musicians as far back as the swing era had fought to raise the level of jazz from its "low art" status, and fusion players who incorporated pop music were thought to lower jazz down to the category of pop music, or mere entertainment.

It seems, in general, that the plurality of jazz into other styles of music is expected if not required as the natural "development" of jazz, while at the same time, such plurality has not always been sanctioned by the jazz community. Instead, the jazz community has created an elaborate hierarchy with mainstream jazz at its center. Any study of jazz will reveal that particular stages are fostered throughout the development of a jazz student: first, start learning the blues; follow this with the ii-V-I progression; then one can tackle the progressions of "Now's the Time" or "All the Things You Are." Each level of advancement gained is predicated by how close to bebop traditions and mainstream jazz one adheres. Play like Charlie Parker in "Yardbird Suite," and you are excellent; if you are more limited in technique or a beginning improviser, you transcribe Miles Davis's solo in "Freddie Freeloader." The closer one can get to imitating the fast, dense lines of a bebop musician like Parker or the musical complexity of Coltrane, the higher one's level of performance. Therefore, this line of thinking argues, the closer one gets to the past or the era of Parker and Coltrane, the closer one gets to legitimacy and acknowledgment. Yet, ironically, if the sole agenda is to emulate Parker, then the musician must focus on imitating others instead of honing his or her own skills. Of course, not all practitioners of jazz agree. Training in any discipline requires one to copy or imitate what has come before, but if one wants to advance in the jazz community, one must dare to write or play music unlike the greats. Not only will copycats pale by comparison, but the music will stagnate, become trite, and overused ideas will reduce the world of music to the commonplace.

> . . . a lot of old jazz musicians are lazy motherfuckers, resisting change and holding on to the old ways because they are too lazy to try something different. They listen to the critics, who tell them to stay where they are because that's what *they* like. . . . The old musicians stay where they are and become like museum pieces under glass, safe, easy to understand, playing that tired old shit over and over again. Then they run around talking about electronic instruments and electronic musical voicing fucking up the music and the tradition. Well, I'm not like that and

> neither was Bird or Trane or Sonny Rollins or Duke or anybody who wanted to keep on creating. Bebop was about change, about evolution. It wasn't about standing still and becoming safe.[80]

The role of avant-garde music is to be controversial. As Miles Davis says in the above paragraph, bebop is about change and evolution; jazz, in general, is about change and should not stand still. But how does the jazz community adapt to the infusion of pop music and other idioms into the jazz tradition? What advantage or disadvantages are there through the inclusion of electronic instruments? Davis is known as one of those artists who kept reinventing himself and participated in various new types of jazz, such as the jazz-rock fusion of *Bitches Brew*. He even included pop tunes such as Cyndi Lauper's "Time After Time" and Michael Jackson's "Human Nature" on his 1985 album *You're Under Arrest.* While some critics consider the latter example to be slanderous to the name of jazz, the point Davis was making is that jazz, as a music of change, should adapt to current happenings in music. Davis embraced American popular tunes of the 1980s as well as the 1930s, and incorporated them into a jazz setting.

Why does the jazz community resist ~~free jazz~~ and experimental music since the 1960s? One of the reasons for this, I believe, is that the traditional sound of jazz as we know it with Charlie Parker or Count Basie's big band is lost to the pulsating world of popular music. E. Taylor Atkins suggests, like Scott DeVeaux, that jazz history was constructed according to those who benefit from the retelling of history.

> The primary purpose of jazz history was to identify significant figures and words, thus facilitating the construction of a canon, and establishing standards of taste for judging future works. The resulting narratives detailed a natural stylistic evolution, guided by a select handful of "geniuses" who captivated the world with the sounds they produced. Such approaches have undoubtedly succeeded in conferring aesthetic respectability and a sense of national accomplishment on the idiom, but too often at the expense of the rich social and cultural crises that concurrently shaped and were shaped by the music.[81]

Jost agrees as he discusses the individual or a small circle of innovators, who are in the front lines (the avant-garde) of musical development and who set new standards that a large army of fellow travelers accepts for their own work.[82] Hence the presentation of jazz historically is a means to rationalize the development of dance music to the level of sophisticated art music. Or as Duke Ellington says, "Let's not worry about whether the result is jazz or this or that type of performance. Let's just say that what we're all trying to create, in one way or another, is music."[83]

Conclusion

The Visual Image of Jazz

> Music is always changing. It changes because of the times and the technology that's available, the material that things are made of, like plastic cars instead of steel. So when you hear an accident today it sounds different, not all the metal colliding like it was in the forties and fifties. Musicians pick up sounds and incorporate that into their playing, so the music that they make will be different. New instruments like synthesizers and all them other things people play make everything different. Instruments used to be wood, then it was metal, and now it's hard plastic. I don't know what it's going to be in the future but I know it's going to be something else.[1]

With statements like this from his autobiography, Miles Davis hypothesizes that the jazz community—musicians, listeners, and critics—should embrace components of music that lie outside of traditional jazz composition, instrumentation, and style, even if the result does not sound like standardized jazz music. In some cases, the audience will not like the music, nor are they required to, as we determined in the last chapter. So how do members of the jazz community like Miles Davis justify developing new music knowing the public will not approve and album sales will suffer? How can new music be cultivated under constant pressure from traditionalists and the market to make jazz a marketable, and at the same time, vibrant item?

This book argues that the answer is found with the image. Both the public and the jazz community are fixated on the image of the jazz musician itself; the nostalgia, the art, and the class found within the *idea* of jazz is much too alluring to leave at this point. In particular, the image of mainstream jazz provides the viewer with a sense of class and style, and this association is often used to further market other styles of jazz. Often the image of the jazz musician, once transferred onto an advertising product, creates the same prestige for that product—such as Rolex watches, jazz documentaries like Ken Burns's *Jazz*, or the cover of *Time*. Marsalis's high-class visual image proved jazz could be marketed. The capital gain, however small, is a commodity, and the jazz community cannot afford to lose this association. Such publicity works both ways, for not only do those musicians who portray a successful musical style gain the greatest notoriety in the jazz community, but those who present a marketable visual image gain an introduction to a general public unfamiliar with jazz—who may not know what jazz sounds like, but through images of Marsalis and other visual stimuli, they know what jazz looks like.

As a mnemonic device within the public sphere, the repeat occurrence of the image in society helps to support, market, teach, and even inspire future jazz musicians. Herman Leonard's photographic depictions of African American jazz musicians created a visual image of black musicians of the 1950s, and became the standard by which the musical style of jazz from 1945 to 1959 would be represented. From the frozen faces of Dexter Gordon and Ella Fitzgerald to the still life of Lester Young's possessions, Leonard provides insight into the lifestyle of the professional jazz musician. Through his use of smoke, black and white film, lighting, framing, and compositional arrangement, Leonard simultaneously exposes the rigorous professionalism, lighthearted humor, improvised musical style, and notorious lifestyle of the jazz artist. His photographs are the epitome of class, and demonstrate the artist in front of the lens as well as behind.

As Ernie Bastin said in an interview, "the music world is now in a tonal pocket; we favor what sounds good."[2] As jazz musicians know, a rhythmic "pocket" describes the groove of the band; the drummer and bass player usually lay down a strong pulse for the other musicians to fall into. So figuratively, musicians dig deep into the rhythmic pocket; the "swing" they put in their music is a major part of the sound of jazz. When applied to tonality, Bastin's statement beautifully summarizes the taste of neoclassicists as preferring tonality to resound comfortably in our ears, much like the rest of the public and its taste for pretty-sounding music. Again, it is the image of the jazz musician that anchors us to mainstream jazz and tonality. The classic photograph represents "classic" jazz, gravitating our ears to the sound that inspired the photograph.

Leonard's photographs have become as necessary in the definition of jazz as is the music itself. His photographs act as musical ID cards of each musician, recalling the "good" time of jazz history, back when musicians fought for justice, equality, respectability, and musical creativity. In this manner, the image cast by Leonard and absorbed into society is well received, and allows the viewer to remember the sound of jazz. It acts as a catalyst for tonal, traditional jazz.

Avant-garde is not considered a style that should fit into any current category or performance practice. But we begin to wonder whether neoclassicism is falling into what Leo Treitler called the "crisis theory" of modern music, according to which a radically new style arises only in response to an impasse in the musical language, which paradoxically has literally used itself up. Is neoclassicism, as Stephan suggests, at an impasse in which the only reaction would be an entirely new formation of music, or the rejuvenation of previous avant-garde musicians such as Ornette Coleman, Eric Dolphy, Cecil Taylor, Muhal Richard Abrams and the AACM, or the Art Ensemble of Chicago? What precisely is the future for jazz? Will there be someone who states "the shape of jazz to come" as Coleman did? Will the jazz community tire of the American songbook and demand a different sound of music? Hardly, for in most instances the musicians and artists are far ahead of the rest of society. New music is already being created in various corners of the globe, but North America appears slow to latch on. Seemingly our young American ears, conditioned to what we have been taught, cannot accommodate or keep up with the new sounds available overseas. It will take time for the pendulum to swing from neoclassicism to something new, and as it did with bebop, ~~free jazz~~, fusion, and so on.

It remains to be seen whether the jazz community will embrace new components in the twenty-first century, as Miles Davis says it should, even if the results are a radical change from what had once been acceptable music. Jazz is one musical form that cannot remain stagnant; it is a music of change. Its very nature is one of extemporaneity. Yet, many seek to define jazz by a set of standards and other musical conventions that run counter to the integrity of jazz, its need for innovation, its irregularity in any production, and its hunger for variety. Jazz cannot escape its imagery of the past, as found in Leonard's photography, the musical canon of jazz, or the strong personalities of earlier musicians. One can only wonder if the future of jazz lies in its reconstruction, or if its musicians will renounce the canon and the historical premise jazz is built on in order to create something new? Is jazz relegated to be a museum piece, framed as it once was by those who best represented its vision of change and improvisation?

This study serves to expand the literature on jazz in a new direction by bridging aesthetics, music, and cultural appropriation outside of the more common biographical or stylistic analyses of earlier musical writing. Authors such as Ted Gioia, Scott DeVeaux, Eric Lott, Jim Macnie, Ingrid

Monson, Peter Townsend, Ronald Radano, Stuart Nicholson, and Philip Ford have interpreted one role of jazz as a social function in the United States. This type of scholarship expands the lens of jazz to include more than the improvisation or the musician's background; it includes the environment that jazz currently has, as well as the history, resources, and culture of musicians. Similarly, as an interdisciplinary approach, this book has explored both music and photography in an effort to expand upon their ideas. Much like Abrams's recordings, the jazz image has involved nonmusical elements to gain a greater perspective on how jazz is seen in our society.

Leonard's visual images reflect the musical sound of jazz, yet there remain many more avenues with which to explore this correlation. As Leonard grows in popularity, one may examine his other commercial photographs not directly pertaining to jazz. His professional career far exceeds the duration from 1945 to 1959; therefore, further explorations could be considered from his other photographs. Also, this investigation has focused on the images from the bebop era. A similar relationship between picture and sound could prove valuable with any style in jazz or, in fact, other musical genres.

Other areas of research lie outside the narrow scope of Leonard's photography. There are dozens of very talented jazz photographers and photojournalists who have not received the recognition they deserved. Leonard has been chosen for his popularity and for the clarity of his images. However, there are hundreds of images from which to choose, and the breadth of this correlation between visual image and jazz is endless. The jazz image itself contains hundreds of interpretations, many of which could not be addressed within the limited scope of this book. It is my hope, however, that this area of research continues to be part of the growing literature on jazz, and that through the combined efforts of scholars, including those who have training outside of music, we can reach a greater understanding of jazz and the jazz image in our society.

APPENDIX A

Herman Leonard Timeline 1923 to 2008

Provided by Geraldine Baum

1912	Leonard's parents, Joseph Leonorvich and Rose Morrison, immigrate from Yassi, Romania, to New York City.
1913	Leonard's brother Ira born.
1918	Leonard's sister Francesca born.
1920	The Leonard family moves from New York to Allentown, Pennsylvania. Leonard's father establishes Charis Corporation, manufacturer of women's undergarments.
1923	Herman Leonard born on March 6, Allentown, Pennsylvania.
1929–40	Attends Allentown Secondary and High School. High school yearbook photographer.
1935	Receives his first camera, a gift from his brother Ira, and takes his first photographs.
1935–38	Lives in Palestine with his mother and sister.
1938	First hears jazz music on the radio: "Flat Foot Floogie" by Slim Galliard and Slam Stuart.
1940–43	Attends Ohio University in Athens, Ohio; studies photography, yearbook photographer.
1943–45	Serves with the United States Army in Burma with the 13th Mountain Medical Battalion as an anesthetist. Travels in Burma and Calcutta, India.

1945	Honorably discharged from the army and resumes his college studies.
1947	Attends one of Norman Granz's traveling Jazz at the Philharmonic concerts in Columbus, Ohio, with Buck Clayton, Illinois Jacquet, Helen Humes, and Trummy Young. Takes first photographs of jazz musicians.
1945–47	Completes his Bachelors in Fine Art in Photography at Ohio University.
1947–48	Apprentice to master portrait photographer Yousuf Karsh in Ottawa, Canada. Assists Karsh in the darkroom and with sittings including Albert Einstein, Harry Truman, Martha Graham, and Clark Gable.
1948	Opens studio in New York City at 220 Sullivan Street in Greenwich Village.
1948–56	Images appear regularly on album covers and promotional material for record companies including RCA Victor, Decca, Capitol, Mercury, and Verve. Freelances for popular magazines *Look*, *Life*, *Esquire*, and *Cosmopolitan* and music magazines including *Downbeat* and *Metronome*.
1948–65	Photographs recording sessions for Norman Granz of Verve Records, who becomes a lifelong friend.
1950	Moves studio and residence to 38 East 50th Street, New York City. The special edition *Metronome Yearbook* 1950 features a sixteen-page tribute to Leonard's jazz photography, heralding him as "the favorite photographer of jazzmen."
1954–65	One of the first photographers for Hugh Hefner's new magazine *Playboy*; shoots in New York and as European correspondent.
1955	Photographs Newport Jazz Festival, including Miles Davis, Count Basie, Gerry Mulligan, Percy Heath, and Dinah Washington.
1956	Travels with actor Marlon Brando as his personal photographer, to Hawaii, Guam, the Philippines, Hong Kong, Thailand, Singapore, and Indonesia. Moves from New York to Paris. Frequents Parisian jazz clubs including Club Saint Germaine, Le Chat Qui Peche, and Club La Huchete. Photographs French musicians, including Jacques Brel and Edith Piaf, and American jazz musicians visiting Paris.
1956–60	Works as photographer for Barclay Records.

1960 Son, Mikael Leonard, born in Paris, France to mother Attika ben-Dridi.

Opens studio at 82 bis Rue Charles Lafitte, Neuilly-sur-Seine, Paris. Continues to photograph musicians while expanding his freelance career to include fashion, advertising, and film.

Works for Parisian fashion houses including Christian Dior, Yves St. Laurent and Chanel. Images published in *Elle* and *Marie Claire*. Shoots first catalogue for Girbaud.

Photographs the movie sets of *Dr. No* and *Paris Blues*, the latter featuring American musicians including Louis Armstrong and Duke Ellington.

Marries Jacqueline Fauvreau.

1961 Shoots fashion in Morocco, Tunisia, Spain, Seychelles, Canary Islands, and Greece.

1962 Daughter, Valerie Leonard, born in Paris to mother Jacqueline Leonard.

1964 Travels to Warsaw, Prague, Vienna, and London to shoot *Playboy* features: *Behind the Iron Curtain, The Girls of the Riviera*, and *The Prostitutes of Paris*.

1965 Separates from Jacqueline Fauvreau, whom he divorces some years later.

1968 Meets Elisabeth Braunlich, who becomes longtime partner. Leonard and Braunlich travel to Tunisia, Morocco, and the Canary Islands.

1970–72 Travels extensively shooting for *ER* Magazine: Hong Kong, Thailand, Indonesia, Bali, India, Kashmir, Afghanistan, Iran, Turkey, Ethiopia, Kenya, and Tanzania.

1971 Leonard and Braunlich move from Paris to London.

1972 Daughter, Shana, born in London to mother Elisabeth Braunlich.

1974 Leonard and Braunlich move from London to Paris.

1977 Son, David, born in Paris to mother Elisabeth Braunlich.

1980 Leonard and family move from Paris to the island of Ibiza. Spain.

1985 Publishes first monograph, *L'oeil du Jazz*, Editions Filipacchi, France. Receives Music Book of the Year award from the French Literary Society.

1987 Leonard and family move from Ibiza to London. Braunlich and Leonard separate.

1988 First exhibition of Leonard's jazz photographs at the Special Photographers Company, London.

1989 Moves from London to San Francisco, California.

1989 Publishes *The Eye of Jazz*, the English edition of *L'oeil du Jazz*, Viking Press.

1990 First United States exhibition tours major cities. First visit to New Orleans; attends opening at A Gallery for Fine Photography.

1991 Moves from San Francisco to New Orleans.

Extensive product line published by Graphique de France featuring jazz images.

1992–2006 Establishes a full service archive with images appearing in publications and exhibitions worldwide. Continues to shoot and expand his archive.

1995 Publishes *Jazz Memories*, Editions Filipacchi, France.

Receives Honorary Masters of Science in Photography from The Brooks Institute of Photography.

1997 Premiere of the film *Frame After Frame: The Images of Herman Leonard*, by Louisiana Public Broadcasting.

1999 Receives Milt Hinton Award for Excellence in Jazz Photography, Jazz Photographers Association.

2000 Receives Excellence in Photography award, Jazz Journalists Association.

2001 Extensive image use in *Jazz: A Film By Ken Burns* and the accompanying book and CD, *Jazz: A History of America's Music* and *Ken Burns JAZZ Collection*, respectively.

2002 Fifth of January decreed Herman Leonard Day by New Orleans Mayor Marc Morial.

Publishes *Herman Leonard: Jazz Portraits*, Fotofolio, USA.

2004 Receives Lifetime Achievement Award, *Down Beat*.

2005 Exhibits *Passport: The Known and Unknown Photographs of Herman Leonard*, Ogden Museum of Southern Art, New Orleans.

2005 New Orleans home and business destroyed during the flood after Hurricane Katrina.

2006 Moves from New Orleans to Studio City, California.

2007 Establishes the Herman Leonard Jazz Archive.

2008 The Herman Leonard Jazz Archive is awarded a Grammy Foundation grant for archiving and preservation.

Receives Lucie Award for Outstanding Achievement in Portraiture.

List of Exhibitions for Herman Leonard's Photography

Provided by Geraldine Baum

DATE	LOCATION
Jun 1988	Special Photographers Company, London, England
Feb 1989	Southampton Art Gallery, Southampton, England
Apr 1989	The Woods Gallery, Leicester, England
Jun 1989	The Old Museum of Transport, Glasgow, Scotland
Jul 1989	Royal Festival Hall, London, England
	The Concert Hall, Aarhus, Denmark
Sep 1989	The Gallery of Photographs, Dublin, Ireland
	Triskel Art Center, Cork, Ireland
Oct 1989	Gallerie Lafrache, Cannes, France
Nov 1989	City of Aberdeen Art Gallery, Aberdeen, Scotland
Dec 1989	The Corner House, Manchester, England
Apr 1990	G. Ray Hawkins, Santa Monica, California
May 1990	Barbara Gillman Gallery, Miami, Florida
Jun 1990	Fay Gold Gallery, Atlanta, Georgia
	North Sea Jazz Festival, The Hague, Netherlands

Jul 1990	Catherine Edelman, Chicago, Illinois
	Jane Corkin Gallery, Toronto, Canada
	Robert Klein Gallery, Boston, Massachusetts
Aug 1990	Robert Koch Gallery, San Francisco, California
Sep 1990	Addison Ripley Gallery, Washington, D.C.
Oct 1990	A Gallery for Fine Photography, New Orleans, Louisiana
	Camera Obscura, Denver, Colorado
Dec 1990	Brent Sikkema Gallery, New York, New York
Jan 1991	Central Cultural Caixa de Valencia, Valencia, Spain
Mar 1991	Kimballs East, Emeryville, California
May 1991	Morgan Gallery, Kansas City, Kansas
Jun 1991	Special Photographers Company, London, England
Oct 1991	Blitz Corporation, Tokyo, Japan
	Barcelona Gallery, Barcelona, Spain
Dec 1991	Morgan Gallery, Kansas City, Kansas
Apr 1992	A Gallery for Fine Photography, New Orleans, Louisiana
	Barcelona Gallery, Barcelona, Spain
	Robert Koch Gallery, San Francisco, California
Aug 1992	G. Ray Hawkins, Santa Monica, California
Sep 1992	Parco Galleries, Tokyo, Japan
Dec 1992	Kirin Plaza, Osaka, Japan
Mar 1993	A Gallery for Fine Photography, New Orleans, Louisiana
Apr 1993	Brooks Institute of Photography, Santa Barbara, California
Oct 1993	Museum of American Art, Athens, Ohio

Dec 1993 Nagoya Galleries, Nagoya, Japan

Jan 1994 De Roca Sastra Gallery, Madrid, Spain

Mar 1994 Kirin Gallery, Kyoto, Japan

Jun 1994 S. K. Josefsberg Gallery, Portland, Oregon

Oct 1994 Ven Norman Gallery, Covington, Louisiana

Aug 1994 Special Photographers Company, London, England

Sep 1996 Govinda Gallery, Washington, D.C.

Mar 1997 Louisiana State University, Baton Rouge, Louisiana

May 1997 Tatar Alexander Gallery, Toronto, Canada
Ven Norman Gallery, Covington, Louisiana

Jul 1997 S. K. Josefsberg Gallery, Portland, Oregon

Sep 1997 Carla Sozzani Gallery, Milan, Italy

Oct 1997 Fahey/Klein Gallery, Los Angeles, California
Visual Blues Jazz Galerie, Berlin, Germany

Jan 1998 Jackson Fine Art, Atlanta, Georgia

Apr 1998 Austin Jazz Festival, Austin, Texas

Sep 1998 Northwestern State University, Natchitoches, Louisiana

Oct 1998 Ohio University, Athens, Ohio

Jan 1999 Hastings College, Hastings, Nebraska

Jun 1999 Marshall Artist Series, Huntington, West Virginia

Jul 1999 Etherton Gallery, Chicago, Illinois
New Zealand Jazz Festival, Wellington, New Zealand

Dec 1999 S. K. Josefsberg Gallery, Portland, Oregon

Jan 2000	Creative Allies, Boston, Massachusetts
Apr 2000	Louisiana Center for the Book, Baton Rouge, Louisiana
	Stephen Bulger Gallery, Ontario, Canada
Oct 2000	Jazz at Lincoln Center, New York, New York
Nov 2000	High Museum of Art, Atlanta, Georgia
Mar 2001	Missouri History Museum, St. Louis, Missouri
Apr 2001	Sandra Byron Gallery, Sydney, Australia
Jun 2001	Monterey Jazz Festival, Monterey, California
Oct 2001	Walnut Street Gallery, Fort Collins, Colorado
Jan 2002	Candace Perich Gallery, Katonah, New York
Oct 2002	Commune de Padova, Padova, Italy
Nov 2002	*We Always Swing* Jazz Series, Colombia, Missouri
Jan 2003	Rupertinum Museum of Modern Art, Salzburg, Austria
Jan 2003	Oswald Gallery, Austin, Texas
Oct 2003	Andrew Smith Gallery, Santa Fe, New Mexico
Mar 2004	King Tisdell Cottage Foundation, Atlanta, Georgia
Apr 2004	North Sea Jazz Festival, Cape Town, South Africa
	Duque Arts Center, New Orleans, Louisiana
May 2004	New Orleans Jazz & Heritage Festival, New Orleans, Louisiana
Jun 2004	Ven Norman Gallery, Covington, Louisiana
Jul 2004	Gallery of the Auditorio Nacional of Mexico, Mexico City, Mexico
Aug 2004	Gallery 270, Jersey City, New Jersey

Nov 2004	Howard Luntz Photography, Palm Beach, Florida
Jan 2005	Utah Museum of Fine Art, Salt Lake City, Utah
Apr 2005	Ogden Museum of Southern Art, New Orleans, Louisiana
Nov 2005	Catherine Edelman Gallery, Chicago, Illinois
Mar 2006	Gallery One, Dubai, United Arab Emirates
Nov 2007	Fahey Klein Gallery, Los Angeles, California
Feb 2008	Morrison Hotel Gallery, La Jolla, California
May 2008	Morrison Hotel Gallery, New York, New York
	Polk Museum of Art, Lakeland, Florida
Sep 2008	Santa Monica College, Santa Monica, California
Nov 2008	Richter Gallery of Photography, Nashville, Tennesee
Oct 2009	Jazz at Lincoln Center, New York, New York
	Maison da Festival Rio Tinto Alcan, Montreal, Canada

SELECTED PERMANENT EXHIBITIONS

Smithsonian Institution National Museum of American History

Smithsonian Institution Traveling Exhibition Services (SITES), Washington, D.C.

Jazz at Lincoln Center, New York, New York

Ogden Museum of Southern Art, New Orleans, Louisiana

Houston Museum of Modern Art, Houston, Texas

American Jazz Museum, Kansas City, Missouri

Lyman Allyn Art Museum, New London, Connecticut

Pensacola Museum of Art, Pensacola, Florida

Louisiana State Museum Traveling Exhibition, Baton Rouge, Louisiana

Kennedy Museum of Art, Ohio University, Athens, Ohio

George Eastman House, *Gershwin to Gillespie: Portraits in American Music*, Rochester, New York

One Hundred Photographs: A Collection, by Bruce Bernard

His Majesty King Bhumibol Adulyadej of Thailand

Sir Elton John's photography collection

Joshua Pailet, A Gallery for Fine Photography, New Orleans, Louisiana

Barbara Gillman Gallery, Miami, Florida

The Children's Museum, Miami, Florida

Notes

INTRODUCTION

1. For example, see Mark C. Gridley, *Jazz Styles: History and Analysis*. 9th ed. Upper Saddle River, NJ: Pearson, 2006.
2. "The Images of Herman Leonard: Herman Leonard Biography," accessed, 3 June 2006, lpb.org/programs/frame/leonard.html.
3. At the Granz concert in Columbus, Ohio, Leonard heard Buck Clayton, Illinois Jacquet, Helen Humes, and Trummy Young.
4. "Images of Herman Leonard."
5. For an extensive list of Leonard's exhibitions see Appendix B.
6. *Ibid.*
7. Telephone interview with Geraldine Baum, 31 July 2008.
8. *Ibid.*
9. Herman Leonard and Philippe Carles, *The Eye of Jazz: The Jazz Photographs of Herman Leonard* (London: Viking, 1989); Herman Leonard, *Jazz Memories* (Paris: Levallois-Perret, 1995); and David Houston and Jenny Bagert, eds., *Jazz, Giants, and Journeys: The Photography of Herman Leonard* (London: Scala, 2006).
10. Geraldine Baum interview. For more information see Jennifer Odell, "The Beat: Leonard Loses Thousands of Prints, Saves Negatives in New Orleans Floods," *Down Beat* 72.12 (December 2005): 26; or Howard Reich, "Thousands of Famed Photos Ruined," Chicagotribune.com (September 12, 2005), chicagotribune.com/news/nationworld/chi-0509120262sep12,0,7792959.story, accessed 2 August 2008. Another documentary, directed by Leslie Woodhead, was released in the UK entitled *Saving Jazz*. A co-production between Sundance Channel and BBC, *Saving Jazz* chronicles Leonard's efforts to recover his materials from the flood in New Orleans.
11. Geraldine Baum interview. To aid in this process, Leonard's studio will use Microsoft-based programs, and to gain some feedback on the catalogue system, Microsoft will do a case study of Leonard's catalogue and Microsoft software that will provide a reference and further use for both parties.
12. Leonard was even honored by former President Bill Clinton, who presented a portfolio of Leonard's prints as an official gift from the United States government to a fellow musician, the King of Thailand.
13. Telephone interview with Herman Leonard's agent, Jenny Bagert, 11 September 2006.
14. Liner notes by Charles Mingus for his album *Let My Children Hear Music*, Columbia Records, 1972.

15. Peter Townsend, *Jazz in American Culture* (Edinburgh, Scotland: Edinburgh University Press, 2000), 166.
16. See for example, Roland Barthes, *Camera Lucida: Reflections on Photography* (New York: Hill and Wang, 1981); Roland Barthes, *Image, Music, Text*, Stephen Heath, trans. (New York: Hill and Wang, 1977); Susan Sontag, *On Photography* (New York: Anchor, 1989); Bernard Shaw, *Bernard Shaw on Photography* (Salt Lake City, UT: Peregrine Smith, 1989); David Liebman, *Self Portrait of a Jazz-Artist: Musical Thoughts and Realities* (Rottenburg, West Germany: Advance Music, 1988); Michel Foucault, *The Order of Things: An Archaeology of the Human Sciences*, a translation of *Les Mots et les choses* (New York: Vintage, 1970); Michel Foucault, *This is Not a Pipe*, James Harkness, trans. and ed. (Berkeley: University of California Press, 1983); Wynton Marsalis, "What Jazz Is—and Isn't," *New York Times* (31 July 1988, Arts & Leisure) 21, 24; Scott DeVeaux, "Constructing the Jazz Tradition: Jazz Historiography," *Black American Literature Forum* 25.3 (Fall 1991): 525–60; Scott DeVeaux, "Struggling with Jazz," *Current Musicology* 71–73 (Spring 2001–Spring 2002): 353–74; Scott DeVeaux, *The Birth of Bebop: A Social and Musical History* (Berkeley: University of California Press, 1997); George E. Lewis, "Improvised Music after 1950: Afrological and Eurological Perspectives," *Black Music Research Journal* 22 (2002): 215–46; George E. Lewis, "Taste Cultures and Musical Stereotypes: Mirrors of Identity?" *Popular Music and Society* 19.1 (Spring 1995): 37–58; Ingrid Monson, "The Problem with White Hipness: Race, Gender, and Cultural Conceptions in Jazz Historical Discourse," *Journal of the American Musicological Society* 48 (1995): 396–422; Ingrid Monson, *Saying Something: Jazz Improvisation and Interaction* (Chicago: University of Chicago Press, 1996); Ted Gioia, *The History of Jazz* (New York: Oxford University Press, 1997); and Ted Gioia, *The Imperfect Art: Reflections on Jazz and Modern Culture* (New York and Oxford: Oxford University Press, 1988).
17. For example, Houston A. Baker Jr., *Black Studies, Rap, and the Academy* (Chicago: University of Chicago Press, 1993); Houston A. Baker Jr., *Blues, Ideology, and Afro-American Literature: A Vernacular Theory* (Chicago: University of Chicago Press, 1984); Greg Tate, ed., *Everything But the Burden: What White People Are Taking from Black Culture* (New York: Broadway, 2003), and Kimberly W. Benston, *Performing Blackness: Enactments of African-American Modernism* (London and New York: Routledge, 2000).
18. For an example, see Gioia, *The Imperfect Art.*
19. Philip Ford, "Somewhere/Nowhere: Hipness as an Aesthetic," *Musical Quarterly* 86.1 (Spring 2002): 49–81; Monson, "The Problem with White Hipness."
20. Scott DeVeaux, "Constructing the Jazz Tradition: Jazz Historiography," *Black American Literature Forum* 25.3 (Fall 1991): 525–60; DeVeaux, "Struggling with Jazz."
21. Imamu Amiri Baraka (Leroy Jones), *Black Music* (New York: William Morrow, 1967); Imamu Amiri Baraka (Leroy Jones), *Blues People: Negro Music in White America* (New York: William Morrow, 1999); Stanley Crouch, *Considering Genius: Writings on Jazz* (New York: Basic Civitas, 2006); Frank Kofsky, "Black Nationalism in Jazz: the Forerunners Resist Establishment Repression, 1958–1963," *Journal of Ethnic Studies* 10.2 (1982): 1–27; Frank Kofsky, *Black Music, White Business: Illuminating the History and Political Economy of Jazz* (New York:

Pathfinder, 1998); Frank Kofsky, *John Coltrane and the Jazz Revolution of the 1960s*, 2nd ed. (New York: Pathfinder, 1998); Frank Kofsky, *Black Nationalism and the Revolution in Music* (New York: Pathfinder, 1970); Albert Murray, *The Hero and the Blues* (Columbia: University of Missouri Press, 1973); Albert Murray, *The Omni-Americans: New Perspectives on Black Experience and American Culture* (New York: Outerbridge and Dienstfrey, 1970); Eric Porter, *"Out of the Blue": Black Creative Musicians and the Challenge of Jazz, 1940–1995*, diss., University of Michigan, 1997; Eric Porter, *What Is This Thing Called Jazz: African American Musicians as Artists, Critics, and Activists* (Berkeley: University of California Press, 2002).

22. Baker, *Black Studies, Rap, and the Academy*; Baker, *Blues, Ideology, and Afro-American Literature*; Tate, ed., *Everything But the Burden*; and Benston, *Performing Blackness*.

CHAPTER 1

1. This activity took place on the first day of "Rock and Rhetoric: Popular Music as Communication" class before any word was spoken in the classroom. The students filled out a pre-test on different areas of music history. One of the eight questions was: "Can you describe what you think a jazz musician looks like? (instrument, clothing, appearance, etc.)." Of the twenty-eight students who answered, twenty-two gave the instrument associated with jazz as saxophone, eight trumpet, three mentioned "brass instruments," and two drums. In addition, ten provided sunglasses as part of the attire, nine mentioned that the musician was wearing a suit, and many others said they would be wearing nice or professional clothing. Six gave the gender as male, and three said he would be "older." The pre-test was taken on 25 August 2008 and continues to be utilized in each new section of this class.
2. Evidence of Leonard's popularity can be seen from his list of clients, which range from Apple Computers to Sir Elton John, his many awards, two documentaries about him, and the naming January 5th as Herman Leonard Day in 2002 by New Orleans Mayor Marc Morial.
3. Nicholas Mirzoeff, *An Introduction to Visual Culture* (New York: Routledge, 1999), 13.
4. Cawthra, *Blue Notes in Black and White*, 5.
5. Mirzoeff, *An Introduction to Visual Culture*, 5.
6. *Ibid.*
7. Martin Heidegger, "The Age of the World Picture," in *The Question Concerning Technology and Other Essays*, trans. William Lovitt (New York and London: Garland, 1977), 130; quoted in Mirzoeff, *An Introduction to Visual Culture*, 5.
8. Mirzoeff, *An Introduction to Visual Culture*, 6.
9. Much can be said of the allegory between death and university study. By the time art in any form is canonized enough to be included as a chapter in a textbook, its creative spirit is divorced from the practice of creating; it has deceased, because it no longer flourishes in its original from.
10. Sontag, *On Photography*, 21.
11. The history of photography began in 1826 in France. Joseph Nicephore Niépce found a way to produce a permanent image in a camera obscura by coating a metal plate with a light-sensitive chemical and exposing the plate in the camera for

approximately eight hours. The resulting picture, showing the view from Niépce's window, was the world's first photograph. Niépce's technique was perfected during the 1830s by another French experimenter, Louis Daguerre, who exposed an image to a sheet of silver-coated copper and saved the image onto the sheet with table salt. The process named after him, the daguerreotype, required a relatively short exposure of fifteen to thirty seconds and produced sharp, detailed images. In 1839 the French Academy of Sciences first became aware of the daguerreotype, which was not yet fully available to the public. Photography took a sharp turn York in 1840, when the first portrait studio opened in New, allowing for wide circulation and a relatively easy method of production.

12. Mirzoeff, *An Introduction to Visual Culture*, 65.
13. Cawthra, *Blue Notes in Black and White*, 21.
14. By 1896 the Columbia Phonograph Company listed a catalogue of prerecorded cylinders that contained thousands of titles ranging from marches by the Marine Band and John Atlee, to popular songs and musical comedy by Dan Quinn, love ballads by George J. Gasken, monologues by Russell Hunting, and novelty songs, or coon songs, that exploited negative stereotypes of African Americans. Reebee Garofalo, *Rockin' Out: Popular Music in the USA* (Boston: Pearson Prentice Hall, 2008), 15–18.
15. Taylor Atkins, ed., *Jazz Planet* (Jackson: University Press of Mississippi, 2003), xiv.
16. Burton W. Peretti, "Emerging from America's Underside: The Black Musician from Ragtime to Jazz," in Kenneth, J. Bindas, ed., *America's Musical Pulse: Popular Music in Twentieth-Century Society* (Westport, CT: Greenwood, 1992), 23.
17. In the 1910s, airplanes, automobiles, movie theaters, skyscrapers, vaudeville houses, dance halls, and amusement parks such as New York's Coney Island "were drawing urban Americans away from books, parlor games, and other private leisure they had enjoyed in their homes." The outbreak of the war, or course, stifled much of the joyous atmosphere and nightly celebration. Peretti, *Jazz in American Culture*, 7–8.
18. Peretti, *Jazz in American Culture*, 41.
19. *Ibid.*
20. *Ibid.*, 32.
21. Gioia, *The History of Jazz*, 31. Although it is well known that jazz originated from New Orleans, there is little documentation that jazz, or jas, came from the red light district. This common myth was probably attributed to jazz because of its provocative rhythms and negative stereotyping.
22. Jed Rasula, "Jazz and American Modernism," in Walter Kalaidjian, ed., *The Cambridge Companion to American Modernism*, 158.
23. For more information see Frederick J. Spencer, *Jazz and Death: Medical Profiles of Jazz Greats* (Jackson: University Press of Mississippi, 2002).
24. "Where The Etude Stands on Jazz," *The Etude* (August 1924): 515; "Where Is Jazz Leading America?" *The Etude* (August 1924): 517–18, 520; "Where Is Jazz Leading America?" Part II, *The Etude* (September 1924): 595, quoted in Robert Walser, ed., *Keeping Time: Readings in Jazz History* (New York: Oxford University Press, 1999), 49.
25. Reproduced on the cover of Walser, *Keeping Time: Readings in Jazz History.* The quotation can be found on page 49.

26. Another comment: "I don't object to the dances as such, for I have always enjoyed dancing; but the infernal racket that usually accompanies them, and the monkey shines of some of the performers, are enough to give even a musician of my type a chronic case of the 'jim-jams,'" Robert M. Stults, quoted in Walser, ed., *Keeping Time: Readings in Jazz History*, 41–54.
27. Peretti, *Jazz in American Culture*, 55.
28. Peretti, "Emerging from America's Underside," 70.
29. Ibid., 65.
30. Ibid., 69.
31. Interview with the author, 11 February 2009.
32. Reginald Twigg explains in his essay entitled "The Performative Dimension of Surveillance: Jacob Riis' *How the Other Half Lives*," in Lester C. Olson, Cara A. Finnegan, and Dana S. Hope, eds., *Visual Rhetoric: A Reader in Communication and American Cultur*, (Los Angeles: Sage, 2008), 21–40.
33. Peretti, "Emerging from America's Underside," 64.
34. Kenneth J. Bindas, "Race, Class, and Ethnicity of Swing Musicians," in Bindas, ed., *America's Musical Pulse: Popular Music in Twentieth-Century Society* (Westport, CT: Greenwood, 1992).
35. Cawthra, *Blue Notes in Black and White*, 25.
36. Photography also became a way of making a stronger social statement, as with Jacob Riis and Lewis Hine, or a means of altering an image to best illustrate a story for publication, a process that hardened into photojournalism. Photojournalists could now have the freedom of depicting a subject in any guise they wanted, while at the same time claiming the authenticity of the subject in real life. In 1935 the Associated Press became the world's first wire service for photographs, allowing anyone to send a photo to newspapers by telegraph or telephone. Thus, photojournalism emerged as a primary form of documentation, including the photographer's own stance or portrayal of the subject. Through an awkward start by Jacob Riis and Lewis Hine, photography grew into a voyeuristic trade by issuing photographs as documentary keepsakes of curiosity.
37. Cawthra, *Blue Notes in Black and White*, 22.
38. This remains the case today with streets and buildings named after Armstrong; postage stamps featuring his likeness have been issued in at least ten countries (Chad, Senegal, Mali, Niger, Gabon, Rwanda, Upper Volta, Dominica, St. Vincent, and the United States). The U.S. Postal Service issued a stamp in his honor in 1971, and a commemorative stamp was issued in New Orleans in 1995. Duke Ellington received his first stamp in 1986 as a part of the Black American series issued by the U.S. Postal Service. And in July 2008 the U.S. Postal Service issued a series of stamps featuring Ellington and other African American icons of jazz. On May 23, 2008, Washington, D.C., residents voted for a Duke Ellington design to go on the face of a new quarter to be released in circulation in 2009.
39. Several of these pictures were collected and later included in museums, such as the Louisiana State Museum Jazz Collection, which contains over 10,000 photographs, posters, and prints of the local music scene in New Orleans from about 1950 to the present.
40. Herman Gray, "Black Masculinity and Visual Culture," in Thelma Golden, ed., *Black Representations of Masculinity in Contemporary American Art* (New York:

Whitney Museum of American Art, distributed by Harry N. Abrams, 1994), 175–76.

41. bell hooks, "Feminism Inside: Toward a Black Body Politic," in Thelma Golden, *Black Representations of Masculinity in Contemporary American Art* (New York: Whitney Museum of American Art: Distributed by Harry N. Abrams, 1994), 131.
42. In his research, Benjamin Cawthra explains several instances in which articles in the magazine contained racial slurs, inflammatory stereotypes, and generalizations especially aimed toward jazz. See Cawthra, *Blue Notes in Black and White*, 38–106.
43. Cawthra, *Blue Notes in Black and White.* Cawthra has written on several examples of the jazz image with visual representations of jazz musicians from 1936 to 1965, and provides a phenomenal amount of historical iconography that constructs a pattern of images into a visual rhetoric of jazz. He traces the development of the jazz image in its first exposures, previously left out as historical artifacts by many other scholars.
44. Cawthra, *Blue Notes in Black and White*, 71.
45. Mili continued his dedication to jazz by making a short film in 1944, *Jammin' the Blues*, which displays his ability to project physical motion (the Lindy Hop) and music (jazz) together on film. Mili also filmed several jam sessions, including footage with Charlie Parker, Hank Jones, Ray Brown, and Buddy Rich.
46. Cawthra, *Blue Notes in Black and White*, 56.
47. Peretti, "Emerging from America's Underside," 68.
48. Cawthra, *Blue Notes in Black and White*, 41.
49. The exceptions are more memorable; one may recall the abstract drawings found on the cover art of Miles Davis's *Bitches Brew.* The sky, people, water, and flower that collide with each other sharply connect with the seriousness of the music that lies within the cover.
50. Other examples include saxophonist Benny Golson's appearance in the 2004 Steven Spielberg film *The Terminal*, swing musicians who revolted against German Nazism in *Swing Kids*, and Django Reinhardt's hovering presence in Woody Allen's *Sweet and Lowdown.*
51. More typically, jazz is used in the background of a film. But there are rare appearances of jazz musicians in movies, such as *Indecent Proposal* (1993), where Robert Redford brings Herbie Hancock aboard his yacht to provide alluring music for his guest.
52. For an excellent discussion on black presence and anti-presence in film, see Krin Gabbard, *Black Magic: White Hollywood and African American Culture* (New Brunswick, NJ: Rutgers University Press, 2004), and Krin Gabbard, *Jammin' at the Margins: Jazz and the American Cinema* (Chicago: University of Chicago Press, 1996).
53. This list is limited and does not include magazines or journals from other countries.
54. Cawthra, *Blue Notes in Black and White*, 10.
55. Sontag, *On Photography*, 8.
56. Cawthra, *Blue Notes in Black and White*, 3.
57. For more information, see Anders S. Lunde, "The American Federation of Musicians and the Recording Ban," *Public Opinion Quarterly* 12.1 (Spring 1948): 45–56.

58. John S. Wilson, *Jazz: The Transition Years, 1940–1960* (New York: Appleton Century Crofts, 1966), 13.
59. David Borgo, *Sync or Swarm: Improvising Music in a Complex Age* (New York: Continuum, 2005), 15.
60. Lester Young, Roy Eldridge, Jimmy Blanton, Jo Jones, and Charlie Christian are the main transitional figures typically identified as bridging the music from swing to bebop. Wilson, *Jazz: The Transition Years*, 7, 13.
61. Other additions from the songwriting pool began to surface, such as Richard Rodgers and Lorenz Hart, Hoagy Carmichael, Harold Arlen, Johnny Mercer, Duke Ellington, and Richard Rodgers and Oscar Hammerstein II.
62. One of the main differences in bebop occurred in the transition from singer to instrumentalist. The instrumental leader of the small group would play the melody of the song, which was followed by an improvised musical section over the same chord changes heard under the melody. The result adapted the song to be played instrumentally and with some alterations to the chord changes.
63. Every jazz musician is familiar with the literature from this era. The verses and chord changes of these songs are collected into Real or Fake books, which remain the primary source material for all performing jazz musicians.
64. DeVeaux, *The Birth of Bebop: A Social and Musical History*, 2.
65. *Ibid.*, 7.
66. Milt Hinton, David G. Berger, and Holly Maxson, *Over Time: The Jazz Photographs of Milt Hinton* (Petaluma, CA: Pomegranate, 1991), 9.
67. These photographers are well documented, and are considered by many as artists in their own right. For examples of their work see Joachim Ernest Berendt, *Jazz: A Photo History*, trans. William Odom (London: Deutsch; New York: Schirmer, 1979); Ole Brask, *Jazz People: Photographs by Ole Brask* (Englewood Cliffs, NJ: Prentice Hall, 1976); Carol Friedman, *A Moment's Notice: Portraits of American Jazz Musicians* (New York: Schirmer, 1983), William P. Gottlieb, *The Golden Age of Jazz* (New York: Simon and Schuster, 1979), and Lee Tanner, *Jazz Address Book* (Studio City, CA: Pomegranate, 1991).
68. See also W. Royal Stokes, *Swing Era New York: The Photographs of Charles Peterson* (Philadelphia: Temple University Press, 1994), and Valerie Wilmer, *The Face of Black Music: Photographs by Valerie Wilmer* (New York: Da Capo, 1976).
69. Jerry Jazz Musician, "Herman Leonard Interview," accessed 10 March 2006, jerryjazzmusician.com/linernotes/hleonard.html.
70. Ed Enright, "'Down Beat' Lifetime Achievement Award: Herman Leonard—Eye for the Music," *Down Beat* 71.10 (October 2004): 60–62.
71. Telephone interview with Jenny Bagert, 11 September 2006.
72. In an interview with the author, 11 February 2009.
73. The information on this Herman Leonard timeline was provided by Jenny Bagert in 2006 and from Geraldine Baum in 2009.
74. Cawthra says, "photography tells us more about the photographers as it does about the subject." Cawthra, *Blue Notes in Black and White*, 12.
75. Upon graduation, Bacher worked at Campbell-Ewald Advertising in Detroit allowing him to create his initial contacts in the jazz world.
76. Bacher especially supported musicians who embraced the avant-garde, like Andrew Hill and Pharoah Sanders.

77. For promotion, Bacher invited musicians such as Bobby Hutchinson to perform for the National Entertainment Conference. In this manner, other agents and those who attended the conference would hear Hutchinson, creating more contacts and future gigs. Lutz Bacher, Personal Interview, July 31, 2008.
78. Lutz Bacher, interview with the author, 15 October 2006.
79. As his first serious client, Bacher put an advertisement and a photo of Andrew Hill in the Musical America guide directory.
80. Catherine Moore, "A Picture Is Worth 1000 CDs: Can the Music Industry Survive as a Stand-Alone Business?" *American Music* 22.1 (Spring 2004): 178–79.
81. Cawthra, *Blue Notes in Black and White*, 14.
82. Telephone interview with Jenny Bagert, 20 September 2006.
83. *Ibid.*
84. Mirzoeff, *An Introduction to Visual Culture*, 5.
85. Telephone interview with Jenny Bagert 20 September 2006.
86. DeVeaux, *The Birth of Bebop*, 15.
87. John Fordham, *Jazz*; quoted in DeVeaux, *The Birth of Bebop*, 15.
88. Charles Nanry as quoted by Townsend, *Jazz in American Culture*, 41.
89. Leonard Feather, *Inside Be-bop* (New York: J.J. Robbins, 1949), 45; quoted in DeVeaux, *The Birth of Bebop*, 14.
90. In my own classroom, twenty-eight college students filled out a pre-test for class which included the question, "Can you describe what you think a jazz musician looks like? (instrument, clothing, appearance, etc.)." Of the twenty-eight students who answered, twenty-two gave the instrument associated with jazz as saxophone, eight wrote trumpet, three mentioned "brass instruments," two said "drums." The pre-test was taken on 25 August 2008.
91. David Ake, *Jazz Cultures* (Berkeley: University of California Press, 2005), 156.
92. Charles Johnson, in foreword to Fredrik Stromberg, *Black Images in Comics: A Visual History* (Seattle, WA: Fantagraphics, 2003), 10.
93. hooks, "Feminism Inside: Toward a Black Body Politic," 131.
94. *Ibid.*
95. See Greg Tate, "Preface to a One-Hundred-and-Eighty-Volume Patricide Note: Yet Another Few Thousand Words on the Death of Miles Davis and the problem of the Black Male Genius," in Gina Dent, ed., *Black Popular Culture: A Project by Michele Wallace* (Seattle: Bay Press, 1992) 243–48.
96. Cawthra, *Blue Notes in Black and White*, 6.
97. In the Renaissance, it was in Northern Europe rather than in Italy that this idea of genius was first applied to the visual arts. Alberti, Piero della Francesca, and Da Vinci were influenced by the concept of genius that arrived simultaneously in Ficino's Neoplatonic philosophy. Erwin Panofsky, *Studies in Iconology: Humanistic Themes in the Art of the Renaissance* (Bolder: Westview, 1972), 140, 209.
98. The importance of the name of the jazz musician can be seen in radio. Jazz radio stations most often announce the name of each musician after the recording has been played. This is in contrast to pop music radio stations that only announce the band and occasionally the name of the song.
99. Ake, *Jazz Cultures*, 159.
100. Michel Foucault, "What Is an Author?" trans. Josue V. Harari, in Paul Rabinow, ed., *The Foucault Reader* (New York: Pantheon, 1984) 106–7.

101. With respect to Davis, one imagines the soft, muted trumpet that is typical of his playing style, a sound so representative of Davis that many parodies have been made. At one point in Charles Mingus's recording "Scenes of the City" retelling the history of jazz, the narrator mentions Davis's name, and immediately a muted trumpet sounds in the background as a spoof of his style.
102. True to the fashion at the time, Davis had long hair and wore shades, producing a tough exterior. For an excellent example, compare Leonard's photo of Miles Davis in New York City taken in 1949, code #MLD08, to the "scary" Miles Davis in London taken in 1989, code #MLD09.
103. In particular, myths accumulate around certain jazz musicians whose lifestyles became intriguing to the jazz community as a form of gossip: Miles Davis's "Buddha on the mountain" image, who spoke little and created much; Thelonious Monk's drug-free antics on stage and lack of social skills; John Coltrane's exaggerated practice time of twelve hours every day; Tony Williams's questionable sexuality; Bix Beiderbecke's serious approach to both music and alcohol; and all jazz musicians' association with sex, drugs, alcohol, smoking, and womanizing that is perpetuated by the fact that musicians play in bars and other unorthodox venues.
104. Obviously this myth also depicts all artists, musicians, and actors whose identification with their art allows the free license of their personality to creatively mirror the production of their art.
105. David Liebman, *Self Portrait of a Jazz-Artist: Musical Thoughts and Realities* (Rottenburg, West Germany: Advance Music, 1988), 37.
106. For more on the hipster image, see Norman Mailer, "The White Negro: Superficial Reflections on the Hipster," *Dissent* 4.3 (1957): 276–93; Philip Ford, "Somewhere/Nowhere: Hipness as an Aesthetic," *The Musical Quarterly* 86.1 (Spring 2002): 49–81; Roy Carr, Brian Case, and Fred Dellar, *The Hip: Hipsters, Jazz and the Beat Generation* (London: Faber and Faber, 1986); and Monson, "The Problem with White Hipness," 396–422.
107. Ronald Radano, "Myth Today: The Color of Ken Burns's *Jazz*," *Black Renaissance* 3, no. 3 (2001): 45.
108. Townsend, *Jazz in American Culture*, 161.
109. Barthes, *Mythologies*, 143, quoted in Townsend, *Jazz in American Culture*, 161.
110. Radano, "Myth today," 45.
111. *Ibid.*, 54.
112. Gabbard, *Jammin' at the Margins*, 1.

CHAPTER 2

1. Dizzy Gillespie, quoted in Dan Morgenstern's foreword, Ole Brask, *Jazz People*, 10.
2. Ake, *Jazz Cultures*, 159.
3. Barthes, *Image, Music, Text*, 17.
4. For example, Leonard uses several photogenic techniques to create an "artistic" photograph, such as setting, black and white film, smoke, and position of the musician. Each of these elements is used to enhance the mythical appearance of the jazz musician.
5. Michel Frizot, "Introduction: The Age of Light," in Michel Frizot, ed., *A New History of Photography* (Köln: Könemann Verlagsgesellschaft, 1998), 9.

6. "While a painting or a prose description can never be other than narrowly selective interpretation, a photograph can be treated as a narrowly selective transparency." Sontag, *On Photography*, 6.
7. Julia Thomas, ed., *Reading Images* (New York: Palgrave, 2000), ix.
8. Thomas, ed., *Reading Images*, ix.
9. Sontag, *On Photography*, 3.
10. In terms of theoreticians, there are Ferdinand de Saussure, *Course in General Linguistics*, trans. Wade Baskin (New York: McGraw-Hill, 1969); Foucault, *The Order of Things*; Michel Foucault, *Language, Counter-Memory, Practice: Selected Essays and Interviews* (Ithaca: Cornell University Press, 1977); Foucault, *This is Not a Pipe*; Hans-Georg Gadamer, *Philosophical Hermeneutics*, trans. and ed. David E. Linge (Berkeley: University of California Press, 1976); Barthes, *Image, Music, Text*; Barthes, *S/Z*; and Barthes, *Camera Lucida*. Many of these theorists find new meanings for images, and in turn disassemble age-old views on truth and reality as they have been understood from the Enlightenment until the twentieth century. Many of these scholars feel terms such as *truth, reality, image, icon, subject, history, identity, code*, and *sign* need to be re-evaluated. Through an expanding sense of self-consciousness and social construction, these theorists explore identification and representation in society.
11. Little information can be adequately gathered on the reception of images in society; it is difficult to poll subjects according to what one can "read" from an image. The data would be inconclusive because perception of images is influenced by social background, previous experiences, tastes, political leanings, and education, not to mention race, gender, sexual preference, and class.
12. Stuart Hall, ed. *Representation: Cultural Representations and Signifying Practices* (London: Sage, 1998), 35. Hall suggests that our theory of representation has been changed to include three methods of interpretation: (1) the *reflective* or *mimetic* approach proposes a direct relationship of imitation or reflection between words as signs and things; (2) the *intentional* theory reduces representation to the intentions of its author or subject; (3) the *constructionist* theory proposes a mediated relationship between things in the world and our concepts in thought and language. All three of these approaches are used in the study of semiotics.
13. The "sign," according to Vincent M. Colapietro's *Glossary of Semiotics*, is a term traditionally defined as "aliquid stat pro aliquo" or something that stands for something else. Sign is used along side of other terms with similar meanings such as "symbols," "icons," and "myths" (New York: Paragon House, 1993), 179–80. Charles S. Pierce specified three types of signs according to the relationship between the sign and the object. The grouping of three types of signs (or Trichotomy) includes: the icon, index, and symbol. The icon designates a sign that specifically resembles the object or produces a mental image of the object such as a map that represents a region or territory. If the sign that points to something, indicates it, or directly relates to an object by physical or actual connection as smoke escaping from a fire, the sign is called an index or indexical sign. If a sign stands in place of an object like a single red rose as the symbol for affection, it is a symbol. For further information see Vincent M. Colapietro, *Glossary of Semiotics* (New York: Paragon House, 1993); Max H. Fisch, *Pierce, Semiotic, and Pragmatism*, eds. Kenneth Laine Ketner and Christian J. W. Kloesel (Bloomington: Indiana

University Press, 1986); and C. M. Smith, "The Aesthetics of Charles S. Peirce," *Journal of Aesthetics and Art Criticism* 31.1 (Fall 1972): 21–29.

14. Take for example, the internationally broadcast images of clamoring civilians on their rooftops during Hurricane Katrina , insinuating that the United States of America is not prepared for disasters, nor is it as strong a country as once thought. Other images of the disaster capture the stunned victims wading through water carrying food and fresh drinking supplies. These images were indirectly used by the press to project society's prejudice toward African Americans and highlight the racial inequalities still present in the United States. Thus, the transfer of power moves from the marginalized African American presented in the image to the viewer, and embodies one with awareness and social injustice. Not only did this invite further generalizations of black and white communities, but it also generalized the disaster as that which happened only to New Orleans, Louisiana. The rest of the destruction on the Gulf Coast, including Mississippi, Alabama, and Florida, has been less reported by the media.
15. Foucault views discourse as "the inscription of a specific knowledge in a language usage that is bound up with power." Thomas, ed., *Reading Images*, 5.
16. If (sign = signified/signifier) or (n = d/r), then [(n = d/r) + (x = d/n) + (y = d/x) + (z = d/y), etc.]. This post-structuralist process can be repeated endlessly, building a layered discourse of an image. Signs that are repeated so extensively that they lose their meaning as a highly conventionalized sign are called codes. The visual image, in general, is layered with coded messages.
17. Bernard Shaw, "The Unmechanicalness of Photography: An Introduction to the London Photographic Exhibitions, 1902," in *Bernard Shaw on Photography* (Salt Lake City: Peregrine Smith, 1989), 82.
18. Colin Osman, *Histoire de la Photographie* (Paris: Bordas, 1986), 169, quoted in Frizot, ed., *A New History of Photography*, 619.
19. Thomas, ed., *Reading Images*, 4.
20. Kalamu ya Salaam, "Herman Leonard: Making Music with Light," *African American Review* 29.2 Special Issues on the Music (Summer 1995): 242.
21. Ruth A. Solie, "Defining Feminism: Conundrums, Contexts, Communities," 8.
22. John Berger, *Ways of Seeing* (Harmondsworth, UK: Penguin, 1972), 45–64, quoted in Philip Alperson, ed., *The Philosophy of the Visual Arts* (New York: Oxford University Press, 1992), 248–59.
23. Thomas, ed., *Reading Images*, 3. Of course, not everyone in Western society has the opportunity to look. bell hooks uses Foucault's ideas that ways of seeing are complicit with power and this explains the marginalization of African Americans by presenting "whiteness" as the norm and refusing blacks the right to look. The act of looking is constituted as dangerous, something threatening. The black male gaze was long subject to punishment by the white-controlled society. The danger of looking, says bell hooks, is found in the example of fifteen-year-old Emmett Till's murder, which was caused by Till's "look" at a white woman, perceived as a violation punishable by his death. See Thomas, ed., *Reading Images*, 125.
24. Joanna Lowry, "Negotiating Power," in Mark Durden and Craig Richardson, eds., *Face On: Photography as Social Exchange* (London: Black Dog, 2000), 13.
25. *Ibid.*, 15.
26. Interview with the author, 11 February 2009.

27. *Ibid.*
28. Barthes, *Image, Music, Text*, 20.
29. *Ibid.*, 19.
30. Miles Orvell, *American Photography* (Oxford: Oxford University Press, 2003), 188.
31. Color in photography was first introduced in 1907 with autochrome; however, it was not until the 1930s that color could be printed from a negative. Color photographs have been available ever since, yet many photographers choose black and white film instead of color to provide a sense of historic, artful quality to the photograph.
32. Milt Hinton, in Hinton, Berger, and Maxson, *The Jazz Photographs of Milt Hinton*, 9.
33. Dizzy Gillespie, quoted in Dan Morgenstern and Ole Brask, *Jazz People*, 10.
34. Interview with the author, 11 February 2009.
35. Leonard's response to the question, "What does jazz look like to you?" Interview with the author, 11 February 2009.
36. Salaam, "Herman Leonard: Making Music with Light," 242.
37. Barthes, *Image, Music, Text*, 21.
38. This was an advertisement used from 1954 to 1999 of a masculine young cowboy holding a Marlboro cigarette.
39. Hinton, Berger, and Maxson, *The Jazz Photographs of Milt Hinton*, 9.
40. Carol Friedman, in Hinton, Berger, and Maxson, *The Jazz Photographs of Milt Hinton*, 9.
41. Barthes, *Image, Music, Text*, 28.
42. Liebman, *Self Portrait of a Jazz-Artist*, 30.
43. Lee Friedlander, *The Jazz People of New Orleans* (New York: Pantheon, 1992), 42.
44. Interview with the author, 11 February 2009.
45. Friedlander, *The Jazz People of New Orleans*, 42.
46. As indicated by Charles Buchanan in a telephone conversation with the author, 14 January 2007.
47. Michel Frizot, "Body of Evidence: The ethnophotography of difference," in Frizot, ed., *A New History of Photography*, 259.
48. Margaret Olin, "Gaze," in Robert Nelson and Richard Shiff, eds., *Critical Terms for Art History* (Chicago: University of Chicago Press, 1996).
49. W. Eugene Smith in Duane Michals, *Real Dreams: Photo Stories* (Danbury, NH: Addison House; Rochester, NY: distributed by Light Impressions, 1976), quoted in Orvell, *American Photography*, 168.
50. Frizot, ed., *A New History of Photography*, 620.
51. Sontag, *On Photography*, 4.
52. Barthes, *Image, Music, Text*, 43.
53. Sontag, *On Photography*, 6.
54. E. H. Gombrich, "The Mask and the Face: The Perception of Physiognomic Likeness in Life and in Art," in E. H. Gombrich, Julian Hochberg, and Max Black, *Art, Perception, and Reality* (Baltimore: The Johns Hopkins University Press, 1972), 17.
55. Sontag, *On Photography*, 5.
56. Sontag, *On Photography*, 77.
57. *Ibid.*, 9.
58. Sontag, "From Plato's Cave," in *On Photography*, 3–14.

59. Gombrich, "The Mask and the Face," in Gombrich, Hochberg, and Black, *Art, Perception, and Reality*, 13.
60. Louis Althusser, "Ideology and Ideological State Apparatuses," *Lenin and Philosophy and Other Essays*, trans. Ben Brewster (London: Monthly Review Press, 1977), 11, quoted in Thomas, ed., *Reading Images*, 7.
61. Gombrich, "The Mask and the Face," in Gombrich, Hochberg, and Black, *Art, Perception, and Reality*, 3.
62. Interview with the author, 14 February 2009.
63. Collier, *The Making of Jazz*, 470.
64. Barthes, *Image, Music, Text*, 34.
65. *Ibid.*
66. *Ibid.*
67. *Ibid.*, 35.
68. *Ibid.*, 39.
69. Orvell, *American Photography*, 192.
70. Leonard describes the setting of the legendary shot in an interview for *ABC News with Charles Gibson* segment entitled "Jazz Giants: Photographer's Iconic Images of Legendary Jazz Artists," shown on June 6, 2008. abcnews.go.com/Video/playerIndex?id=5016845, accessed 1 September 2008.
71. Barthes, *Image, Music, Text*, 44.
72. *Ibid.*, 45.
73. Barthes, *Camera Lucida*, in Thomas ed., *Reading Images*, 58.
74. Sontag, *On Photography*, 16.
75. This April 1998 interview with Herman Leonard by Anatoly Kiryushkin, editor and interviewer, appears in *Jazz News*, an English web supplement to the Russian web site *Jazz-Quad* (nestor.minsk.by/jz/), home.nestor.minsk.by/jazz/articles/2005/06/0039.html, accessed 19 September 2006.
76. Telephone interview with Jenny Bagert, 11 September 2006.
77. April 1998 interview with Herman Leonard by Anatoly Kiryushkin.
78. Sontag, *On Photography*, 28.

CHAPTER 3

1. Neoclassicism is also referred to as Neo-mainstream, as described in the NEA: Jazz in the Schools website, neajazzintheschools.org/lesson4/essay4.php?uv=s, accessed 2 January 2009.
2. Ben Sidran begins his 1986 interview with "Wynton, you're not just a trumpet player. You're a cause célèbre. For better or worse, that's a big part of your story. You came to us, of course, a man dedicated to the jazz tradition, but then were vaulted into this other position, that of spokesperson for all of jazz." In *Talking Jazz: An Illustrated Oral History* (San Francisco: Pomegranate, 1992), 336.
3. Paul Lopez, "Diffusion and Syncretism: The Modern Jazz Tradition," *Annals of the American Academy* 566.1 (November 1999): 35.
4. Some personalities, like Dizzy Gillespie and the earlier Cab Calloway did lean toward a dynamic showmanship during concerts, but this is the exception in jazz.
5. Ed Enright, "Bebop Emergence," *Down Beat's Jazz* 101, on the *Down Beat* website, downbeat.com/default.asp?sect=education&subsect=jazz_09, accessed 6 March 2007.

6. David Andrew Ake, *Being Jazz: Identities and Images*, diss., University of California at Los Angeles (1998), 225.
7. There are several printed music books, often dubbed "real" or "fake" book, that list the chord changes and melody lines of jazz standards.
8. William Weber, "The History of Musical Canon," in Nicholas Cook and Mark Everist, eds., *Rethinking Music* (Oxford: Oxford University Press, 1999), 338.
9. Ake, *Jazz Cultures*, 149, 151.
10. Larry Kart, *Jazz in Search of Itself* (New Haven, CT: Yale University Press, 2004), 9.
11. *Ibid.*
12. *Ibid.*
13. Roger Braun, email to the author, 12 March 2007.
14. Porter, *What Is This Thing Called Jazz?* 30.
15. While he was in school, Ellington excelled in mechanical and freehand drawing, so much so that he won a scholarship from the NAACP to study art at the Pratt Institute of Applied Arts in Brooklyn, which he turned down in order to pursue music. Similar in method to Toulouse-Lautrec, Ellington likely painted posters as artworks, disguised as advertisements, which allowed him to be creative and financially stable, while at the same time to develop his business sense at an early age.
16. Charles Gerard, *Jazz in Black and White: Race, Culture, and Identity in the Jazz Community* (Westport, CT: Praeger, 1998), 3.
17. William Weber, "The History of Musical Canon," in Nicholas Cook and Mark Everist, eds., *Rethinking Music* (Oxford: Oxford University Press, 1999), 349.
18. Christopher Porter, editorial in *Jazz Times* April 2003, in Stuart Nicholson, *Is Jazz Dead? Or Has It Moved to a New Address* (New York: Routledge, 2005), 3.
19. "As I say, let my children have music. Jazz—the way it has been handled in the past—stifles them so that they believe only in the trumpet, trombone, saxophone, maybe a flute now and then or a clarinet could play. But it is not enough. I think it is time our children were raised to think they can play bassoon, oboe, English horn, French horn, lull percussion, violin, cello. The results would be—well the Philharmonic would not be the only answer for us then. If we so-called jazz musicians who are the composers, the spontaneous composers, started including these instruments in our music, it would open everything up, it would get rid of prejudice because the musicianship would be so high in caliber that the symphony couldn't refuse us." Liner notes by Charles Mingus for the album *Let My Children Hear Music* (Columbia Records, 1971).
20. The first generation of these musicians, such as Anthony Braxton, Joseph Jarman, Kalaparush(a) Maurice McIntyre, Julius Hemphill, Muhal Richard Abrams, and Lester Bowie, experimented with layers of sound, especially with the treatment of space and time in music. To these artists, music is found in the distribution of tension and release of sound, suggesting that any music, including jazz, contains the possibility of more complex and varied musical expression by creating greater tension within the traditional barriers of musical performance. In fact, members of the AACM began their own revolution by performing without the constraints of time or tonality.
21. This quotation comes from the website "NEA: Jazz in the Schools," which is dedicated to providing material to those who will teach jazz in the classroom. This website is supported in part by Jazz at Lincoln Center. "The curriculum, an

initiative of the National Endowment for the Arts, is produced by Jazz at Lincoln Center, a not-for-profit arts organization dedicated to enriching the artistic substance and perpetuating the democratic spirit of America's music, and is supported by a $100,000 grant from the Verizon Foundation." neajazzintheschools.org/lesson4/essay4.php?uv=s, accessed 19 March 2009. The quote comes from Lesson 4, entitled "From the New Frontier to the New Millennium: Back to the Future," insinuating that jazz had died in the 1960s with electronic music and free jazz and was reborn in the late 1980s by those who pursue "traditional jazz." Although no author is listed for each historical essay on jazz, there is a list of contributing authors for the lessons, including Stanley Crouch, David Kastin, John Szwed, and Geoffrey C. Ward.

22. Geoffrey C. Ward and Ken Burns, *Jazz: A History of America's Music* (New York: Alfred A. Knopf, 2000), 458.
23. *Ibid.*
24. Nicholson, *Is Jazz Dead?*, 7.
25. neajazzintheschools.org/timeline/index.php?uv=s, accessed 12 December 2008.
26. Ward and Burns, *Jazz: A History of America's Music*, 432.
27. Sidran, "Wynton Marsalis," in *Talking Jazz*, 345.
28. Larry Kart, "Provocative Opinion: The Death of Jazz?" *Black Music Research Journal* 10.1 (Spring 1990): 76–77.
29. Several universities offer degrees in jazz studies, and a few universities (such as the University of North Texas and Berklee School of Music) offer undergraduates an intensive jazz-based foundation, providing the market a steady stream of young but accomplished players.
30. Stanley Crouch, David Kastin, John Szwed, and Geoffrey C. Ward, "From the New Frontier to the New Millennium: Back to the Future," NEA: Jazz in the Schools, neajazzintheschools.org/lesson4/essay4.php?uv=s, accessed 11 July 2009.
31. Nate Chinen, "Wynton Marsalis: The Once and Future King of Jazz at Lincoln Center," *New York Times*, 26 September 2006. www.nytimes.com/2006/08/27/arts/music/27chin.html?pagewanted=prin t.
32. The website for this program is neajazzintheschools.org.
33. Ward and Burns, *Jazz: A History of America's Music*, 459.
34. It was estimated that 13 million viewers saw the first episode, and when calculated over the entire ten episodes, 23 million viewers tuned in for the series, which is double the typical public television audience. Gary R. Edgerton, *Ken Burns's America* (New York: Palgrave/St. Martin's, 2001), 213. The five-CD boxed set from the series sold more than 500,000 copies, and in January 2001, sixteen of the twenty-five spots on *Billboard's* Top Jazz Albums chart came from the series. Michael Kauffman indicated that jazz sales were up 20 percent. Edgerton, *Ken Burns's America*, 213. Even longtime rival labels Columbia/Legacy and Verve decided to combine their available jazz recordings into a compilation for the series, later joined by Blue Note, RCA, and Rhino.
35. Nicholson, *Is Jazz Dead?* 6.
36. The National Endowment for the Arts funded three surveys on public participation in the arts during the years 1982, 1985, and 1992. Harold Horowitz evaluated the results of the first survey in 1982 and presented his findings in David Baker, ed., *New Perspectives on Jazz* (Washington: Smithsonian Institution Press, 1990),

1–8; Scott DeVeaux's evaluation of the results of the third survey done in 1992 were published in Scott DeVeaux, "Jazz in America: Who's Listening?" *Research Division Report #31*, National Endowment for the Arts (Carson, California: Seven Locks, 1995): 1–4, 36–37, and 56–57. The conclusions from the surveys indicated a sharp growth in the jazz audience over this span. DeVeaux, "Jazz in America: Who's Listening?" 1–4, 36–37, and 56–57. Of American adults, 33 percent reported that they "liked jazz," which was higher than the 26 percent affirmative responses in 1982. The same percentage of adult Americans (10 percent) stated that they attended a jazz performance in 1982 and in 1992. Another increase was found in the 1992 survey, in which 22 percent of people watched jazz on television in some form compared to 18 percent in 1982. Similarly, 28 percent listened to jazz on the radio in 1992 compared to 18 percent in 1982. The results of the "most popular musical genre" as indicated by the survey ranked jazz fifth, country being the most preferred musical genre and folk being the last. Jazz went down one rank to number six for those respondents who "liked a musical genre best of all." The jazz base group, comprised mostly of educated, middle income listeners, runs the gamut in terms of race. Perhaps predictably, more men acknowledged an interest in jazz, 54 percent.

37. He is interviewed frequently for his opinion of the handling of the disaster by FEMA, especially because of Marsalis's own family ties to the city. He was asked to play live from the Allen Room at Jazz at Lincoln Center on national television's *NBC Nightly News with Brian Williams*. He spoke with Williams about the state of his hometown and the birthplace of jazz on the second Mardi Gras after Hurricane Katrina, and closed the segment by playing a second line tune with Wycliffe Gordon, Victor Goines, Carlos Henriquez, and Ali Kackson. The video clip of this performance can be viewed on Wynton Marsalis's fan club website, wyntonmarsalis.org/2007/02/21/wynton-played-and-spoke-live-for-nbc-nightly-news/, accessed 7 March 2007.
38. Brown, "Marsalis and Baraka," 243.
39. Roger Braun telephone conversation with the author, 13 May 2007.
40. Ronald L. Jackson and Elaine B. Richardson, eds., *Understanding African American Rhetoric: Classical Origins to Contemporary Innovations* (New York: Routledge, 2003), xvi.
41. Sherrie Tucker, AMS 650: Jazz and American Culture, course, Spring 2003, University of Kansas, Lawrence, people.ku.edu/~sjtucker/650.html, accessed 2 April 2004.
42. Wynton Marsalis, "What Jazz Is—and Isn't," *New York Times* (31 July 1988, Arts & Leisure) 21, 24.
43. For complete article, sections, and chapters dedicated to Marsalis's reference to jazz as black music, see Lee Brown, "Marsalis and Baraka: An Essay in Comparative Cultural Discourse," *Popular Music* 23.3 (2004): 241–55; Stuart Nicholson's chapters "Where Do We Go From Here? The Jazz Mainstream 1990 to 2005," "Between Image and Artistry: The Wynton Marsalis Phenomenon," and "Prophets Looking Backward: Jazz at Lincoln Center," in *Is Jazz Dead?*; and Scott DeVeaux, "Constructing the Jazz Tradition: Jazz Historiography," *Black American Literature Forum* 25.3 (Fall 1991): 525–60.

44. Ornette Coleman used white bassists Charlie Haden and Scott LaFaro during the Black Nationalist movement in the mid-1960s to justify presence of whites.
45. Gerard, *Jazz in Black and White*, 10.
46. *Ibid.*, 36–37.
47. DeVeaux, "Constructing the Jazz Tradition," 528–29, and Joel Rudinow, "Race, Ethnicity, Expressive Authenticity: Can White People Sing the Blues?" *Journal of Aesthetics and Art Criticism* 52.1 The Philosophy of Music (Winter 1994): 127–37.
48. Lee B. Brown discusses this issue in his article, "Marsalis and Baraka: An Essay in Comparative Cultural Discourse," *Popular Music* 23.3 (2004): 241–55.
49. DeVeaux, "Constructing the Jazz Tradition," 527–28.
50. Sidran, "Herbie Hancock," in *Talking Jazz*, 269–70.
51. Rafi Zabor and Vic Garbarini, "Wynton Vs. Herbie: The Purist and the Crossbreeder Duke it Out," *Musician* 77 (March 1985): 52–64, also quoted in Walser, ed., *Keeping Time: Readings in Jazz History*, 345, 347.
52. Brown, "Marsalis and Baraka," 252, and Nicholson, *Is Jazz Dead?* 26.
53. Lopez, "Diffusion and Syncretism: The Modern Jazz Tradition," 27.
54. The following is a select list of actual occurrences listed in Ingrid Monson's "The Problem with White Hipness," 408–9.
55. Reported in "Carter v. Crow," *Metronome* 61 (August 1945): 7.
56. "Jim Crow Stuff Still Spreading! Girl Trumpeter Tastes Southern Chivalry and Color Ousts Mab's Men," *Down Beat* 13 (29 July 1946): 1.
57. "Kansas City Court Makes Just Ruling," *Down Beat* 13 (14 January 1946): 10.
58. "Eckstine, Band, Lose Job after Brawl in Boston," *Down Beat* 14 (15 January 1947): 4.
59. Samuel Floyd, *The Power of Black Music* (New York: Oxford University Press, 1995), quoted in Lopez, "Diffusion and Syncretism: The Modern Jazz Tradition," 29.
60. Valerie Wilmer, *As Serious As Your Life* (Westport, CT: Lawrence Hill, 1980), 225, quoted in Ronald M. Radano, "The Jazz Avant-Garde and the Jazz Community: Action and Reaction," *Annual Review of Jazz Studies* 3 (1985): 75.
61. Lopez, "Diffusion and Syncretism: The Modern Jazz Tradition," 30.
62. Theodore Gracyk, *I Wanna Be Me: Rock Music and the Politics of Identity* (Philadelphia: Temple University Press, 2001), 115, quoted in Brown, "Marsalis and Baraka," *Popular Music* 23.3 (2004): 250.
63. Rudinow, "Can White People Sing the Blues?" 127–37.
64. See also Kwame Anthony Appiah, "Race," in Frank Lentricchia and Thomas McLaughlin, eds., *Critical Terms for Literary Study* (Chicago: University of Chicago Press, 1990).
65. "A lot of musicians would come into his store looking for their own recordings. And being on the West Coast, there were a ton of musicians living here. And friendships ensued, and they invited him down to their recording sessions, and all of a sudden they'd discover that he is also a photographer, so they have him photograph their sessions." Cynthia Sesso telephone interview with the author, 18 March 2009.
66. She currently represents seventeen different photographers.
67. Cynthia Sesso telephone interview with the author, 18 March 2009.

68. The fact that his entire collection is in the permanent archives of musical history in the Smithsonian Institution in Washington, D.C., and examples are housed in the permanent collection of several other museums such as the Kennedy Museum of Art, Athens, Ohio, and the Ogden Museum of Southern Art, New Orleans, Louisiana, attest to their importance in preserving some kind of imprint of this elusive jazz image. (A complete list of permanent collections and exhibitions is provided in Appendix A.)
69. Similar to a conductor as the front face of a symphony orchestra, the lead singer draws more appeal than other members in the band. More tickets are sold to see Bono performing rather than The Edge even though they perform in the same band, U2.
70. Leonard's 11" x 14" open edition prints sell for $950 and his 16" x 20" limited edition prints start at $1,200. The beginning price to be photographed by Leonard himself is $5,000. He also offers exhibition rentals, lectures, slide shows, and workshops, all of which start at $25,000 plus airfare and accommodation for two. Leonard's listings for lectures and portrait sessions are located under "Services" on his webpage, hermanleonard.com/services.html, accessed 7 March 2007.
71. Provided by an online interview by Aurora Rodriguez, *Ledger Online*, theledger .com/apps/pbcs.dll/article?AID=/20060821/NEWS/608210302/1326, accessed 15 September 2006.
72. Interview with the author, 2 February 2009.
73. Telephone interview with Jenny Bagert, 20 September 2006.
74. Amiri Baraka, "Jazz and the White Critic," in *The Leroi Jones/Amiri Baraka Reader*, ed. William J. Harris (New York: Thunder's Mouth, 1999), 179.
75. Andrew Ross, *No Respect: Intellectuals and Popular Culture* (New York: Routledge, 1989), 85, quoted in Monson, "The Problem with White Hipness," 403.
76. Steve Shoemaker, "Norman Mailer's 'White Negro': Historical Myth or Mythical History?" *Twentieth Century Literature* 37 (1991): 343–60.
77. Imamu Amiri Baraka, (LeRoi Jones), *Blues People*, 219, quoted in Monson, "The Problem with White Hipness," 401–2.
78. Winthrop Sargeant, *Jazz, Hot and Hybrid*, quoted in Gioia, *The Imperfect Art*, 32–33.
79. Gioia, *The Imperfect Art*, 31.
80. Charles Gerard, *Jazz in Black and White*, 14.
81. E. Taylor Atkins, "Toward a Global History of Jazz," in Atkins, ed., *Jazz Planet*, xii.
82. Gary Giddins, *Ryhthm-a-ning: Jazz Tradition and Innovation in the '80s* (New York: Oxford University Press, 1985), 161.
83. Nicholson, *Is Jazz Dead?* 1.
84. *Ibid.*, 7.
85. Wynton Marsalis, "What Jazz Is—and Isn't," *New York Times* 31 July 1988 (Arts & Leisure), 21 and 24, quoted in DeVeaux, "Constructing the Jazz Tradition," 510, fn 28.
86. Kart, *Jazz in Search of Itself*, 258.
87. Gioia, *The Imperfect Art*, 33.
88. Townsend, *Jazz in American Culture*, 37.
89. Benny Green, *The Reluctant Art: The Growth of Jazz* (Plainview, NY: Books for Library Press, 1962), 14.

90. DeVeaux, "Constructing the Jazz Tradition," 552.
91. Bruton W. Peretti, *Epilogue: Jazz as American History*, quoted in Nicholson, *Is Jazz Dead?* 18.
92. Giddins, *Ryhthm-a-ning*, 169–70.
93. *Ibid.*
94. Shaw, "The Unmechanicalness of Photography," in *Bernard Shaw on Photography*, 82.
95. *Ibid.*, 84.
96. Ironically, at the same time that neoclassicists have valued older music traditions with bebop, younger musicians like Dave Holland, Bill Bruford, David Murray, Kenny Wheeler, and Henry Threadgill have broadened the boundaries of jazz to include styles of playing that exist outside of the mainstream. In other words, the tonality, instrumental arrangements, and chord structures of neoclassical musicians have remained somewhat cohesive, while the rhythm, technique, and style of playing has changed drastically. The technical aptitude has become harder for all musicians, the mixture of other styles of music is all-encompassing between pop, jazz, blues, hip-hop, and "indie," and new rhythms and sounds burn into the eclectic ear of jazz musicians. Today's musicians search for further inspiration just as the beats of the 1950s were acting out the American desire for cultural multiplicity.
97. Foucault, *The Order of Things*, 168.
98. DeVeaux, "Constructing the Jazz Tradition," 525.
99. DeVeaux, "Constructing the Jazz Tradition," quoted in Walser, ed. *Keeping Time: Readings in Jazz History*, 417.
100. *Ibid.*
101. From the creation of jazz to about 1970, jazz history texts mainly consist of biographies, stylistic analysis, harmonic analysis (such as transcriptions), and explanations of jazz development. In order to teach an oral tradition such as jazz through lectures and books, one must consolidate the history of jazz into steadfast stylistic developments, thus confining the range and scope of each musical style. The majority of jazz texts provide the history of jazz chronologically, according to stylistic developments that push traditional models of music to the breaking point, which occurs with free jazz and Ornette Coleman.
102. Paul F. Berliner, *Thinking in Jazz: The Infinite Art of Improvisation* (Chicago: University of Chicago Press, 1994), 485.
103. Weber, "The History of Musical Canon," quoted in Cook and Everist, eds., *Rethinking Music*, 337.
104. George E. Lewis, "Experimental Music in Black and White: The AACM in New York, 1970–1985," *Current Musicology* 71–73 (Spring 2001–Spring 2002): 31.
105. Radano, "The Jazz Avant-Garde and the Jazz Community," 74.
106. Archie Shepp, "An Artist Speaks Bluntly," 11, quoted in Radano, "The Jazz Avant-Garde and the Jazz Community," 75.
107. Radano, "The Jazz Avant-Garde and the Jazz Community," 75.
108. Ferdinand Jones, "Jazz and the Resilience of African Americans," in *The Triumph of the Soul: Cultural and Psychological Aspects of African American Music* (Westport, CT: Praeger), 133; Adelbert H. Jenkins, *Psychology and African-Americans: A Humanistic Approach*, 2nd ed. (Boston: Allyn and Bacon, 1995), 42–43; Henry Louis Gates Jr., "Thirteen Ways of Looking at a Black Man," *The New Yorker* 23 October 1995: 56–65.

109. Jazz is not a part of university training for a musicologist, who is assumed to study classical music.
110. An analysis into the European jazz image is beyond the efforts of this book. However, I imagine that Europeans would agree that their contribution to the development of jazz has been misplaced for decades.
111. Atkins, "Toward a Global History of Jazz," xi and xii.
112. *Ibid.*, xiii.
113. *Ibid.*
114. For examples, see Ekkehard Jost, *Free Jazz* (New York: Da Capo, 1994); E. Taylor Atkins, ed., *Jazz Planet* (Jackson: University Press of Mississippi, 2003); and Stuart Nicholson, *Is Jazz Dead? Or Has It Moved to a New Address* (New York: Routledge, 2005).
115. Atkins, "Toward a Global History of Jazz," xi.
116. For more information on the stereotyping of African Americans, see Ronald L. Jackson and Elaine B. Richardson, eds., *Understanding African American Rhetoric: Classical Origins to Contemporary Innovations* (New York: Routledge, 2003); Henry Louis Gates Jr., *The Signifying Monkey: A Theory of African-American Literary Criticism* (New York: Oxford University Press, 1988); and Greg Tate, ed., *Everything But the Burden: What White People Are Taking from Black Culture* (New York: Broadway Books, 2003).
117. Thomas, ed., *Reading Images*, 8.
118. Susan McClary, *Feminine Endings: Music, Gender, and Sexuality* (Minneapolis: University of Minnesota Press, 1991), 7–8, 17, 57, quoted in Porter, *What Is This Thing Called Jazz?*, 30.
119. *Ibid.*
120. For example in music theory, the masculine cadence of V to I always dominates the weaker feminine cadence IV to I. Marcia Citron in *Gender and the Musical Canon* discusses nineteenth-century societal-construct stereotypes of femininity. Theorists A. B. Marx, in *Die Lehre von der musikalischen Komposition* in 1845, and Hugo Riemann, in *Katechismus der Musik (Allegemeine Musiklehre)* first issued in 188 both use the metaphor to describe the two themes of the sonata form: the dominant theme as masculine and the weaker secondary theme as feminine.
121. Marcia Citron, *Gender and the Musical Canon* (Cambridge, UK: Cambridge University Press, 1993), 133.
122. Ward and Burns, *Jazz: A History of America's Music*, 99.
123. When discussing the "othering" of women, Foucault comes to mind through his discussions of the body in society. Often, the physical body is used as a source of power or as a source for determining where the power should be.
124. For further information on women in jazz, see the scholarship of Sherrie Tucker.
125. Citron, *Gender and the Musical Canon*, 122.
126. Eduard Hanslick, *The Beautiful in Music* (New York: Liberal Arts, 1957), 57, quoted in Gioia, *The Imperfect Art*, 103. For Kant's views see *The Critique of Judgment* (New York: Hafner, 1966), 173–75.
127. Gioia, *The Imperfect Art*, 105.
128. Karl Marx, "Excerpts from James Mills Elements of Political Economy," in *Early Writings* (Harmondsworth, UK: Penguin, 1974), 266; found in Pierre

Bourdieu, *Distinction: A Social Critique of the Judgment of Taste*, trans. Richard Nice (Cambridge, MA: Harvard University Press, 1984), 280.

129. Gabbard, *Jammin' at the Margins*, 1.
130. The blues is another genre that is easy to recognize, but lies outside the limits of this particular study.
131. For example in the lower art form of daytime television, many soap operas use jazz as background music in expressing a romantic scene for a heterosexual relationship. This scene usually occurs in a restaurant or in a bedroom, obviously laden with sexual implications.
132. Interview with trumpet player and educator Ernie Bastin, 4 May 2006.
133. Bourdieu, *Distinction: A Social Critique of the Judgment of Taste*, 280–81.
134. Anne Friedberg's essay "A Denial of Difference: Theories of Cinematic Identification" describes the word "identification" as that which is recognizable, representing an "implicit confirmation of the ideology of the status quo." bell hooks, quoted in Thomas, ed., *Reading Images*, 126.
135. Translator James Harkness's Introduction in Foucault, *This Is Not a Pipe*, 5.
136. Zabor and Garbarini, "Wynton Vs. Herbie," also quoted in Walser, ed., *Keeping Time: Readings in Jazz History*, 346.

CHAPTER 4

1. Jost, *Free Jazz*, 17.
2. *Ibid.*, 10.
3. The "NEA Four" was four performance artists—Karen Finley, Tim Miller, John Fleck, and Holly Hughes—who won grants from the National Endowment for the Arts (NEA), but an attempt to revoke the grant money was made by John Frohnmayer and Senator Jesse Helms in June 1990 due to the sexual nature of each artwork. The artists won their money back through a decision made in 1993 by the United States Supreme Court in *National Endowment for the Arts v. Finley*.
4. Mayor Rudolph Giuliani of New York withheld funding and attempted to sue the museum for housing the exhibit *Sensation: Young British Artists from the Saatchi Collection*, which included Chris Ofili's *The Holy Virgin Mary*. And in response to the rising controversy surrounding artworks by Robert Mapplethorpe and Andrea Serrano, the U.S. Congress cut NEA funding by 40 percent and added the Decency Clause to NEA regulations.
5. The ninety cans of Merda d'artista or Artist's Shit were first exhibited in the Galleria Pescetto (Albisola Marina) on 12 August 1961 as part a show. For an online collection of Manzoni's work, see the website pieromanzoni.org/EN/index_en.htm>, accessed 7 March 2007.
6. Musicians of any style seem to function under a conservative understanding about what music actually is and how it should be performed. In order to distinguish "sound" from Western "music" for example, "music" should utilize the rules of Western music theory and tonality in some form, and it must be organized in a manner rhythmical and temporally, depending on the ideas of the composer or instigator of sound. Over the years classical composers such as Wagner, Debussy, Prokofiev, and then Schoenberg, Stockhausen, Messiaen, Cage, and Partch

stretched these restrictions. Even if stipulations of time and organization do not appear to hold back the creativity of a particular artist, in actuality some find it difficult to write music that does not follow these rules. When Arnold Schoenberg dismantled tonality, he had to contrive a new way to organize the production of sound. The establishment of a twelve-tone row completed his idea, and that system became a new method of composition in Western music. Likewise, John Cage's composition 4'33" challenged all musicians to rethink their definition of music. It provided an example of sound created at a certain time and place, but determined by someone else other than the performer/composer. Cage's instructions required no instrument to play nor voice to sing, so the "music" produced came from the ambient noises of the attending audience, implying that sounds in everyday life can also be music.

7. *Times Square* is an invisible block of sound coming from a large underground vault covered by a grating. The sound emerges from the middle of a pedestrian island in Times Square, and once the unsuspecting listener steps over the metal grating, one is surrounded by a wall of sound, simultaneously housing and shielding the listener from the noises of New York City. In this manner, *Times Square* acts more as a feature of architecture rather than of art created by sound. The computer-generated sounds were played continuously from 1977 to 1992 and were restarted in 2002; they have been playing ever since.
8. Radano, "The Jazz Avant-Garde and the Jazz Community," 77.
9. Jost, *Free Jazz*, 10, 17.
10. Further discussion of this can be found in Radano, "The Jazz Avant-garde and the Jazz Community," 71–81.
11. *Ibid.*
12. "Avant-garde jazz," in Barry Kernfeld, ed., *The New Grove Dictionary of Jazz*, 2nd ed. Grove Music Online (Oxford Music Online), oxfordmusiconline.com/subscriber/article/grove/music/J019200, accessed 6 January 2009.
13. J. Bradford Robinson, "Free Jazz," *Grove Music Online*, ed. L. Macy, grovemusic.com, accessed 11 March 2006.
14. Lewis, "Experimental Music in Black and White," 104.
15. Muhal Richard Abrams, interview with the author, 17 March 2006.
16. Martin Heidegger originally used the term "erasure" or "sous rature." He crossed out a word in a text which allowed the reader to still see the word but implied that its use was challenged. For Derrida, the term is a visual reference that stresses the limitations of language and syntax. For more information on "erasure," see Jacques Derrida, *Margins of Philosophy* trans. Alan Bass (Chicago: University of Chicago Press, 1984).
17. Jost, *Free Jazz*, 9.
18. Lincoln T. Beauchamp Jr. ed., *Art Ensemble of Chicago: Great Black Music—Ancient to the Future* (Chicago: Art Ensemble of Chicago, 1998), quoted in Lewis, "Experimental Music in Black and White," 101.
19. William Parker quoted in David Borgo, *Reverence for Uncertainty: Chaos, Order, and the Dynamics of Musical Free Improvisation*, diss., University of California in Los Angeles, 1999 (UMI: Microform 9947057), 83.
20. Roscoe Mitchell's statement from Terry Martin, "Blowing Out in Chicago: Roscoe Mitchell," *Down Beat* (6 April 1967): 47, quoted in Ronald M. Radano,

"Jazzin' the Classics: The AACM's Challenge to Mainstream Aesthetics," *Black Research Journal* 12.1 (1992): 90.

21. Radano, "Jazzin' the Classic," 90.
22. Jost, *Free Jazz*, 12.
23. Racial relations linked with free jazz is a frequently debated topic. For a much fuller discussion, see Radano, "Jazzin' the Classics," 79–95; and Lewis, "Experimental Music in Black and White," 100–154.
24. Radano, "Jazzin' the Classics," 90.
25. For more information on the Black Power movement's relationship with jazz, see Jason Robinson, "The Challenge of the Changing Same: The Jazz Avant-garde of the 1960s, the Black Aesthetic, and the Black Arts Movement," *Critical Studies in Improvisation/Études critiques en improvisation* vol. 1, no. 2 (2005); and John D. Baskerville, *The Impact of Black Nationalist Ideology on American Jazz Music of the 1960s and 1970s* (Lewiston, NY: Edwin Mellen, 2003).
26. Baskerville, *The Impact of Black Nationalist Ideology on American Jazz Music of the 1960s and 1970s*, 7.
27. *Ibid.*, 43.
28. *Ibid.*, 73.
29. Even the publication information for his book apparently was created by Sun Ra. Sun Ra, *Sun Ra: The Immeasurable Equation* (Enterplanetary Koncepts [printed in] "Old" Europe: Waitawhile Books, 2005) 79.
30. Wilmer, *As Serious as Your Life*, 71, quoted in the footnotes of Radano, "The Jazz Avant-Garde and the Jazz Community," 71–81.
31. After becoming a forceful presence on the jazz scene, John Coltrane catered to the second generation of ~~free jazz~~ musicians. His constant experimentation with harmony and common tones, as with *Giant Steps*, pushed the act of soloing to the breaking point, even if it meant adding more notes, creating asymmetrical phrasing, or more diverse rhythmic units. Coltrane became more interested in creating a texture in his sound, a change echoed by ~~free jazz~~ musicians. His mystic persona, heightened by his spiritual dedication, also imitated the spiritual nature found in some ~~free jazz~~ musicians. His most famous album, *A Love Supreme*, was dedicated to God during the troubled times Coltrane had when quitting heroin and alcohol in 1957.

    Monk's rhythmic and chromatic style influences much current jazz, and his place among mainstream musicians remains a debatable issue. Obviously his infamous solos are not typical of what was happening around him, and that was bebop. Mingus and Coltrane forged a path toward the breaking point of tonal jazz. In addition, Mingus composed music with ~~free jazz~~ in mind as seen in the album Charles Mingus Presents Charles Mingus, but never considered himself a ~~free-jazz~~ musician. Realizing that musical notation was inadequate for his approach to composition, Mingus transmitted the details of his works by dictating lines to each player. Once he had created a "lick" on the keyboard, he often asked his band at rehearsals to fill in the gaps for the rest of the tune. In this manner, he composed collectively and layered motifs over each other. Thus, rehearsals were used as an experimental ground to create songs by ear, challenging the members to improvise from the conception of the composition. His rhythmic contrasts—such as double-, half-, or stop-time passages, shifting tempos or meters, and irregular style patterns, as with *Fables*, *Praying with Eric*, and *Pithecanthropus Erectus*—often prefigured rhythmical characteristics associated with free jazz. Mingus also demonstrated his opinions of racism and political activism through the titles of compositions such as *Free Cell Block F*, *'Tis Nazi U.S.A.*, *Work Song*, *Haitian Fight Song*, and *Oh Lord, Don't Let Them Drop That Atomic Bomb on Me*.

32. Ronald Radano points out that the performances at the Five Spot represented the early efforts that would eventually lead to a more abstract sound, while at the same time, the concerts introduced a new, revolutionary method of playing to an intrigued New York jazz community. Radano, "The Jazz Avant-Garde and the Jazz Community," 72.
33. George Hoefer, "The Hot Box," *Down Beat* 21 January 1960: 42; John Tynan, "Ornette: The First Beginning," *Down Beat* 12 July 1960: 32. Both statements are quoted in Radano, "The Jazz Avant-Garde and the Jazz Community," 73.
34. Jost, *Free Jazz*, 51.
35. One remarkable production at Lincoln Center in 1997 consisted of four nights of performances including the entire original band (Don Cherry, Charlie Haden, and Billy Higgins) rejoining Coleman onstage, with additional concerts featuring the New York Philharmonic with Prime Time. The performances funded by the grant were huge events, almost Wagnerian in scope, and allowed a rejuvenation of Coleman's music.
36. Tynan in "Ornette: The First Beginning," *Down Beat* 21 July 1960, quoted in Gioia, *The Imperfect Art*, 42.
37. John Tynan, "Record Review," *Down Beat* 18 January 1962: 28, quoted in Radano, "The Jazz Avant-Garde and the Jazz Community," 73.
38. Gioia, *The Imperfect Art*, 47.
39. James Lincoln Collier, *The Making of Jazz: A Comprehensive History* (New York: Doubleday, 1978), 463, quoted in Gioia, *The Imperfect Art*, 37.
40. Gioia, *The Imperfect Art*, 37.
41. *Ibid.*, 44.
42. Leo Tolstoy, *What Is Art?* trans. Aylmer Maude (Indianapolis: Bobbs-Merrill, 1960), 42–53.
43. Pete Welding and John A. Tynan, "Double View of a Double Quartet," *Down Beat* 18 January 1962: 28, quoted in Walser, ed., *Keeping Time: Readings in Jazz History*, 254.
44. John Litweiler, *The Freedom Principle: Jazz after* 1958 (New York: William Morrow, 1984), 43.
45. Vivien Goldman, ed., Ornette Coleman homepage, harmolodic.com/ornette/frameset_then.html, accessed 2 May 2006.
46. Robert Palmer, liner notes, *Beauty Is a Rare Thing: The Complete Atlantic Recordings*, Rhino Records boxed set, 1993.
47. Ornette Coleman, "Prime Time for Harmolodics," *Down Beat* (July 1983): 54–55, quoted in Gioia, *The Imperfect Art*, 43.
48. For an even more detailed explanation of the term "harmolodic" by Coleman see his homepage, harmolodic.com/philosophy/index.htm.
49. Vivien Goldman, ed., Ornette Coleman homepage, harmolodic.com/ornette/frameset_then.html, accessed 1 May 2006.

50. Vivien Goldman, ed., Ornette Coleman homepage, harmolodic.com/ornette/frameset_then.html, accessed 2 May 2006.
51. This approach can also be found in other African-based music groups.
52. Gioia, *The Imperfect Art*, 43.
53. Jost, *Free Jazz*, 17.
54. The Art Ensemble of Chicago (which included Jarman, Mitchell, Bowie, Favors, and later Don Moyle) grew out of the AACM organization of Paris in 1969 and continued to tour and travel throughout Western Europe. The Art Ensemble's popularity grew in the 1970s and gained fame largely as a result of the release of four albums in the 1980s. The Black Artists Group (BAG) began in 1968 and included Lake, Yakub, altoist Hemphill, trumpeter Floyd LeFlore, and drummer Charles Bobo Shaw; BAG quickly added actors, dancers, poets, and visual artists from St. Louis. The National Endowment for the Arts heavily supported BAG until 1972 when it dissolved.
55. The goals of the AACM have remained unchanged for forty years and have been codified into these nine pursuits:

    1. To cultivate young musicians and to create music of a high artistic level through programs designed to magnify creative music.
    2. To create an atmosphere conducive to artistic endeavors for the artistically inclined.
    3. To conduct free training for disadvantaged city youth.
    4. To encourage sources of employment for musicians.
    5. To set an example of high moral standards for musicians and to uplift the image of creative musicians.
    6. To increase respect between creative musicians and musical tradespersons.
    7. To uphold the tradition of cultured musicians handed down from the past.
    8. To stimulate spiritual growth in musicians.
    9. To assist other complementary charitable organizations.

    AACM (Association for the Advancement of Creative Musicians), Fidelio Online, fidelio.hu/nevjegy.asp?id=280&p=&cat=int, accessed 5 March 2006.
56. John B. Litweiler, "AACM's 20th Anniversary—An Interview with Muhal Richard Abrams," (Chicago) *Reader* (9 May 1975), quoted in Litweiler, *The Freedom Principle*, 196.
57. Radano, "Jazzin' the Classics," 80.
58. *Ibid.*
59. Jost, *Free Jazz*, 163.
60. Although much of the development and cultivation of ~~free jazz~~ is the result of European interest and devotion, such European elements remain beyond the scope of this paper. However, the European influence in jazz is undeniable, and recent scholarship is filling in large gaps of history formerly absent from the historical account of the development of ~~free jazz~~ in Europe.
61. Jost, *Free Jazz*, 163.
62. Lester Bowie, quoted in Sun Ra, *Sun Ra: The Immeasurable Equation* (blank page before table of contents).
63. Litweiler, *The Freedom Principle*, 100.

64. Nate Chinen, "Outward Bound: An Interview with Muhal Richard Abrams," from *Philadelphia City Paper*, February 5–12, 1998. Accessed 18 January 2009, citypaper.net/articles/020598/musld.shtml.
65. Litweiler, *The Freedom Principle*, 178.
66. The conjoining of jazz with poetry developed out of the Harlem Renaissance, through such poetry giants as Langston Hughes and Paul Dunbar. It extended through the Beat poets of the bebop era like Jack Kerouac and Alan Ginsberg, continued with Afrocentrists like Amiri Baraka in the 1960s and 1970s, and finally culminated in some of the dynamic spoken-word experimentalists of today. However, some of the best synesthetic examples of jazz and poetry occur in the work of Langston Hughes, especially in such poems as "The Weary Blues," with Leonard Feather conducting the music as performed and written by Charles Mingus, "Jazzonia," "Harlem Night Club," "The South," and *Montage of a Dream Deferred*, a book-length suite of poems illustrating Harlem life. Hughes conjures up images of Harlem streets, bars, dancing, and singing, and he echoes the sound of the music expressed in the language the poem.
67. Other albums of original music by Abrams around the same time are *Young At Heart, Wise in Time* (Delmark, 1969), *Things to Come from Those Now Gone* (Delmark, 1972), *Afrisong* (India Navigation, 1975), and *Sightsong* (Black Saint, 1975).
68. Radano, "Jazzin' the Classics," 91.
69. Chinen, "Outward Bound: An interview with Muhal Richard Abrams."
70. Radano, "Jazzin' the Classics," 91.
71. Steven Smith, liner notes, *Bap-Tisum*, Art Ensemble of Chicago.
72. Barthes, *Image, Music, Text*, 142–48.
73. Borgo, *Reference for Uncertainty*, 85–86.
74. Gunther Schuller, *Early Jazz* (New York: Oxford University Press, 1968) x, quoted in Jost, *Free Jazz*, 13.
75. Liebman, *Self Portrait of a Jazz-Artist*, 37.
76. Muhal Richard Abrams, interview with the author, 17 March 2006.
77. Postmodernity cannot be boiled down to a specific set of principles and is not necessarily the focus of this paper; however, the influence of postmodernity needs greater study in the field of jazz in order to determine the future of the music itself.
78. For more information on musical correlations found in postmodernism, see Jonathan D. Kramer, "The Nature and Origins of Musical Postmodernism," *Current Musicology* 66 (Spring 1999): 7–20; George Lipsitz, *Dangerous Crossroads: Popular Music, Postmodernism, and the Poetics of Place* (London: Verso, 1997); Judy Lochhead and Joseph Auner, eds., *Postmodern Music, Postmodern Thought* (New York: Routledge, 2002); and Peter Manuel, "Music as Symbol, Music as Simulacrum: Postmodern, Pre-modern, and Modern Aesthetics in Subcultural Popular Musics," *Popular Music* 14.2 (May 1995): 227–39.
79. Jonathan D. Kramer, "The Nature and Origins of Musical Postmodernism," *Current Musicology* 66 (Spring 1999): 9–10.
80. Miles Davis, *Miles: The Autobiography* (New York: Simon & Schuster, 1989), 394.
81. Atkins, "Toward a Global History of Jazz," in *Jazz Planet*, xii.
82. Jost, *Free Jazz*, 10.

83. Duke Ellington in 1962, from Mark Tucker, ed., *The Duke Ellington Reader* (New York: Oxford University Press, 1993), 326, quoted in Lewis, "Experimental Music in Black and White," 128.

CONCLUSION

1. Davis, *Miles: The Autobiography*, 393.
2. Ernie Bastin, interview with the author, 4 May 2006.

Bibliography

Abrams, Muhal Richard. Personal interview. 17 March 2006.

Ake, David Andrew. *Being Jazz: Identities and Images*. Diss., University of California at Los Angeles, 1998.

———. *Jazz Cultures*. Berkeley: University of Los Angeles Press, 2005.

Alperson, Philip, ed. *The Philosophy of the Visual Arts*. New York: Oxford University Press, 1992.

Althusser, Louis. *Essays in Self-Criticism*. Trans. Grahame Lock. London: NLB; Atlantic Highlands, NJ: Humanities Press, 1976.

Anderson, Iain. "Jazz Outside the Marketplace: Free Improvisation and Nonprofit Sponsorship of the Arts, 1965–1980." *American Music* 20.2 (Summer 2002): 131–67.

———. *"This is our music": Free Jazz, the Sixties, and American Culture*. Philadelphia: University of Pennsylvania Press, 2007.

Appel, Alfred, Jr. *Jazz Modernism: From Ellington and Armstrong to Matisse and Joyce*. New Haven and London: Yale University Press, 2004.

Atkins, E. Taylor, ed. *Jazz Planet*. Jackson: University Press of Mississippi, 2003.

Attali, Jacques. *Noise: The Political Economy of Music*. Minneapolis: University of Minnesota Press, 1996.

Audi, Robert, ed. *The Cambridge Dictionary of Philosophy*. 2nd ed. Cambridge: Cambridge University Press, 1999.

Ayer, Alfred Jules. *Language, Truth and Logic*. New York: Dover, 1936.

Bacher, Lutz. Personal interview. 15 October 2006.

———. Personal interview. 31 July 2008.

Bagert, Jenny. Telephone interview. 19 September 2006.

Baker, David, ed. *New Perspectives on Jazz*. Washington: Smithsonian Institution Press, 1990.

Baker, David. "Improvisation: A Tool for Music Learning." *Music Educators Journal* 66 (January 1980): 42–50.

———. *Roots II*. St. Louis: MMB Music, 1992.

Baker, David N., Lida M. Belt, and Herman C. Hudson, eds. *The Black Composer Speaks*. Metuchen, NJ: Scarecrow, 1978.

Baker, Houston A., Jr. *Black Studies, Rap, and the Academy*. Chicago: University of Chicago Press, 1993.

———. *Blues, Ideology, and Afro-American Literature: A Vernacular Theory*. Chicago: University of Chicago Press, 1984.

Balara, Lawrence Matthew. *The Personal and Social Dimensions of Creativity in Collective Jazz Improvisation*. Diss., California Institute of Integral Studies, 2000.

Baraka, Imamu Amiri (Leroy Jones). *Black Music*. New York: William Morrow, 1967.

———. *Blues People: Negro Music in White America.* New York: William Morrow, 1999.

Baraka, Amiri Imamu (LeRoi Jones), Nat Hentoff, Frank Kofsky, Steve Kuhn, Archie Shepp, Robert F. Thompson, and George Wein. "Jazz and Revolutionary Black Nationalism." *Jazz* (April 1966–July 1967).

Barrett, Terry. *Criticizing Photographs: An Introduction to Understanding Images.* 3rd ed. Mountain View, CA: Mayfield, 2000.

Barthes, Roland. *Camera Lucida: Reflections on Photography.* New York: Hill and Wang, 1981.

———. *Image, Music, Text.* Trans. Stephen Heath. New York: Hill and Wang, 1977.

———. "Myth Today." *Visual Culture: The Reader.* Eds. Jessica Evans and Stuart Hall. London: Sage, 1998.

———. *Roland Barthes S/Z.* Trans. Richard Miller. New York: Hill and Wang, 1974.

Baskerville, John D. *The Impact of Black Nationalist Ideology on American Jazz Music of the 1960s and 1970s.* Lewiston, NY: Edwin Mellen, 2003.

Basin, Yevgeny. *Semantic Philosophy of Art.* Trans. by Christopher English. Moscow: Progress Publishers, 1979.

Bastin, Ernie. Personal interview. 4 May 2006.

Baudrillard, Jean. *Simulations.* New York: Semiotext(e), 1983.

Baum, Geraldine. Telephone interview. 31 July 2008.

Belgrad, Daniel. *The Culture of Spontaneity: Improvisation and the Arts in Postwar America.* Chicago: University of Chicago Press, 1998.

Bellman, Jonathan, ed. *The Exotic in Western Music.* Boston: Northeastern University Press, 1998.

Belton, Don, ed. *Speak My Name: Black Men on Masculinity and the American Dream.* Boston: Beacon, 1995.

Benston, Kimberly W. *Performing Blackness: Enactments of African-American Modernism.* London and New York: Routledge, 2000.

Berger, Martin A. *Sight Unseen: Whiteness and American Visual Culture.* Berkeley: University of California Press, 2005.

Berger, John. *The Sense of Sight: Writings by John Berger.* New York: Vintage, 1993.

———. *Ways of Seeing.* Harmondsworth, UK: Penguin, 1972.

Bernotas, Robert W. *Critical theory, jazz, and politics: A critique of the Frankfort School.* Diss., Johns Hopkins University, 1987. Ann Arbor: UMI, 1987.

Berendt, Joachim Ernest. *Jazz: A Photo History.* Trans. William Odom. London: Deutsch; New York: Schirmer, 1979.

Berliner, Paul F. *Thinking in Jazz: The Infinite Art of Improvisation.* Chicago: University of Chicago Press, 1994.

Borgo, David. *Reverence for Uncertainty: Chaos, Order, and the Dynamics of Musical Free Improvisation.* Diss., University of California in Los Angeles, 1999. Los Angeles: UMI Microform, 1999. 9947057.

———. *Sync or Swarm: Improvising Music in a Complex Age.* New York: Continuum, 2005.

Bourdieu, Pierre. *Distinction: A Social Critique of the Judgment of Taste.* Trans. Richard Nice. Cambridge: Harvard University Press, 1984.

Brask, Ole. *Ole Brask . . . Photographs, Jazz.* Nieswand, Norway: Verlag, 1995.

———. *Jazz People: Photographs by Ole Brask.* Englewood Cliffs, NJ: Prentice Hall, 1976.

Braxton, Anthony. *Forces in Motion: The Music and Thoughts of Anthony Braxton*. New York: Da Capo, 1988.

Brown, Lee B. "The Theory of Jazz Music 'It Don't Mean a Thing . . .'" *Journal of Aesthetics and Art Criticism* 49 (1991): 115–27.

———. "Musical Works, Improvisation, and the Principle of Continuity." *Journal of Aesthetics and Art Criticism* 54 (1996): 353–69.

———. "Feeling My Way: Jazz Improvisation and Its Vicissitudes—A Plea for Imperfection." *Journal of Aesthetics and Art Criticism* 58.2 (2000): 113–23.

———. "Marsalis and Baraka: An Essay in Comparative Cultural Discourse." *Popular Music* 23.3 (2004): 241–55.

Brown, Matthew P. "Funk Music as Genre: Black Aesthetics, Apocalyptic Thinking and Urban Protest in Post-1965 African-American Pop." *Cultural Studies* 8.3 (1994): 484–508.

Brown, Robert L. "Classical Influences on Jazz." *Journal of Jazz Studies* 3 (1975): 19–35.

Broyard, Anatole. "Portrait of the Hipster." *Partisan Review* 15.6 (1948): 721–27.

Buchanan, Ian, and Marcel Swiboda, eds. *Deleuze and Music*. Edinburgh: Edinburgh University Press, 2004.

Budds, Michael J. *Jazz in the Sixties: The Expansion of Musical Resources and Techniques*. Iowa City: University of Iowa Press, 1990.

Burke, Patrick. "Oasis of Swing: The Onyx Club, Jazz, and White Masculinity in the Early 1930s." *American Music* vol. 24, no. 3 (Fall 2006): 320–436.

Butterfield, Matthew W. "Music Analysis and the Social Life of Jazz Recordings." *Current Musicology* 71–73 (Spring 2001–Spring 2002): 324–52.

Carner, Gary. "Jazz Photography: A Conversation with Herb Snitzer." *Black American Literature Forum* 25.3, Literature of Jazz Issue (Autumn 1991): 561–92.

Carr, Roy, Brian Case, and Fred Dellar. *The Hip: Hipsters, Jazz and the Beat Generation*. London: Faber and Faber, 1986.

Cassidy, Donna M. *Painting the Musical City: Jazz and Cultural Identity in American Art, 1910–1940*. Washington: Smithsonian Institution Press, 1997.

Cawthra, Benjamin Scott. *Blue Notes in Black and White: Photography, Race and the Image of Jazz, 1936–1965*. Diss., Washington University in St. Louis, 2007. Ann Arbor: UMI Dissertation Services, 2008. 3268014.

Chambers, Jack. *Milestones: The Music and Times of Miles Davis*. New York: Beech Tree, 1983.

Charters, Samuel Barclay, and Leonard Kunstaft. *Jazz: A History of the New York Scene*. Garden City, NY: Doubleday, 1962.

Chomsky, Noam. *Language and Responsibility*. Trans. John Viertel. New York: Pantheon, 1977, 1979.

Citron, Marcia. *Gender and the Musical Canon*. New York: Cambridge University Press, 1993.

Clark, Andrew, ed. *Riffs and Choruses: A New Jazz Anthology*. London, New York: Continuum, 2001.

Collier, James Lincoln. *The Making of Jazz: A Comprehensive History*. New York: Doubleday, 1978.

———. *The Reception of Jazz in America: A New View*. Brooklyn: Institute for Studies in American Music, Brooklyn College of the City University of New York, 1988.

Conyers Jr., James L., ed. *African American Jazz and Rap: Social and Philosophical Examinations of Black Expressive Behavior*. Jefferson, NC: McFarland, 2001.

Cook, Nicholas, and Mark Everist, eds. *Rethinking Music*. Oxford: Oxford University Press, 1999.

Crouch, Stanley. *Considering Genius: Writings on Jazz*. New York: Basic Civitas, 2006.

Crow, Bill. *From Birdland to Broadway: Scenes from a Jazz Life*. New York: Oxford University Press, 1992.

———. *Jazz Anecdotes*. New York: Oxford University Press, 1990.

Dahlhaus, Carl. *The Idea of Absolute Music*. Trans. Roger Lustig. Chicago: University of Chicago Press, 1989.

Danto, Arthur C. *After the End of Art: Contemporary Art and the Pale of History*. Princeton: Princeton University Press, 1997.

Davis, Angela. *Blues Legacies and Black Feminism: Gertrude 'Ma' Rainey, Bessie Smith, and Billie Holiday*. New York: Pantheon, 1998.

Davis, Francis. *Bebop and Nothingness: Jazz and Pop at the End of the Century*. New York: Schirmer; London: Prentice Hall International, 1996.

———. *In the Moment: Jazz in the 1980s*. New York: Oxford University Press, 1986.

Davis, Miles. *Miles: The Autobiography*. New York: Simon and Schuster, 1989.

Day, William. "Knowing as Instancing: Jazz Improvisation and Moral Perfectionism." *Journal of Aesthetics and Art Criticism* 58.2 (Spring 2000): 99–111.

DeCarava, Roy. *The Sound I Saw: Improvisations on a Jazz Theme*. London: Phaidon, 2001.

Demsey, David. "Chromatic Third Relations in the Music of John Coltrane." *Annual Review of Jazz Studies* 5 (1991): 145–80.

Denora, Tia. *Music in Everyday Life*. Cambridge: Cambridge University Press, 2000.

DeVeaux, Scott. "Constructing the Jazz Tradition: Jazz Historiography." *Black American Literature Forum* 25.3 (Fall 1991): 525–60.

———. "Jazz in America: Who's Listening?" *Research Division Report* #31, National Endowment for the Arts (Carson, CA: Seven Locks, 1995): 1–4, 36–37, 56–57.

———. "Struggling with Jazz." *Current Musicology* 71–73 (Spring 2001–Spring 2002): 353–74.

———. "American Musics: What Did We Do to Be So Black and Blue?" *Musical Quarterly* 80:3 (Fall 1996): 392–430.

———. *The Birth of Bebop: A Social and Musical History*. Berkeley: University of California Press, 1997.

Dewey, John. *Art as Experience*. New York: Capricorn, 1934.

Dunham, D. J. *Will in Jazz: Schopenhauer's Philosophy on Music and the Aesthetics of Miles Davis*. Masters thesis, Wright State University, 1999.

Dunkley, Leon Latimer, Jr., *The Icarus Endeavor: Jazz, Narrative History and the Idea of Race*. Diss., University of Pittsburgh, 1997.

Durden, Mark, and Craig Richardson, eds. *Face On: Photography as Social Exchange*. London: Black Dog, 2000.

Edgerton, Gary R. *Ken Burns's America*. New York: Palgrave/St. Martin's, 2001.

Enright, Ed. "'Down Beat' Lifetime Achievement Award: Herman Leonard—Eye for the Music." *Down Beat* 71.10 (Oct 2004): 60–62.

Erlmann, Veit. "How Beautiful Is Small? Music, Globalization and the Aesthetics of the Local." *Yearbook for Traditional Music* 30 (1998): 12–21.

Feather, Leonard. *The Encyclopedia of Jazz*. New York: Horizon, 1960.

Fischlin, Daniel, and Ajay Heble, eds. *The Other Side of Nowhere: Jazz, Improvisation, and Communities in Dialogue*. Middletown, CT: Wesleyan University Press, 2004.

Floyd, Samuel A., Jr., *The Power of Black Music.* New York: Oxford University Press, 1995.

Ford, Philip. "Somewhere/Nowhere: Hipness as an Aesthetic." *The Musical Quarterly* 86.1 (Spring 2002): 49–81.

Foster, Audrey Gwendolyn. *Performing Whiteness: Postmodern Re/Constructions in the Cinema.* Albany: State University of New York Press, 2003.

Foucault, Michel. *The Order of Things: An Archaeology of the Human Sciences.* A Translation of *Les Mots et les choses.* New York: Vintage, 1970.

———. *This Is Not a Pipe.* Trans. and ed. James Harkness. Berkeley: University of California Press, 1983.

Francesconi, Robert. "Free Jazz and Black Nationalism: A Rhetoric of Musical Style." *Critical Studies in Mass Communication* vol. 3, no. 1. (March 1986): 36–49.

Friedlander, Lee. *The Jazz People of New Orleans.* New York: Pantheon, 1992.

Friedman, Carol. *A Moment's Notice: Portraits of American Jazz Musicians.* New York: Schirmer, 1983.

Frizot, Michel, ed. *A New History of Photography.* Köln: Könemann Verlagsgesellschaft, 1998.

Gabbard, Krin. *Black Magic: White Hollywood and African American Culture.* New Brunswick, NJ: Rutgers University Press, 2004.

———. *Jammin' at the Margins: Jazz and the American Cinema.* Chicago: University of Chicago Press, 1996.

Gabbard, Krin, ed. *Jazz Among the Discourses.* Durham, NC: Duke University Press, 1995.

———, ed. *Representing Jazz.* Durham: Duke University Press, 1995.

Gates, Henry Louis, Jr., *The Signifying Monkey: A Theory of African-American Literary Criticism.* New York: Oxford University Press, 1988.

———. *Thirteen Ways of Looking at a Black Man.* New York: Random House, 1997.

Gerard, Charley. *Jazz in Black and White: Race, Culture, and Identity in the Jazz Community.* Westport, CN: Praeger, 1998.

Gennari, John. *The Politics of Culture and Identity.* Diss., University of Pennsylvania, 1993.

Giddins, Gary. *Ryhthm-a-ning: Jazz Tradition and Innovation in the '80s.* New York: Oxford University Press, 1985.

———. *Riding on a Blue Note: Jazz and American Pop.* New York: Oxford University Press, 1981.

Gilman, Sander L., and Zhou Xun. *Smoke: A Global History of Smoking.* London: Reaktion, 2004.

Gioia, Ted. *The History of Jazz.* New York: Oxford University Press, 1997.

———. *The Imperfect Art: Reflections on Jazz and Modern Culture.* New York and Oxford: Oxford University Press, 1988.

Goldberg, Alan. "The Jazz Musician as Preacher: Afro-American Music and Social Change." *Proceedings of the Central States Anthropological Society, selected papers* 3 (1977): 23–30.

Golden, Thelma. *Black Representations of Masculinity in Contemporary American Art.* New York: Whitney Museum of American Art/Harry N. Abrams, 1994.

Gombrich, E. H., Julian Hochberg, and Black. *Art, Perception, and Reality.* Baltimore: Johns Hopkins University Press, 1972.

Goodheart, Matthew. "The 'Giant Steps' Fragment." *Perspectives of New Music* 39:2 (Summer 2001): 63–95.

Gottlieb, Robert, ed. *Reading Jazz: A Gathering of Autobiography, Reportage, and Criticism from 1919 to Now.* New York: Pantheon, 1996.

Gottlieb, William P. *The Golden Age of Jazz.* New York: Simon and Schuster, 1979.

Green, Benny. *The Reluctant Art: The Growth of Jazz.* Plainview, NY: Books for Library Press, 1962.

Greenblatt, Stephen J. "Improvisation and Power." *Literature and Society.* Ed. Edward W. Said. Baltimore: Johns Hopkins University Press, 1980.

Hall, Stuart. "Ethnicity: Identity and Difference." *Radical America* 23.4 (1998).

———. *Stuart Hall: Critical Dialogues in Cultural Studies.* Eds. D. Morley and K. H. Chen. London and New York: Routledge, 1996.

———, ed. *Representation: Cultural Representations and Signifying Practices.* London: Sage, 1998.

Harrison, Max. *A Jazz Retrospect.* Boston: Crescendo, 1976.

Haskins, James. *Black Music in America: A History Through Its People.* New York: Thomas Y. Crowell, 1987.

Hentoff, Nat. *The Jazz Life.* New York: Dial, 1961.

Hester, Karlton E. *The Melodic and Polyrhythmic Development of John Coltrane's Spontaneous Composition in a Racist Society.* Lewiston, NY: Edwin Mellen, 1997.

Hinton, Milt, David G. Berger, and Holly Maxson. *Over Time: The Jazz Photographs of Milt Hinton.* Petaluma, CA: Pomegranate, 1991.

Hobsbawm, Eric. *The Jazz Scene.* New York: Pantheon, 1993.

Hodeir, André. *Toward Jazz.* Trans. Noel Burch. New York: Da Capo, 1976.

hooks, bell. *We Real Cool: Black Men and Masculinity.* New York and London: Routledge, 2004.

Horowitz, Irving Louis. "Authenticity and Originality in Jazz: Toward a Paradigm in the Sociology of Music." *Journal of Jazz Studies* 1.1 (October 1973).

Houston, David, and Jenny Bagert, eds. *Jazz, Giants, and Journeys: The Photography of Herman Leonard.* London: Scala, 2006.

Houser, Craig. "I Abject." *Abject Art: Repulsion and Desire in American Art.* New York: Whitney Museum of American Art, 1993.

Huggins, Nathan, ed. *Voices from the Harlem Renaissance.* Oxford: Oxford University Press, 1971.

Jackson, Jeffrey H. "Music-Halls and the Assimilation of Jazz in 1920s Paris." *Journal of Popular Culture* 34.2 (Fall 2000): 69–82.

Jackson, Ronald L. II, ed. *African American Communication and Identities: Essential Readings.* Thousand Oaks, CA: Sage, 2004.

Jackson, Ronald L. (Ronald L. Jackson II), and Elaine B. Richardson, eds. *Understanding African American Rhetoric: Classical Origins to Contemporary Innovations.* New York: Routledge, 2003.

Jang, Jon. "We Don't All Sound Alike." *Views on Black American Music* 3 (1985–88): 33–38.

Jarrett, Michael. *Drifting on a Read: Jazz as a Model for Writing.* Albany: State University of New York Press, 1999.

Jones, Max. *Talking Jazz.* New York: W.W. Norton, 1988.

Jost, Ekkehard. *Free Jazz.* New York: Da Capo, 1994.

Joyner, David. "Analyzing Third Stream." *Contemporary Music Review* 19.1 (2000): 63–87.

Kalaidjian, Walter, ed. *The Cambridge Companion to American Modernism*. Cambridge, UK: Cambridge University Press, 2005.

Kart, Larry. "Provocative Opinion: The Death of Jazz?" *Black Music Research Journal* 10.1 (Spring 1990): 76–81.

———. *Jazz in Search of Itself*. New Haven, CT: Yale University Press, 2004.

Kaur, Raminder, and Partha Banerjea. "Jazzgeist: Racial Signs of Twisted Times." *Theory, Culture and Society* 17.3 (2000): 159–80.

Kebede, Ashenafi. *Roots of Black Music: The Vocal, Instrumental, and Dance Heritage of Africa and Black Music*. Trenton, NJ: Africa World Press, 1995.

Kelly, Robin D. G. "Dig They Freedom: Meditations on History and the Black Avant-Garde." *Lenox Avenue* 3 (1997).

Kitwana, Bakari. *Why White Kids Love Hip-Hop: Wankstas, Wiggers, Wannabes, and the New Reality of Race in America*. New York: Basic Civitas, 2005.

Klotman, Phyllis Rauch, ed. *Humanities through the Black Experience*. Dubuque, IA: Kendall and Hunt, 1977.

Kofsky, Frank. *Black Music, White Business: Illuminating the History and Political Economy of Jazz*. New York: Pathfinder, 1998.

———. *John Coltrane and the Jazz Revolution of the 1960s*. 2nd ed. New York: Pathfinder, 1998.

———. "Black Nationalism in Jazz: The Forerunners Resist Establishment Repression, 1958–1963." *Journal of Ethnic Studies* 10.2 (1982): 1–27.

———. *Black Nationalism and the Revolution in Music*. New York: Pathfinder, 1970.

Kramer, Jonathan D. "The Nature and Origins of Musical Postmodernism." *Current Musicology* 66 (Spring 1999): 7–20.

Kramer, Lawrence. *Musical Meaning: Toward a Critical History*. Berkeley: University of California Press, 2002.

———. "Musicology and Meaning." *Musical Times* 144.1883 (Summer 2003): 6–12.

Kynaston, Trent P., and Robert J. Ricci. *Jazz Improvisation*. Englewood Cliffs, NJ: Prentice Hall, 1978.

LaBelle, Brandon, and Steve Roden, eds. *Site of Sound: of Architecture and the Ear*. Los Angeles: Errant Bodies, 1999.

LaRue, Jan. *Guidelines for Style Analysis: A Comprehensive Outline of Basic Principles for the Analysis of Musical Style*. New York: W. W. Norton, 1970.

Larson, Steve. "Schenkerian Analysis of Modern Jazz: Questions about Method." *Music Theory Spectrum* 20.2 (Fall 1998): 209–41.

Latour, Bruno. *We Have Never Been Modern*. Trans. Catherine Porter. Cambridge, MA: Harvard University Press, 1993.

Leggio, James, ed. *Music and Modern Art*. New York: Routledge, 2002.

Leonard, Herman. Personal interview. 11–14 February 2009.

Leonard, Neil. *Jazz and the White American: The Acceptance of a New Art Form*. Chicago: University of Chicago Press, 1962.

———. *Jazz: Myth and Religion*. New York: Oxford University Press, 1987.

Lewis, George E. *A Power Stronger Than Itself: The AACM and American Experimental Music*. Chicago and London: University of Chicago Press, 2008.

———. "Experimental Music in Black and White: The AACM in New York, 1970–1985." *Current Musicology* 71–73 (Spring 2001–Spring 2002): 100–157.

———. "Improvised Music after 1950: Afrological and Eurological Perspectives." *Black Music Research Journal* 22 (2002): 215–46.

———. "Purposive Patterning: Jeff Donaldson, Muhal Richard Abrams, and the Multidominance of Consciousness." *Lenox Avenue* 5 (1999): 63–69.

———. "Taste Cultures and Musical Stereotypes: Mirrors of Identity?" *Popular Music and Society* 19:1 (Spring 1995): 37–58.

Liebman, David. *Self Portrait of a Jazz-Artist: Musical Thoughts and Realities*. Rottenburg, West Germany: Advance Music, 1988.

Ligon, Bert. *Jazz Theory Resources: Tonal, Harmonic, Melodic and Rhythmic Organization of Jazz*. Milwaukee, WI: Houston, 2001.

Lipsitz, George. *Dangerous Crossroads: Popular Music, Postmodernism, and the Poetics of Place*. London: Verso, 1997.

Litweiler, John. *The Freedom Principle: Jazz after 1958*. New York: William Morrow, 1984.

Lochhead, Judy, and Joseph Auner, eds. *Postmodern Music, Postmodern Thought*. New York: Routledge, 2002.

Lock, Graham. *Blutopia: Visions of the Future and the Revisions of the Past in the Work of Sun Ra, Duke Ellington, and Anthony Braxton*. Durham, NC: Duke University Press, 1999.

Lopes, Paul. *The Rise of a Jazz Art World*. Cambridge, UK: Cambridge University Press, 2002.

———. "Diffusion and Syncretism: The Modern Jazz Tradition." *Annals of the American Academy* 566.1 (November 1999): 25–36.

Mailer, Norman. "The White Negro: Superficial Reflections on the Hipster." *Dissent* 4.3 (1957): 276–93.

Mandel, Howard. *Future Jazz*. Oxford and New York: Oxford University Press, 1999.

Manuel, Peter. "Music as Symbol, Music as Simulacrum: Postmodern, Pre-modern, and Modern Aesthetics in Subcultural Popular Musics." *Popular Music* 14.2 (May 1995): 227–39.

Mark, Michael L. "The Acceptance of Jazz in the Music Education Curriculum: A Model for Interpreting a Historical Process." *Bulletin of the Council for Research in Music Education* 92 (Summer 1987): 15–21.

Martin, Henry. "Jazz Harmony: A Syntactic Background." *Annual Review of Jazz Studies* 4 (1986): 9–30.

Martin, Henry, and Keith Waters. *Jazz: The First 100 Years*. Belmont, CA: Wadsworth, 2002.

Marsalis, Wynton. "What Jazz Is—and Isn't." *New York Times* (31 July 1988, Arts & Leisure): 21, 24.

Matheson, Carl. "The Metaphysics of Jazz." *Journal of Aesthetics and Art Criticism* 58.2 (Spring 2000): 125–33.

McClary, Susan. *Feminine Endings: Music, Gender, and Sexuality*. Minneapolis: University of Minnesota Press, 1991.

McRae, Rick. "'What Is Hip?' and Other Inquiries in Jazz Slang Lexicography." *Notes* 57.3 (March 2001): 574–84.

Meltzer, David, ed. *Writing Jazz*. San Francisco: Mercury House, 1999.

Merriam, Alan P., and Raymond W. Mack, "The Jazz Community." *Social Forces* 38.3 (March 1960): 211–22.

Mezzrow, Mezz, and Bernard Wolfe. *Really the Blues*. New York: Random House, 1946.

Mitchell, W. J. T. *What Do Pictures Want? The Lives and Loves of Images*. Chicago: University of Chicago Press, 2005.

Mirzoeff, Nicholas. *An Introduction to Visual Culture*. New York: Routledge, 1999.

Monson, Ingrid. *Saying Something: Jazz Improvisation and Interaction*. Chicago: University of Chicago Press, 1996.

———. "The Problem with White Hipness: Race, Gender, and Cultural Conceptions in Jazz Historical Discourse." *Journal of the American Musicological Society* 48.3 (Fall 1995): 396–422.

———. "Doubleness and Jazz Improvisation: Irony, Parody, and Ethnomusicology." *Critical Inquiry* 20 (1994): 283–313.

———. *Musical Interaction in Modern Jazz: An Ethnomusicological Perspective*. Diss., New York University, 1991.

———, ed. *The African Diaspora: A Musical Perspective*. New York: Garland, 2000.

Moore, Catherine. "A Picture Is Worth 1000 CDs: Can the Music Industry Survive as a Stand-Alone Business?" *American Music* 22.1 (Spring 2004): 176–86.

Murray, Albert. *The Hero and the Blues*. Columbia: University of Missouri Press, 1973.

———. *The Omni-Americans: New Perspectives on Black Experience and American Culture*. New York: Outerbridge and Dienstfrey, 1970.

Nakayama, Thomas K., and Judith N. Martin, eds. *Whiteness: The Communication of Social Identity*. Thousand Oaks, CA: Sage, 1999.

Nicholson, Stuart. *Is Jazz Dead? Or Has It Moved to a New Address*. New York: Routledge, 2005.

———. *Jazz Rock: A History*. New York: Schirmer Books, 1998.

———. *Jazz: The 1980s Resurgence*. New York: Da Capo, 1995.

———. *Jazz: The Modern Resurgence*. London: Simon and Schuster, 1990.

Nielsen, Aldon Lynn. *Black Chant: Languages of African American Post-Modernism*. Cambridge, UK: Cambridge University Press, 1997.

Nisenson, Eric. *Blue: The Murder of Jazz*. New York: St. Martin's, 1997.

Norris, Christopher, ed. *Music and the Politics of Culture*. New York: St. Martin's, 1989.

Olson, Lester C., Cara A. Finnegan, and Dana S. Hope, eds. *Visual Rhetoric: A Reader in Communication and American Culture*. Los Angeles: Sage, 2008.

O'Meally, Robert, ed. *The Jazz Cadence of American Culture*. New York: Columbia University Press, 1998.

O'Meally, Robert G., Brent Hayes Edwards, and Farah Jasmine Griffin, eds. *Uptown Conversation: The New Jazz Studies*. New York: Columbia University Press, 2004.

Orvell, Miles. *American Photography*. Oxford: Oxford University Press, 2003.

Owens, Thomas. *Bebop: The Music and Its Players*. New York: Oxford University Press, 1995.

Panish, Jon. *The Colour of Jazz: Race and Representation in Postwar American Culture*. Jackson: University Press of Mississippi, 1997.

Peretti, Burton W. *Jazz in American Culture*. Chicago: Ivan R. Dee, 1997.

———. *The Creation of Jazz: Music, Race and Culture in Urban America*. Urbana: University of Illinois Press, 1992.

Phinney, Kevin. *Souled America: How Black Music Transformed White Culture*. New York: Billboard Books, 2005.

Placksin, Sally. *Jazzwomen, 1900 to the Present: Their World, Lives, and Music*. London: Wideview, 1982; New York: Pluto Press, 1987.

Porter, Eric. *What Is This Thing Called Jazz: African American Musicians as Artists, Critics, and Activists*. Berkeley: University of California Press, 2002.

———. *"Out of the Blue": Black Creative Musicians and the Challenge of Jazz, 1940–1995*. Diss., University of Michigan, 1997.

Potter, Gary. "Analyzing Improvised Jazz." *College Music Symposium* 30 (1990): 64–74.

Rabinow, Paul, ed. *The Foucault Reader*. New York: Pantheon, 1984.

Radano, Ronald M. "Myth Today: The Color of Ken Burns' Jazz." *Black Renaissance* 3, no. 3 (2001): 43–54.

———. *New Musical Figurations: Anthony Braxton's Cultural Critique*. Chicago: Chicago University Press, 1993.

———. "Jazzin' the Classics: The AACM's Challenge to Mainstream Aesthetics." *Black Research Journal* 12.1 (1992): 79–95.

———. "The Jazz Avant-Garde and the Jazz Community: Action and Reaction." *Annual Review of Jazz Studies* 3 (1985): 71–81.

Reinelt, Janelle G., and Joseph R. Roach, eds. *Critical Theory and Performance*. Ann Arbor: University of Michigan Press, 1992.

Remonko, Guy. Personal interview. 28 June 2006.

Robinson, Jason. "The Challenge of the Changing Same: The Jazz Avant-Garde of the 1960s, the Black Aesthetic, and the Black Arts Movement." *Critical Studies in Improvisation/Études critiques en improvisation* vol. 1, no. 2 (2005).

Rose, Tricia. *Black Noise: Rap Music and Black Culture in Contemporary America*. Hanover, NH: Wesleyan University Press, 1994.

Rosenthal, David H. *Hard Bop: Jazz and Black Music 1955–1965*. New York: Oxford University Press, 1992.

Ross, Andrew. *No Respect: Intellectuals and Popular Culture*. New York: Routledge, 1989.

Rudinow, Joel. "Race, Ethnicity, Expressive Authenticity: Can White People Sing the Blues?" *Journal of Aesthetics and Art Criticism* 52.1, The Philosophy of Music (Winter 1994): 127–37.

Rugg, Linda Haverty. *Picturing Ourselves: Photography and Autobiography*. Chicago: University of Chicago Press, 1997.

Russell, Ross. *Jazz Styles in Kansas City and the Southwest*. Berkeley: University of California Press, 1971.

Rustin, Nichole T. *Mingus Fingers: Charles Mingus, Black Masculinity, and Postwar Jazz Culture*. Diss., New York University, 1999.

Said, Edward. *Musical Elaborations*. New York: Columbia University Press, 1991.

Salamone, Frank A. "Africa as a Metaphor for Authenticity in Jazz." *Studies in Third World Societies* 46 (1991): 1–20.

Salaam, Kalamu ya. "Herman Leonard: Making Music with Light." *African American Review* 29.2, Special Issues on The Music (Summer 1995): 241–46.

Saul, Scott. *Freedom Is, Freedom Ain't: Jazz and the Making of the Sixties*. Cambridge, MA: Harvard University Press, 2003.

Sawyer, Keith. "Improvisation and the Creative Process: Dewey, Collingwood, and the Aesthetics of Spontaneity." *Journal of Aesthetics and Art Criticism* 58.2 (2000): 149–61.

Schuller, Gunther. "Third Stream Flow." *Jazziz* 17 (January 2000): 401.

———. *The Swing Era: The Development of Jazz, 1930–1945*. New York: Oxford University Press, 1989.

———. *Musings: The Musical World of Gunther Schuller*. New York: Oxford University Press, 1986.

———. *Early Jazz: Its Roots and Musical Development*. New York: Oxford University Press, 1968.

———. "Third Stream Music." *The New Yorker*, 9 December 1961: 42–44.

———. "We Start with Music." *Newsletter of the American Symphony Orchestra League* 10, nos. 3–4 (1959): 5.

———. "Is Jazz Coming of Age?" *Musical America* 79 (February 1959): 8–9, 166–67.

Schwartz, Elliott, and Daniel Godfrey. *Music since 1945: Issues, Materials, and Literature*. New York: Schirmer, 1993.

Scruggs, T. M. "Come On In North Side, You're Just In Time": Musical-Verbal Performance and the Negotiation of Ethnically Segregated Social Space." *Current Musicology* 71–73 (Spring 2001–Spring 2002): 179–99.

Sesso, Cynthia. Telephone interview. 18 March 2009.

Shadwick, Keith. *Jazz: Legends of Style*. Edison, NJ: Chartwell, 1998.

Shaw, Bernard. *Bernard Shaw on Photography*. Salt Lake City, UT: Peregrine Smith, 1989.

Shipton, Alyn. *A New History of Jazz*. London and New York: Continuum, 2002.

Sidran, Ben. *Talking Jazz: An Illustrated Oral History*. San Francisco: Pomegranate, 1992.

Solie, Ruth A. "Defining Feminism: Conundrums, Contexts, Communities." *Women and Music: A Journal of Gender and Culture* 1.1 (1997): 1–12.

Sontag, Susan. *On Photography*. New York: Anchor, 1989.

Spencer, Lloyd, ed. *The Sense of Sight: Writings by John Berger*. New York: Vintage, 1993.

Spencer, Jon Michael. *Re-Searching Black Music*. Knoxville: University of Tennessee Press, 1996.

Stanbridge, Alan. "From the Margins to the Mainstream: Jazz, Social Relations, and Discourses of Value." *Critical Studies in Improvisation/Études critiques en improvisation*, vol. 4, no. 1 (2008).

Steinberger, Peter J. "Culture and Freedom in the Fifties: The Case of Jazz." *Virginia Quarterly Review* 74.1 (1998): 118–34.

Strunk, Steven. "Linear Intervallic Patterns in Jazz Repertory." *Annual Review of Jazz Studies* 8 (1996): 63–111.

Sukla, Ananta Ch., ed. *Art and Representation: Contributions to Contemporary Aesthetics*. Westport, CT: Praeger, 2001.

Sun Ra. *Sun Ra: The Immeasurable Equation*. Enterplenatary Koncepts (printed in) "Old" Europe: Waitawhile Books, 2005.

Tanner, Lee. *The Jazz Image: Masters of Jazz Photography*. New York: Abrams, 2006.

———. *Jazz Address Book*. Studio City, CA: Pomegranate, 1991.

Tate, Greg, ed. *Everything But the Burden: What White People Are Taking from Black Culture*. New York: Broadway, 2003.

Taylor, Yuval, ed. *The Future of Jazz*. Chicago: A Cappella, 2002.

Thomas, Julia, ed. *Reading Images*. New York: Palgrave, 2000.

Thomas, Lorenzo. "Ascension: Music and the Black Arts Movement." *Jazz Among the Discourses*. Ed. Krin Gabbard. Durham, NC: Duke University Press, 1995.

Tirro, Frank. *Jazz: A History.* 2nd ed. New York: W. W. Norton, 1993.

———. "Constructive Elements in Jazz Improvisation." *Journal of the American Musicological Society* 27.2 (Summer 1974): 285–305.

Tolstoy, Leo. *What Is Art?* Trans. Richard Pevear and Larissa Volokhonsky. London: Penguin, 1995.

Tomlinson, Gary. "Cultural Dialogics and Jazz: A White Historian Signifies." *Black Music Research* 11.2 (Fall 1991): 229–64.

Townsend, Peter. *Jazz in American Culture.* Edinburgh: Edinburgh University Press, 2000.

Turner, Victor. *The Anthropology of Performance.* New York: Performing Arts Journal, 1988.

Vincent, Ted. *Keep Cool: The Black Activists Who Built the Jazz Age.* London: Pluto, 1995.

Wakefield, Dan. *New York in the Fifties.* New York: Houghton Mifflin, 1992.

Walker, John A., and Sarah Chaplin. *Visual Culture: An Introduction.* Manchester, UK: Manchester University Press, 1997. (Distributed in the USA by St. Martin's, New York.)

Wallin, Nils L., Bjorn Merker, and Steven Brown, eds. *The Origins of Music.* Cambridge: MIT Press, 2000.

Walser, Robert, ed. *Keeping Time: Readings in Jazz History.* New York: Oxford University Press, 1999.

Ward, Geoffrey C., and Ken Burns. *Jazz: A History of America's Music.* New York: Alfred A. Knopf, 2000.

Watkins, Glenn. *Soundings: Music in the Twentieth Century.* New York: Schirmer, 1988.

Werner, Craig Hansen. *Playing the Changes: From Afro-Modernism to the Jazz Impulse.* Urbana: University of Illinois Press, 1994.

West, Cornel. *Keeping Faith: Philosophy and Race in America.* New York: Routledge, 1993.

Whaley, Preston, Jr. *Blows Like a Horn: Beat Writing, Jazz, Style, and Markets in the Transformation of U.S. Culture.* Cambridge, MA: Harvard University Press, 2004.

Williams, Martin, and Ira Gitler, selected and annotated by. *The Smithsonian Collection of Classic Jazz.* Washington, DC: The Smithsonian Collection of Recordings, 1973 first edition, 1987, 1997.

Wilmer, Valerie. *As Serious As Your Life: The Story of the New Jazz.* Westport, CT: Lawrence Hill, 1980.

Wilson, John S. *Jazz: The Transition Years, 1940–1960.* New York: Appleton Century Crofts, 1966.

Wragg, David. "Or any art at all?: Frank Zappa Meets Critical Theory." *Popular Music* 20.2 (May 2001): 205–22.

Yanow, Scott. *Bebop.* San Francisco: Miller Freeman, 2000.

Young, James O., and Carl Matheson. "The Metaphysics of Jazz." *Journal of Aesthetics and Art Criticism* 58.2 (Spring 2000): 125–33.

Zorn, John, ed. *Arcana: Musicians on Music.* New York: Granary, 2000.

Index

Page numbers in **bold** indicate illustrations.